Death Dust

Death Dust

THE RISE, DECLINE, AND FUTURE OF RADIOLOGICAL WEAPONS PROGRAMS

William C. Potter,
Sarah Bidgood,
Samuel Meyer, and
Hanna Notte

STANFORD UNIVERSITY PRESS
Stanford, California

Stanford University Press
Stanford, California

©2024 by William C. Potter, Sarah Bidgood, Samuel Meyer, and Hanna Notte. All rights reserved.

No part of this book may be reproduced or transmitted in any form or by any means, electronic or mechanical, including photocopying and recording, or in any information storage or retrieval system, without the prior written permission of Stanford University Press.

Printed in the United States of America on acid-free, archival-quality paper

ISBN 9781503636668 (cloth)
ISBN 9781503637658 (paperback)
ISBN 9781503637665 (electronic)

Library of Congress Control Number: 2023010747

Library of Congress Cataloging-in-Publication Data available upon request.

Cover design: Martyn Schmoll
Cover photograph: Adobe Stock and iStock, manipulated by Eduardo Fujii and Martyn Schmoll

Contents

	Preface	vii
	INTRODUCTION	1
1	The United States	18
2	The Soviet Union	40
3	The United Kingdom	57
4	Egypt	75
5	Iraq	108
	CONCLUSION Patterns across Cases and Prospects for the Future	134
	Notes	161
	Index	209

Preface

The origins of this book can be traced to a presentation made by the Center for Energy and Security Studies director Anton Khlopkov at Wilton Park in December 2013, which included a slide of North Korean soldiers at a Victory Day parade wearing chest packs festooned with the black and yellow radiation symbol. Reflecting on the slide that evening, one of the authors (William Potter) wondered to himself if the chest packs might contain radiological material of the "dirty bomb" variety usually attributed to non-state actors/terrorists. When he returned to Monterey, he broached the idea with his Center for Nonproliferation Studies colleague Jeffrey Lewis, and the two of them began to research both the possibility of a North Korea radiological weapon (RW) and historical precedents for such a weapon. They were astonished to discover that the United States had begun to contemplate RWs even before it entered World War II, and that British scientists also had explored the potential for RWs in the early 1940s.

Potter and Lewis published an article in *Foreign Policy* in early 2014 about their findings[1] and then secured research grants from the SAGA Foundation and the U.S. Air Force to understand better the nature of RW innovation in the United States, the Soviet Union, and possibly other countries.[2] An extended essay on the life cycle of the U.S. and Soviet RW programs was published in 2020 in *International Security*.[3] Over the course of the project leading to that publication, it became evident that, in addition to the extensive RW research, development, and testing programs in the United States and the Soviet Union, the United Kingdom, Iraq, and quite possibly Egypt also had dedicated RW programs. This book is the culmination of over eight years of research on the rise, evolution, and demise of weapons innovation involving radiological weapons. It also derives lessons from a comparative analysis of past state-level RW programs to assess the likelihood of and conditions under which additional states might pursue RWs in the future.

The book is very much a collective effort and bears the imprint of the four authors. Its overall design was conceived by William Potter, who had primary responsibility for the introduction, the case study on the United Kingdom, and the concluding chapter. He also contributed substantially to the U.S. case study. Sarah Bidgood was the primary author of the Soviet RW experience and provided significant input about the role of popular culture in shaping the U.S. perspectives. Hanna Notte was the last to join the project but made an exceptional contribution as the principal author for the case studies on Egypt and Iraq. Sam Meyer was the lead author for the U.S. case study and contributed to early versions of the chapters dealing with the United Kingdom and Egypt.

The authors benefited tremendously from research assistance provided by Veronica Bedenko, Claudia Deitch, Adam Druckman, Martin Everett, Matthew Goldenberg, Fabian Hinz, Baruchi Malewich, Kayo Oda, Jonathan Pike, Rowen Price, Luisa Roemer, Paul Warnke, and Mara Zarka. They also are grateful to Avner Cohen, Pierce Corden, Chen Kane, Ferenc Dalnoki-Veress, David Holloway, Hassan Elbahtimy, Målfrid Braut-Hegghammer, Jeffrey Lewis, George Moore, and William King for their helpful comments on one or more draft chapters. We also are grateful to many others who provided valuable input but asked to remain anonymous. We incorporated many, but not all, of their suggestions, some of which were contradictory, as one might expect given our research on largely untrodden territory. Naturally, the authors bear full responsibility for the final product.

Death Dust

Introduction

I will show you fear in a handful of dust.

T. S. ELIOT

At best, a fine line separates good science and good science fiction. Nowhere is this more apparent than in the realm of military innovation and novel weapons systems. Who is to say, for example, which is more fanciful or imaginary: a city dusted with synthetic "death sand" particles or a gigantic, nuclear-propelled torpedo packed with radioactive waste?

More than seventy years separates the first "science fiction" account of radioactive death dust attributable to Robert Heinlein and his publisher, John W. Campbell, in 1941[1] and the contemporary "doomsday" weapon depicted on slides held by Russian defense officials meeting with President Vladimir Putin.[2] The concept for the latter weapon, some Russian sources maintain, resembles the idea of a giant, nuclear-powered torpedo outlined a half century earlier by Soviet nuclear weapons designer and subsequent human rights and disarmament activist Andrei Sakharov.[3]

And yet, the concept of radiological weapons (RWs) was introduced to avid science fiction readers at practically the same time that President Franklin D. Roosevelt's science advisors were secretly debating the merits of these novel weapons. Subsequently, defense figures in other countries also became attracted to the idea of easy-to-manufacture but devastatingly lethal radiological munitions whose use would not discriminate between civilian and military targets.[4] Some viewed their development as horrific but inevitable; others regarded the weapons as necessary, at least until they could be replaced by even more powerful nuclear arms that relied on the effects of heat and pressure rather than radiation to do the killing.

The RWs imagined by Heinlein and Campbell were pursued in earnest by the United States and the Soviet Union, as well as several other states. During the Second World War, senior U.S. and British military figures feared that Nazi Germany was intent upon their development, and they took precautions against their employment during the planning of the invasion of Normandy. As early as 1940, the United Kingdom itself had begun to explore RWs. Following the conclusion of hostilities with Germany, it continued a program of research on RWs known only to a handful of British defense officials and scientists—including two Soviet spies: Klaus Fuchs and Alan Nunn May.

Although still shrouded in secrecy and largely ignored by both scholars and diplomats, the efforts to develop radiological weapons by these three World War II allies—all of whom had tested nuclear weapons by 1952—were not isolated events. The UN Special Commission on Iraq discovered that Saddam Hussein's regime developed and tested three prototype RW devices in the mid-1980s. There also is circumstantial evidence that Egypt sought to procure the materials for an RW capability in the early 1960s in tandem with its efforts to develop a ballistic missile program. It would be surprising, moreover, if other past and present would-be nuclear weapons aspirants did not seriously contemplate and possibly invest in the pursuit of what may have been perceived to be a "poor man's nuclear weapon." Israel, for example, conducted civil defense exercises in 2011, motivated by the fear of possible Iranian possession and use of RWs, and was viewed by President Gamal Abdel Nasser of Egypt as seeking such a capability in the early 1960s.[5] Others have suggested that North Korea also may have entertained the idea of RWs for the purpose of impeding U.S. and South Korean military operations.[6] More recently, both shortly before and following the Russian invasion of Ukraine in February 2022, the Kremlin's propagandists produced a flurry of unsubstantiated and intentionally misleading allegations that Ukraine was pursuing an RW program centered on the Chernobyl Exclusion Zone.[7]

Notwithstanding the substantial, if often overlooked, historical record of RW research, development, and, for at least three states, actual testing of radiological weapons, there is no evidence that any country has ever deployed RWs in an operational mode. In fact, since the terrorist attacks of September 11, 2001, most expert commentary on radiological weapons has focused almost exclusively on non-state actors, who are assumed to covet radioactive dispersal devices or "dirty bombs" for the purpose of inflicting nuclear punishment on the cheap. Yet, despite the widespread availability of radiological sources and the relative ease of matching a conventional explosive to a radioactive payload, no terrorist has successfully caried out a dirty-bomb attack.[8]

This paradox raises many unanswered questions. Should one conclude from this history that RWs are a thing of the past, more suitable to pulp fiction than serious military procurement or doctrine? Or has an emphasis on non-state actors obscured the continuing possibility that states may pursue RWs, perhaps in addition to or in lieu of nuclear weapons? Why did so many states express interest in RWs, sometimes invest significant resources in their development and testing, but in all instances ultimately choose not to deploy them? Why is so little known known about these multiple false starts, especially outside the United States? Can one draw more general conclusions about the primary drivers and disincentives to acquire radiological weapons? Does renewed Russian interest in a "super torpedo" with an especially toxic radioactive payload represent an outlier in this respect, or does it herald a possible revival of military interest in more efficient and technologically sophisticated radiological weapons? Is there a norm or taboo against their use comparable to those regarding nuclear or biological weapons? Are there military objectives that could usefully be served by RWs, or are the weapons fundamentally inefficient, easily countered, and dependent on too large an investment to justify their existence? Under what circumstances in the future might more states express interest in and/or introduce RWs into their military arsenals, and if the weapons were to proliferate, what would be the implications for nuclear deterrence policy? Finally, what means—including arms control—exist to mitigate the dangers associated with the production, deployment, and use of radiological weapons?

Methodology

This book addresses these and other questions by employing a comparative analysis of the previously underexplored cases of state-level RW programs in the United States, the Soviet Union, the United Kingdom, and Iraq, as well as the more ambiguous case of Egypt. We draw upon newly available archival material, interview data, and other primary sources to illuminate the drivers of and impediments to weapons innovation in this specific nuclear sector. Although the study is not principally devoted to theory building, it is informed by relevant theoretical and conceptual approaches in the fields of international relations and public policy, and it benefits especially from the literature on organizational change and weapons innovation—a literature to which the authors have previously contributed.[9] Its focused comparative analysis of RW developments across multiple countries, paired with an examination of the relationship between the rise and demise of RW programs and the fate of parallel chemical and/or nuclear weapons programs in the United States, Soviet Union, United Kingdom, Egypt, and Iraq, also enhances the generalizability of its findings—an important but often overlooked dimension of theory construction.

Although eclectic, our approach most closely resembles the method of structured focused comparison pioneered by Alexander George. Its intent is to hone and refine existing theories and conceptual frameworks by assessing their ability to explain the impact of different variables on policy behavior across multiple cases. By asking the same set of specific questions across several cases, one increases the generalizability of findings and the cumulation of knowledge.

Our research design also is informed by the conceptual framework proposed by Matthew Evangelista in his comparative analysis of U.S. and Soviet development of new military technologies, a framework that several of the authors have employed (in a modified form) productively in their own research on Soviet and Russian military innovation.[10] According to Evangelista, one can identify five different stages in the process of weapons innovation peculiar to each country. In the United States, these stages are "technocratic initiative," "consensus building," "promotion," "open window," and "high-level endorsement." Their counterparts in the Soviet Union are "stifled initiative," "preparatory measures," "high-level response," "mobilization," and "mass production."[11] Although this framework was conceived for the purpose of comparing and contrasting military innovation in the two Cold War rivals, it also provides a lens through which to examine alternative drivers of and impediments to the innovation process in other countries.

For example, drawing on Evangelista's hypotheses for the present study raises the following questions: Did the impetus for the pursuit of new weapons systems by the United Kingdom, Iraq, and Egypt more closely resemble the U.S. pattern in which a push for new weapons technology arises from below (i.e., from scientists and the military officials with whom they interact) or the Soviet model in which directives typically come from above in response to technological developments abroad? Similarly, did internal factors involving bureaucratic consensus building and policy advocacy in these states usually precede a formal decision for advanced research and development or production, as is often the case in the United States, or did they more closely resemble the post-adoption mobilization/implementation phase characteristic of the Soviet weapons innovation process? Finally, for purposes of illustration, to what extent and at what stage of the RW innovation cycle in different countries do perceptions of external threat become salient? Do they more closely resemble the case of the United States where the perception of an external RW threat was largely irrelevant to the innovation process or the case of the Soviet Union in which concerns about U.S. interest in RWs precipitated research and development in this area? Or is it the case that the pursuit of RWs in the United Kingdom, Egypt, and Iraq was shaped by factors different from those Evangelista considers in his analysis of U.S. and Soviet military innovation? In short, while it is not our intent to apply Evangelista's framework explicitly in our analysis, his concepts and generalizations provide a useful point of departure for identifying potential drivers and inhibitors behind different national actors' decisions to embark on, develop, and subsequently abandon their respective RW programs.

Given our frequent use of the term *innovation*, it is important to define the concept and to distinguish it from two other terms often used in discussions about the adoption of new weapons systems: *invention* and *diffusion*. Although there is no standard definition of these terms, even within a military context, we treat *invention* as the process by which a new idea or concept is created, *innovation* as the process by which an invention is translated into a tangible product and adopted by an organization, and *diffusion* as the process by which an idea or product spreads to or is emulated by another organization. Invention thus precedes innovation, but diffusion does not presuppose adoption of the new idea for a weapon system. This distinction is important in understanding the rise and abandonment of RWs in the cases under review, as RWs as a concept appear to have diffused from the United States to the Soviet Union (and to other countries), although the innovation never really took hold in either country's military in the form of mass production and deployment.

Another important definitional question is what constitutes a radiological weapon. During the early years of the nuclear age, RWs were often considered a subset of nuclear weapons, but they were never precisely defined. For example, in 1948, the United Nations described "radioactive material weapons" alongside "atomic explosive weapons" and "lethal chemical and biological weapons" as types of weapons of mass destruction, but without elaboration. Thirty years later, ambiguity associated with the term contributed to the difficulty in gaining international support for the draft U.S.-Soviet convention on the prohibition of radiological weapons.[12]

The authors of this volume define a radiological weapon as one designed to disperse radioactive material in the absence of a nuclear detonation. This standard definition encompasses a variety of weapons, which state actors have contemplated, pursued, or in several instances tested, including those intended to produce mass casualties and others designed for area denial and sabotage missions. Although we focus on state-level RW programs, the definition is consistent with devices and techniques usually associated with nonstate actors, including radiological dispersal and emission devices,[13] often misleadingly referred to as "dirty bombs." In all instances, the weapons make use of fission products or irradiated isotopes.

The one instance in which we depart from the standard definition of RWs is in our discussion of some nuclear bomb designs intended primarily to create added radioactive fallout. These include "salted bombs," which enhance the normal nuclear weapon fallout by surrounding the core of the nuclear device with neutron-absorbing metal.[14] They should not be confused with enhanced radiation weapons such as "neutron bombs," which rely on bursts of high energy neutrons rather than radioactive fallout to achieve their lethal effects.[15]

An additional methodological issue that may be obvious but still should be highlighted involves the primary level of analysis in our research—that is the nation state. Although we will have reason to look below this level at individuals and organizations involved in the formulation and implementation of policy related to radiological weapons, we consciously have chosen to avoid an analysis of non-state-actor pursuit of radiological dispersal devices (RDDs). That facet of nuclear terrorism is an important subject but one that has received much attention by scholars and experts in governments and international organizations since September 11, 2001.[16] In contrast, there is a dearth of research on state-level RW programs, which differ significantly from those involving non-state actors with respect to motivations for acquisition and use, technical requisites for production, storage, and delivery, the intended target set, and the magnitude of potential loss of human life. For example, although a non-state actor would have little prospect of employing an RDD to kill large numbers of individuals, it might perceive the device as an effective means to instill mass panic among a civilian target population, assuming that were an objective of the terrorist organization. For that purpose, one would not need a sophisticated dispersal device or a large amount of highly radioactive material. Smaller radioactive sources that are widely used commercially in medicine, industry, agriculture, and scientific research could suffice.[17] In contrast, state actors, who are interested in RWs for military missions such as area denial, will require much more difficult-to-produce radionuclides with very specific characteristics.[18] In other words, while the basic principles of radiological dispersal may be similar for would-be state and non-state actors, the motivations, costs, benefits, and alternative means available to inflict damage are very different. As such, a finding that no national actors to date have elected to deploy RWs, while encouraging, is neither a guarantee that this condition will persist indefinitely nor reason to believe that the factors responsible for state abstinence will have much bearing on the behavior of non-state actors.

A final methodological consideration concerns sources. In the U.S. case study, we relied heavily on unclassified and declassified government documents. An especially valuable resource was the final report of the Advisory Committee on Human Radiation Experiments, released by President Bill Clinton in October 1995 under Executive Order 12958. Other important primary-source materials included correspondence and analyses by early U.S. RW enthusiasts. Much of this material was obtained during visits to the U.S. National Archives in College Park, Maryland, the Library of Congress, the University of California Berkeley's Bancroft Library, and the New York Public Library.

We faced greater challenges in securing comparable information about the Soviet, British, Iraqi, and Egyptian radiological weapons programs, given the relative paucity of accessible primary-source material. We were able to compensate in part for this deficit in the Soviet case by distilling a great deal of relevant information on the program's origins and structure from declassified Russian-language documents on the "USSR Atomic History" section of Rosatom's digital library website. We also benefited from the investigative reports on the Soviet RW program published in Russian by the Bellona Foundation, as well as retrospectives written by Soviet participants in the testing of radiological weapons.

Much of our analysis of the British case is informed by a close reading of declassified documents from the UK National Archives in London, access to which was restricted without explanation in 2018 before being restored just as mysteriously in 2020. These documents were supplemented by newspaper accounts, secondary historical accounts of the British nuclear and other nonconventional weapons programs, and an important recent scholarly publication in the journal *War in History*.[19]

One might have expected it to have been easier to investigate the Iraqi RW program given the extraordinary investigations into Iraq nonconventional programs conducted by the UN Special Commission on Iraq (UNSCOM). While we made use of various UNSCOM reports and declassified U.S. intelligence documents, there is surprisingly little material available directly related to Saddam Hussein's RW efforts. Also, regrettably, some of the UNSCOM and International Atomic Energy Agency inspectors with whom we spoke, including very senior officials, either were unfamiliar with the specifics of the RW program or had poor recollections about Iraq's work in that domain. These factors may explain in part why prior scholarly accounts of Iraqi nuclear activities largely gloss over the RW program.

If well-documented information generally is difficult to come by regarding four indisputable state RW programs, the facts surrounding the Egyptian case are exceptionally hard to distill. In an effort to unravel the many intertwined strands of the story, some of which appear to have been intentionally woven in order to disguise the true nature of the fabric, we have relied on Austrian, German, and Swiss court documents, declassified U.S. intelligence reports, publicly available Israeli government accounts, contemporaneous media accounts, and biographies of some of the relevant actors. While some pertinent facts remain obscure, we have compiled the most comprehensive accounting of Egyptian RW efforts to date.

Prior Scholarship on the Sources of Military Innovation[20]

A major impetus for this book was the paucity of scholarship on, or even descriptive accounts of, prior state actions to pursue RW programs. These efforts ranged from informal consideration of the concept to R & D efforts, to production and testing of the weapons. Although there is no evidence that radiological weapons were ever deployed as operational systems in any country's military arsenal, knowledge to that effect was, as best we can discern, rarely the subject of examination by either government analysts or scholars. It is not surprising, therefore, that prior to the authors' research, no comparative study was undertaken of the dynamics of weapons innovation related to RWs.

More difficult to explain is the paucity of comparative research on the broader topic of military innovation, especially that involving the weapons systems of the relatively small number of nuclear weapons possessors. While perceived limitations of data access may account in part for this research deficit, it also probably results from the preponderance of work on the subject by U.S. scholars, who naturally display a U.S.-Eurocentric bias in terms of case selection.

Despite overall limitations in the scope and variety of scholarship on military innovation, one can identify a robust literature drawn primarily from

U.S. cases. Explanations for the origins, adoption, and retention or termination of different types of weapons can be grouped into at least five categories: international security imperatives, bureaucratic political determinants, scientific and technological breakthroughs, economic resources and organizational capacity, and status and prestige.[21] Insights from these categories of explanations relevant to the subject of radiological weapons are summarized below. Their relative explanatory power for specific instances of RW innovation, as well as their more general applicability across different country cases, are examined in subsequent chapters.

International Security Imperatives

Historically, the dominant explanation for military innovation has focused on the international security environment and is heavily influenced by neorealist assumptions. Perceived threats from adversaries, a need to engage in balancing behavior, and the operation of action-reaction dynamics are among the presumed drivers of decisions to acquire new weapons systems, which may have military rationales as varied as deterrence, compellence, or actual warfighting needs. A common element among most studies emphasizing external security considerations is the insight that contending states will emulate one another's innovations in what often appears to be an action-reaction process. As Stephen Rosen puts it, "innovations in one nation will trigger matching or responsive innovations in another."[22] An important subsidiary thesis governing the military innovation diffusion process noted by Rosen is that "the link between the activities in the competing nations is the network of military technical intelligence."[23]

Bureaucratic Political Determinants

Many security-oriented explanations of foreign policy decisions in general and weapons procurement outcomes in particular are vulnerable to criticism about their neglect of internal factors. In response to this perceived shortcoming, a rich literature on domestic sources of foreign policy—and weapons acquisition—developed, drawing heavily on organizational theory and public policy analysis. Especially influential was the early work on bureaucratic politics and organizational processes by Morton Halperin and Graham Allison.[24] They demonstrated convincingly that policy outcomes often are suboptimal from the standpoint of the government as a whole and cannot be explained adequately without reference to the individual and organizational actors involved in what is fundamentally an intranational political bargaining process. In other words, while technological breakthroughs and perceptions of external threat may influence an organization's interest in considering new weapons systems, the most important factors determining military innovation (or the lack thereof) are the personal and organizational interests, frames of reference, and influence of the key players involved in the decision-making process, including the often-overlooked implementation phase.[25]

Scientific and Technological Breakthroughs

Another explanation for military innovation (and arms racing), which usually emphasizes domestic considerations, focuses on science, scientists, and technology as catalysts for the development of new weapons. Although far from uniform in perspective, this school of thought often highlights supply-side, "technology push" factors.[26] According to one prominent proponent of this category of explanation, "Ideas for a new weapon system derived in the first place, not from the military, but from different groups of scientists and technologists who are concerned to replace or improve old weapon systems."[27] One can regard such scientists as change agents or "technological entrepreneurs" committed to promoting new weapons technologies in the face of both indifference and bureaucratic resistance to change.[28] One of the most important insights derived from this school of thought is the key roles scientists play in giving rise to new ideas for weapons systems and advocating for their development and adoption.[29]

Economic Resources and Organizational Capacity

A number of studies of weapons innovation emphasize the impact of economic factors. These explanations range from the financial resources at the disposal of the organization to the nature of the state's economic system, to the role attributed to the military-industrial complex and defense contractors.[30] They also may focus on less tangible organizational resources such as the capacity of a military organization to change, a capacity that may be influenced by economic factors but also may reflect the size, age, and culture of an organization.[31] According to one of the most well-developed theories emphasizing both economic and other organizational resources, military innovators must possess both the financial capital to acquire new technology and the internal capacity to adopt the innovation, which may involve major changes in operating behavior.[32]

Status and Prestige

A subset of scholarship on weapons proliferation, arms racing, and military innovation highlights the importance of international status and prestige as a motivating factor for weapons acquisition, especially for emerging powers.[33] This literature suggests that states may covet certain military capabilities not so much to counter specific threats as to gain status, which can "increase autonomy and influence, while also helping a nation feel more secure in its environs."[34] Yet, considerations of status have been found to vary in importance, depending on the type of weapon. For example, Brad Roberts observes that they drove the acquisition of conventional weapons by newly decolonized nations in the early 1960s but failed to account for states' pursuit of chemical or biological weapons.[35] In addition, a number of studies indicate that nuclear weapons may be seen by some developing states as symbols of scientific knowhow and modernization and as a way to command the attention of and assistance from industrialized nations.[36] By the same token, other studies have found that would-be great powers may regard nuclear weapons as a prerequisite for that status.[37] Similarly, there is evidence that ballistic missile acquisition has been motivated by a desire to gain prestige—for instance, among states in the Middle East.[38]

Despite the large number and diverse nature of studies undertaken to probe the emergence of and resistance to new weapons, the field still lacks a robust theory of weapons innovation that has broad explanatory and predictive power. Even the most sophisticated theoretical approaches, such as Michael Horowitz's "adoption-capacity" theory, leave some variables underspecified, require more information about organizational capacity than is often available, and are better equipped to explain the interstate diffusion process than the original decision to adopt a new weapon system. Indeed, although there has been a proliferation of excellent case studies of weapons innovation decisions over the past half century, explanations for the origins and outcomes of weapons decisions often are not cumulative and frequently are contradictory.

These same theoretical limitations are apparent with respect to innovation regarding radiological weapons, and no single theory or conceptual framework adequately explains the rise and demise of radiological weapons programs in the five countries we have examined. Collectively, however, they provide numerous insights into the dynamics of policymaking involving what once was regarded as a promising new military technology. Application of the method of structured, focused comparison to the cases of the United States, the Soviet Union, the United Kingdom, Egypt, and Iraq also enables us to tease out the similarities and differences in their life spans.

A Preview

In addition to this introduction, the book consists of five case studies of national RW programs and a forward-looking conclusion. Chapter 1 examines the U.S. experience with radiological weapons. It depicts the unusual parallelism in time and substance between the emergence of RWs in science fiction and U.S. popular culture more generally and the appearance of U.S. governmental interest in RWs. This chapter then follows the evolution of the U.S. RW program during and after the Second World War and analyzes the factors driving the program at different phases of its development. Although scientific-technocratic advocates of RWs were able to persuade key military-technical stakeholders to implement a U.S. RW program, including an active testing phase, they were unsuccessful in securing broader support for the new weapons technology among the military services, Congress, and the executive branch. They also neglected to exploit external threats to justify the new weapon's adoption or to secure high-level endorsement for the novel RW technology, outcomes that were influenced in part by faulty U.S. intelligence about the state of the Soviet RW program. These shortcomings, compounded by technical deficiencies in the production process and the lack of a compelling military mission, resulted in the RW program losing out in the competition for financial resources with the more established chemical weapons program and the rapidly expanding U.S. nuclear-weapons complex.

The book's second case study, chapter 2, examines the Soviet RW experience. Unbeknownst to U.S. intelligence, the Soviet Union actively pursued radiological weapons for approximately a decade beginning in 1947. Drawing extensively on Russian-language sources, we chronicle the underexplored origins and evolution of the Soviet RW program, a novel weapons program that in many ways resembled its U.S. counterpart. As was the case in the United States, it appears that Soviet interest in the possible military applications of radioactive material also can be traced to the early 1940s. Although the contours of the U.S. and Soviet programs did not follow identical paths, both eventually suffered similar fates. Changes in perceived threats, the departure of key RW advocates, competition from chemical and nuclear weapons, bureaucratic barriers to weapons innovation within the Soviet military-industrial complex, and, to a lesser extent, health and safety considerations all contributed to the gradual demise of the Soviet RW program, but not before the Soviet Union had tested prototype radiological weapons. Although we cannot point to a Soviet science fiction counterpart to Robert Heinlein's "Solution Unsatisfactory," at least some members of the Soviet RW testing program were consultants to the 1953 science fiction film *Serebristaya pil'* (Silver dust), a heavy-handed depiction of alleged U.S. efforts to develop radiological air bombs containing a silver-gray radioactive dust that was tested on innocent civilians.

The United States, the Soviet Union, and the United Kingdom were the first three states to develop and successfully test nuclear weapons. Perhaps not surprisingly, they also were the first three countries actively to pursue radiological weapons. As such, the third case study in our book, chapter 3, is an analysis of the largely unknown history of the United Kingdom's RW program.[39] Although there is little evidence the United Kingdom seriously contemplated the pursuit of a radiological weapon during World War II, a small number of British military officials and scientists were aware of the potential military implications of RWs and did not rule out the possibility that Nazi Germany might use radioactive fission products for both offensive and defensive purposes. Interestingly, one of the British scientists involved in reviewing a U.S. report about possible German work on radiological weapons was the Soviet spy Alan Nunn May, who reportedly communicated this information to Soviet intelligence. The more famous Soviet atomic spy, Klaus Fuchs, also was privy to British thinking about RWs in the post–World War

II period prior to his arrest in February 1950, but it is unclear how much importance he attached to this military innovation or if he passed along any intelligence related to RWs to his Soviet handlers.

As in the cases of the United States and the Soviet Union, a few individuals in the United Kingdom played oversized roles in advocating for RWs. Eventually, however, they all acknowledged the shortcomings of RWs when compared to chemical weapons, not to mention nuclear weapons, which the United Kingdom first tested in Western Australia in October 1952. Although there is documentary evidence of discussions within the Atomic Energy Research Establishment about the merits of RWs beyond this date, for all practical purposes, the advent of British nuclear weapons marked the end of the United Kingdom's interest in radiological weapons.

By the end of the 1950s, the large-scale radiological weapons programs of the United States and the Soviet Union had run their course, as had the more modest exploration by the United Kingdom. If any other threshold nuclear state pursued RWs during this period, evidence has not yet come to light. However, at the beginning of the 1960s, interest in RWs emerged in a new region, the Middle East. Chapter 4 examines the rudimentary and short-lived RW program of Egypt (known as the United Arab Republic from 1958 to 1971). It attempts to untangle the complex web of Israeli allegations, U.S intelligence assessments, and Austrian, German, and Swiss police and court records regarding Egyptian efforts to acquire radiological sources from abroad. While much of the evidence regarding an Egyptian RW program remains circumstantial and rests to a large degree on Israeli claims and the testimony of Otto Joklik—an enigmatic, self-proclaimed arms merchant, former military officer in the German army, and likely Israeli intelligence asset—there is no doubt that Gamal Abdel Nasser's Egypt sought to develop nonconventional weapons and means for their delivery. For that purpose, Egypt recruited a large cadre of expatriate German scientists, engineers, and military personnel. According to depositions and documents collected by Swiss investigators outlining Joklik's work in Egypt and reviewed by the authors of this book, he had been involved in two Egyptian weapons projects, one of which—Project Ibis—was intended to produce radiological artillery shells. Although U.S. intelligence was skeptical of both Israeli claims of the Egyptian threat and Joklik's testimony, suspicions about Egyptian intentions lingered and made the headlines in November 1963. In an interview with C. L. Sulzberger of the *New York Times*, former Israeli prime minister David Ben-Gurion voiced concern that Egypt, with India's assistance, was seeking to develop warheads for its rockets.[40] Although the interview published in the *Times* does not specify the kind of warhead being pursued, Sulzberger subsequently reported that Ben-Gurion had in mind a missile equipped with "nuclear garbage."[41] What is perhaps most interesting about the inchoate Egyptian RW program—and what sets it apart from those of other states—is that it was almost entirely dependent on foreign assistance, was conceived of primarily for purposes of countering a regional adversary's military applications of nuclear energy, appeared to have developed as a "special project" driven by an individual technological "entrepreneur," and was abandoned for reasons unrelated to progress in the pursuit of a nuclear weapon.

While the Egyptian RW program was short-lived, made limited headway, and might be mistaken for a convoluted spy movie, Saddam Hussein's pursuit of radiological weapons was very real indeed. The book's last case study, in chapter 5, analyzes the heretofore untold story of Iraq's efforts to develop and test RWs before abandoning the program. It probes the factors behind Iraq's quest for RWs, the relationship of the program to the Iran-Iraq war and perceived Iraqi military requirements, the role played by individual advocates (especially Hussein Kamel, Saddam Hussein's son-in-law and head of Iraq's Military Industrialization Corporation), the influence of bureaucratic-institutional factors—including the unusually welcoming environment for scientific entrepreneurs to pursue novel weapons programs—and the technical and political impediments that ultimately led to the demise of the program. The chapter highlights important similarities and differences between the Iraqi program and the corresponding U.S., Soviet, British, and Egyptian programs. The focus on a non-nuclear weapon state also is important for the lessons it offers to future would-be RW proliferators about the obstacles they are likely to confront should they embark on an RW program. Finally, the study of the advanced but ultimately aborted Iraqi effort to acquire a novel weapon system addresses the question of why the Iraqi endeavor has largely been ignored or, at best, treated as a footnote, whether in declassified intelligence reports, the memoirs of scientists involved in Iraq's nuclear weapons program, or the scholarly accounts of Saddam Hussein's quest for WMD.

Having described and analyzed all known prior cases of state-level radiological weapons programs, the book, in its conclusion, highlights similarities and differences across the programs with an eye to identifying more general explanations for the rise, evolution, and demise of weapons innovation involving RWs. It also explores what future circumstances might encourage additional states to pursue RWs and the how the proliferation of such weapons would impact nuclear deterrence and the international nuclear nonproliferation regime. This discussion takes on special importance in the aftermath of the Russian invasion of Ukraine in 2022 and the need to reexamine a number of prevailing assumptions about the utility of nuclear weapons and the operation of nuclear deterrence in a radically different international security environment. The chapter concludes with a discussion of practical steps that might usefully be taken by members of the international community to reduce the likelihood that there will be a resurgence of interest in and pursuit of radiological weapons.

ONE
The United States

U.S. interest in radiological weapons dates to the early 1940s, when scientists and government officials first grappled with the possible military applications of the rapid developments in nuclear science. Radiological warfare was frequently mentioned alongside nuclear explosive bombs, nuclear-fueled aircraft, and nuclear power generation as one the most promising uses for these new scientific discoveries. Although the Manhattan Project ended up focusing almost entirely on "the bomb" to the exclusion of radiological weapons (RWs), this outcome was by no means inevitable. Rather, the rise and demise of the U.S. RW effort was shaped by individual and institutional preferences as well as chance.

Conceptualization of Radiological Weapons

Writers of fiction often anticipate major innovations in military science, and this is certainly the case with respect to atomic warfare. The first literary reference to nuclear weapons is usually attributed to British author H. G. Wells, whose 1914 novel *The World Set Free* envisaged cities laid waste by atomic explosives decades before their use in Hiroshima and Nagasaki.[1] Radiological weapons, for their part, did not make their science fiction debut until much later, in May 1941. As a result, and in contrast to nuclear weapons, RWs entered the popular discourse at virtually the same time that military planners in the U.S. and elsewhere were beginning to contemplate their actual development and use.

These parallel explorations of radiological weapons in both the public and classified domains were an unusual feature of the U.S. RW experience. Their depiction in speculative fiction appears to have been the brainchild of John W. Campbell, Jr., the prolific but controversial American writer and editor who was responsible for nurturing the careers of some of the best-known science fiction authors in Western literature.[2] Campbell took over as editor of the monthly magazine *Astounding Science Fiction* in 1938, placing him at the forefront of science fiction's emerging golden age just as discoveries by nuclear scientists raised the theoretical possibility of atomic warfare.[3] In this role, he drew frequently upon his undergraduate knowledge of physics to produce stories for a readership that included Albert Einstein, Edward Teller, and Wernher von Braun, among other elites of the U.S. military-scientific community.[4]

Campbell found a willing partner in these efforts in Robert Heinlein, a retired naval engineer who, by 1939, was embarking on a second career as a science fiction writer.[5] Their first foray into nuclear science fiction, Heinlein's short story about workplace tensions at a nuclear reactor, "Blowups Happen," appeared in *Astounding Science Fiction* in September 1940. Inspiration for the plot had struck Campbell after "a half-day up at Columbia," which he spent "talking cyclotrons and atomic power to the nuclear research men up there."[6] He wrote to Heinlein, suggesting a story about the psychological challenges facing the new generation of nuclear engineers, who will "drink heavily, off-duty at any rate," receive "terrific salaries," and "nearly all go mad one way or another after about 10 years of work."[7]

Heinlein was receptive to Campbell's proposal but apprehensive about his lack of knowledge of physics. He felt he was "several years out of date" on the subject and requested "two or three up-to-date books, or other sources, suitable for a quick refresher course."[8] As Campbell was quick to point out, however, the pace at which research on nuclear physics was developing in 1940 was so fast that it was impossible for scientific publishing to keep up.

"No one dares bring out a book that takes six months from beginning writing to finished publication," he informed Heinlein, since "half the remarks made would probably have been proven untrue by that time."[9]

A more ready source of information for both this and other examples of Campbell and Heinlein's early atomic fiction was the circle of close contacts they maintained in the nuclear research community. The two men often probed these individuals for "dope" about the details in their stories, although their efforts became less fruitful as secrecy around the atomic bomb project increased.[10] For Heinlein, help came most dependably from Robert Cornog, a key member of the Manhattan Project who was partially responsible for discovering the radioactivity of tritium and later served as chief engineer of the atomic bomb development team's ordnance division. As Heinlein observed decades later in 1977, it was Cornog who afforded him "first-hand and most recent scientific knowledge" about the military uses of uranium at a time "before security restrictions were placed on the matter."[11]

Campbell, meanwhile, had his own contacts within the atomic energy research community with whom he had at least semi-regular interaction. On October 29, 1940, for instance, he was visited by Jack Hatcher and a Dr. [Don M.] Yost[12]—two researchers whom he described to Heinlein as being "involved in biochemical work with radioactive isotopes" and "closely associated with the work being done on U-235."[13] Although Hatcher was well known to Campbell, having contributed nonfiction essays to *Astounding Science Fiction*,[14] it is not clear to what extent Campbell was familiar with Yost's research agenda. In fact, Yost received several federal contracts between 1940 and 1942 for work on chemical warfare under the auspices of the National Defense Research Council (later the Office of Scientific Research and Development)[15] and directed field research on the dispersal of offensive chemical weapons at the newly established Dugway Proving Ground—where the first radiological weapons effects test would later be carried out.[16]

Perhaps inspired by this visit but just as likely by grim developments in the European theater, Campbell sent Heinlein a new story idea for a "socioeconomic-political situation that looks rather savage and rather apt to come up" in mid-December 1940.[17] He outlined how radioactive dust might be used for area denial purposes over a period from 1940 until 1977, first by Nazis, then by English Communists, then by "democracy lovers," then, ultimately, the entire world.[18] Although he quibbled with some of the non-science-fiction details of the plot, Heinlein was enthusiastic about the idea and, within days of receiving Campbell's letter, had begun to prepare a draft. "The reason for the speed," Heinlein explained to Campbell, was that "this is another one of those stories that is so extremely topical that it must be published as soon as possible after it is written."[19]

The result—"Solution Unsatisfactory"—appeared in the May 1941 issue of *Astounding Science Fiction* under Heinlein's pseudonym, Anson MacDonald. Set in the midst of the Second World War, the story depicts the development by a team of U.S. scientists engaged by the War Department of uranium-derivative "deadly artificial radioactives," research that was pursued after work on nuclear explosives utilizing U-235 was discontinued.[20] For some, the production of this "radioactive dust" was seen as a means by which the United States could put an end to the war and declare a Pax Americana—"a loaded gun held at the head of every man, woman, and child on the globe!"[21] Others, however, foresaw a radioactive dust arms race in which the whole world would resemble "a room full of men, each armed with a loaded .45." According to the protagonist, "They can't get out of the room and each one is dependent on the good will of every other one to stay alive. All offense and no defense."[22]

It is unclear whether the U.S. pursuit of radiological weapons was in any way influenced by Heinlein and Campbell's depiction of RWs and their potential military uses. Yet, according to physicist and science fiction writer Gregory Benford, who spent the early years of his career at Lawrence Livermore National Laboratory, "Solution Unsatisfactory" was well-known among Manhattan Project physicists. Benford recounts how Edward Teller showed him his copy of the story and remarked upon the uncanny accuracy with which Heinlein appeared to predict the events of World War II. According to Benford, Teller and his colleagues saw the tale as a "sobering warning": "ultimate weapons lead to a strategic standoff with no way back—a solution unsatisfactory."[23]

Just two months after Heinlein's story appeared in print, Campbell himself published a nonfiction, if sensationalist, cover story entitled "Is Death Dust America's Secret Weapon?" in the entertainment magazine *PIC*.[24] The article is notable in a number of respects, including its observation of the "world-wide silence on atomic experiments" since the summer of 1940 and its captioned photos of a cyclotron, a Van de Graaff high-voltage "atom breaker," Dr. Harold Urey (described as a researcher at Columbia working on the separation of "heavy water"), and Dr. Ernest O. Lawrence (with the caption "Will Dr. Lawrence succeed in harnessing U-235?").[25] The article also presciently noted that the world war (in which the United States was not yet directly involved) would be dramatically impacted by discoveries in the laboratory and would entail a race for uranium ore. The article's main message, however, was to highlight the potential for development of a synthetic, radioactive "death dust," whose dispersal would paralyze cities. Beneath an artist's conception of a city sprayed with the dust is the caption: "Even rats wouldn't survive the blue, luminescent radioactive dust. Vultures would be poisoned by their own appetites."[26]

Ironically, the first known reference to RWs in a government document is in May 1941—the same month and year as the publication date for the Heinlein story in *Astounding Science Fiction* and seven months before Pearl Harbor. The document identified three possible military aspects of atomic fission, the first of which was "production of violently radioactive materials . . . carried by airplanes to be scattered as bombs over enemy territory."[27] The report estimated that "radioactive dust would need a year's preparation after 'the first successful production of a chain reaction,' which meant 'not earlier than 1943.'"[28] A follow-up report, authored by physicists Eugene Wigner and Henry Smyth the day after Germany's declaration of war against the United States, presented two competing visions of how the Germans might employ fission products in warfare.[29] The first, proposed by Ernest Lawrence, was as "Radioactive Poisons," and it resembled in very broad strokes the sort of weapon eventually developed and tested by the U.S. The second, a more novel proposal by Leo Szilard, involved a radioactive "neutron ship" which would be powered by a dirty-uranium engine that would contaminate the water through which it sailed. Szilard's concept was considered a "less serious menace" than radioactive poisons and is not mentioned further in the U.S. documentary record. Nevertheless, echoes of it rebounded in 2016 with Russia's revelation of the so-called Status-6 or Poseidon nuclear torpedo.

These reports led U.S. scientists, including those at the University of Chicago's Metallurgical Laboratory (Met Lab), to consider the possibility that Nazi Germany might use the fission products of a potential nuclear reactor to breed radioactive isotopes that could be mixed with dust or liquid particles for dispersal in a bomb. The United States decided to initiate further study of the military uses of RWs and possible defenses against them.[30]

Although the precise chronology of events related to the serious consideration of RWs in 1943 is unclear, the assignment fell to a subcommittee of the S-1 Committee, the successor to the Advisory Committee on Uranium. The subcommittee produced a short memo titled "Use of Radioactive Material As a Military Weapon," which foresaw two principal military applications: (1) "as a terrain contaminating material" and (2) "as a gas warfare instrument."[31] In the first case, the subcommittee estimated that spreading radioactive products on the ground might provide area denial for weeks or months. In the second case, it anticipated that radioactive material might be ground into microscopic particles to form dust and smoke, which could be "distributed by a ground-fired projectile, land vehicles, or aerial bombs."[32] The subcommittee, however, pointed to several factors that might offset the effectiveness of radioactive dust or smoke: the potential for rapid dissipation due to wind and the "shielding effects of buildings." Although the subcommittee was divided over the likelihood of German use against Allied forces in the fall of 1943, all members thought it unlikely that a radioactive weapon would be used against the continental United States. Nevertheless, the subcommittee was sufficiently concerned about the use of radioactive material as a weapon in Europe to recommend creation of a special committee to prepare a report on defensive measures.[33] Interestingly, the subcommittee itself did not directly advocate development of RWs by the United States but suggested that, if military authorities wished to be ready to employ radiological weapons in response to enemy first use, then "studies on the topic should be started immediately."[34]

In contrast to this cautious assessment of RWs, Manhattan Project physicists Enrico Fermi and Robert Oppenheimer were enthusiastic about their offensive potential. In April 1943, Fermi privately suggested to Oppenheimer that fission products—most likely strontium-90—be used to poison the German food supply. Oppenheimer swore Fermi to silence and even kept the idea from subcommittee member Arthur Compton, but he discussed the concept with fellow physicist Edward Teller, as well as with General Leslie

Groves, director of the Manhattan Project.[35] In Oppenheimer's view, the plan made sense only if it were able to poison a half million men.[36] There is no indication if he had in mind only combatants.

There is no evidence that anything ever came of Fermi's plan directly. Although Groves was persuaded of the need to study the potential of radiological weapons, he disclaimed interest in their offensive use.[37] There also is no indication that either President Franklin Roosevelt or Secretary of War Henry Stimson were apprised of or were interested in the military applications of radioactive material, although they may have been aware of Operation Peppermint—an Allied plan to counter possible German use of radioactive fission products to defend against the Normandy invasion.[38]

Although most of the limited U.S. research on RWs during the war was defense oriented, the ideas for offensive use broached by Fermi resonated with one individual with whom Oppenheimer interacted: Joseph Gilbert Hamilton. He was an assistant professor of medicine at the University of California's Berkeley Radiation Laboratory, who, since 1942, had been investigating the biological effects of uranium fission products.[39] In the same letter to Fermi in which Oppenheimer cautioned against pursuing the food poison plan unless it could be done on a huge scale, he mentioned his plans to pursue the matter "a little more deeply with Hamilton, although of course only on the psychological side."[40]

Hamilton and Oppenheimer exchanged correspondence, but it is unclear if they ever discussed in person Fermi's plan for radiological poisoning.[41] What is known is that Hamilton, who at the time was conducting radiological experiments on both humans and animals, was excited about the possibilities for offensive use of radiological poisons and communicated his ideas to other scientists, including Robert Stone at the Met Lab. As early as May 27, 1943, in a letter to Stone, Hamilton outlined the purported military virtues of using radioactive material to contaminate the air and poison food stocks. Stone, for his part, requested more detailed information from Hamilton about the effects of the material and the optimal concentrations.[42]

However, despite the enthusiasm shown by a few key personnel for offensive RWs, the consensus of scientists and planners involved with the Manhattan Project assigned them relatively low priority compared to the atom bomb. A case in point is Eugene Wigner and Leo Szilard's memo to

Arthur Compton promoting their proposed reactor design. Wigner and Szilard included "production of radioactive poisons" as one of the advantages of their bismuth-cooled reactor, but they noted in the memo's introductory paragraph that should Compton wish to shorten the memo, the section on radioactive poisons could be removed.[43] The Met Lab included both defensive and offensive radiological warfare on its list of research objectives as late as December 1943,[44] and it is possible that a few scientists working on the Manhattan Project at other facilities also explored different facets of radiological weapons. For all practical purposes, however, research on the subject in the United States was put on hold during the last years of the war. The pause, however, was short.

Development of the U.S. Radiological Weapons Program

The process by which RWs gained traction in the United States is largely consistent with the first two phases of the U.S. weapons innovation process described by Evangelista. In the first, "technocratic initiative" phase, scientists discover new technical possibilities and advocate their military applications; in the second, "consensus building" phase, they collaborate with military associates to build broader bureaucratic support and secure R & D funding.[45] In fact, many of the key early proponents of RWs were scientists who had been engaged in radiochemistry and radiological defense during World War II. Hamilton and Stone, for example, pressed for more work on RWs; Teller was enamored by their possibilities; and Lawrence was an ardent supporter. The circle of proponents grew to include military figures who had previously not been directly involved in discussions about RWs. These included General Curtis LeMay, who, in August 1946, reportedly "urged consideration of the use of radioactive fission products from atomic piles," going so far as to suggest that they might be more effective weapons than atomic bombs.[46]

The period between Japan's defeat and the sunsetting of the Manhattan Project exemplified the technocratic initiative phase of U.S. RW pursuits. As funding for research and development dwindled due to postwar demobilization, prominent scientists jostled for bureaucratic support and military patronage for their research. Among the scientists impacted were those connected to Ernest Lawrence's research team at his sprawling laboratory complex at the University of California at Berkeley, one of the world's leading centers for the study of nuclear physics, radiochemistry, and the biological effects of radiation. In particular, the biological research of Dr. Joseph Hamilton had come under scrutiny as postwar Manhattan Project leadership began to look askance at Hamilton's infamous experiments involving the injection of human subjects with plutonium and other radioactive substances.[47] The documentary record suggests that Colonel K. D. Nichols, the incoming head of the Armed Forces Special Weapons Project (AFSWP), the successor agency to the Manhattan Project, agreed to continue funding Lawrence and Hamilton's research only so long as it would fit with the military mandate of the new organization.[48]

It was in this context that Hamilton sent a long memo to Nichols on December 31, 1946, the day before the Manhattan Project became the responsibility of the civilian Atomic Energy Commission (AEC). This memo would essentially become the foundational document of the U.S. RW program, with Hamilton making grand claims about the potential for RWs to revolutionize warfare. The memo enumerated "the major differences between chemical and radioactive poisons" and made a forceful case for the military advantages of RWs. These were alleged to include effective and persistent means of area denial, the difficulty of neutralizing the agents, and the unique suitability of the weapons to spread "consternation, as well as fear and apprehension" among a targeted civilian population.[49] Notably, while Hamilton's memo kick-started the investigation of the possibilities of RWs, the weapons he imagined in the memo hardly resembled those that would be developed and tested in ensuing years. Instead, the memo reads as a justification for the military applications of Hamilton's ongoing research, including gauging the effects of radiation deposits in human and animal tissue and the effect of radioactive contamination on plant life.

Nonetheless, throughout 1947, the AEC sought to operationalize the concepts described in Hamilton's memo. In April, Colonel William Hutchinson, formerly director of the Declassification Office for the Manhattan Project, made it clear in a memo to General James McCormack, director of Military Applications for the AEC, that the AFSWP was the appropriate organization to coordinate RW exploration and development. Hutchinson proposed an expert committee to begin study of RWs: he suggested himself and Hamilton, as well as John von Neumann, the theoretical physicist and mathematician who had previously studied radiological warfare and consulted on the subject.[50]

It is unclear if the proposed Hamilton–von Neumann committee ever met, but by 1948, the AEC had established its interest in RWs. In January, AEC general manager Carroll Wilson informed Hamilton that the AFSWP had established a staff section devoted to RWs,[51] and this group appointed a panel of civilian and military experts to explore the merits of an offensive RW program. The panel, chaired by Army Chemical Corps scientific advisor Albert Noyes, first met in May 1948. The assembled decision-makers, including AEC director David Lilienthal, Ernest Lawrence, General McCormack, and several scientist veterans of the Manhattan Project, concluded that RWs were worthy of further study to determine their military usefulness. Lawrence was a particularly staunch advocate, urging his fellow panel members to avoid drawing unfavorable comparisons between the nascent category of RWs and established weapons such as chemical and biological weapons.[52] During the subsequent summer, researchers at Oak Ridge National Laboratory conducted field tests addressing the problems of dispersal, diffusion, and dosimetry.[53]

Perhaps not surprisingly, the resurgence of interest in RWs in U.S. military circles during the second half of the 1940s was also reflected in popular culture. Although varying greatly in terms of accuracy, sensationalism, and advocacy, a spate of stories on RWs was published in such mainstream magazines as *Colliers*, *Coronet*, *Popular Science*, and *Time*, as well as several specialized journals such as the *Bulletin of the Atomic Scientists* and *Officer's Call*. These stories on occasion were not polemical,[54] but more often than not they trumpeted either the amazing potential of RWs to transform warfare or alter life on the planet. This tendency is reflected in titles such as "War without Death,"[55] "What Are We Doing about Our Deadly Atomic Garbage?,"[56] and "Our Silent Mystery Weapon: Death Sand."[57]

Probably the most widely read fictional depiction of RWs from this period, however, was a storyline in Al Capp's immensely popular comic strip *Li'l Abner* depicting the unanticipated effects of the aerial dumping of accumulated atomic rubbish on the population of the fictional community of Dogpatch.[58] Running from December 11, 1947, to January 24, 1948, it appeared at virtually the same time that the move toward establishing a dedicated RW program began to accelerate. This renewed interest in RWs displaced scientists with military officials as the prime movers of the program.

As a result of these bureaucratic changes, the proposed modalities and missions imagined for RWs became more limited and grounded in familiar military doctrine. The National Military Establishment's liaison to the AEC drafted a memo in May 1948 that illustrated this dynamic: the military recommended several possible avenues for RW research but stressed "feasibility" and a weapon that could be used when the employment of atomic bombs would be "uneconomical." The memo gives privilege of place to RWs as "limited area denial weapons"—that is, weapons that would be employed similarly to traditional chemical weapons.[59]

In August 1948, after accumulating data from the Oak Ridge tests, the committee led by Albert Noyes released a report to the Department of Defense in which it laid out its recommendations for an RW program. The report did not fully reflect the enthusiasm of Hamilton's earlier memo regarding the effectiveness and feasibility of RWs and completed the drift away from the strategic and mass-casualty weapons originally proposed by Hamilton.[60] It did, however, acknowledge that initial experiments were encouraging enough to recommend that the Defense Department pursue a full-fledged program to design and build radiological weapons. The panel examined various means of delivery and concluded that the most promising path was the use of munitions similar to those employed in the then-active U.S. chemical weapons program. As such, the Defense Department assigned responsibility for the design and testing of radiological dispersal devices to the Army Chemical Corps (ACC).

Proponents of RWs found an enthusiastic military partner in the ACC (formerly the Chemical Warfare Service), an organization that had been marginalized by the nonuse of chemical weapons during World War II and the emergence of the atomic bomb as a decisive weapon. Just days after atomic bombs were dropped on Hiroshima and Nagasaki, a high-ranking officer in the Chemical Warfare Service recommended to the CWS commander, General Alden Waitt, that their unit should "move into the atomic business."[61]

Responsibility for the RW mission offered the ACC a new bureaucratic raison d'être at a time when the atomic bomb posed a challenge to the organization's existence as a separate entity.[62] The new mission also provided the ACC with a greater profile and increased funding, albeit temporarily. In fiscal years 1950–53, RW Agents and RW Munitions were among the most generously funded ACC research and development projects.[63]

Shortly after the ACC was tasked with responsibility for RW development, it set about identifying an appropriate test site. After consideration of several military sites, it settled upon Dugway Proving Grounds, a U.S. Army facility about eighty-five miles from Salt Lake City, Utah.[64] The ACC constructed the necessary facilities for a permanent, large-scale test site, and Dr. Hamilton, Dr. Lawrence, and Glenn Seaborg visited in May 1949 to inspect the grounds and advise the ACC on radiation safety, particularly the danger to "the civilian population, its animal life, plant life, water supplies, etc."[65] Hamilton pointedly advised the ACC to inform the public of the hazards but to also say that the program was being conducted "primarily for setting up proper defense mechanisms for the civilian population."[66]

Having judged the safety precautions and public awareness campaign to be adequate, the ACC conducted its first-ever test of a prototype radiological munition at Dugway on October 22, 1949. The test munition was designated E59 and was dropped from a bomber. Details of the test are unavailable, but the munition apparently exceeded expectations. The "dissemination of particles was uniform and extended over an area 50% greater than anticipated."[67] A second test in December was also deemed "as successful as could be hoped," although the radioactive cloud dissipated much more quickly than in the first test.[68]

These early successful field tests emboldened the ACC and supportive scientists to conduct tests with ever-greater releases of radiation. In 1950, a test was planned that would release 7,500 curies of radiation.[69] In all, dozens of tests were likely conducted, although records of individual tests are spotty. The results of these tests were insufficient to counter the diminution of institutional support during this period for the Army RW program. As early as 1950, the program faced severe pushback: General McCormack considered the program not very promising and urged that the program be reduced in scope, if not entirely abandoned.[70] Powerful advocates in the scientific community, particularly Ernest Lawrence, were able to stave off the program's demise for a time. However, in 1954, the Weapons System Evaluation Group, a technical committee that appraised the effectiveness of weapons systems for the Department of Defense and Joint Chiefs of Staff, recommended a significant downgrade of the RW program given complications related to the "U.S. capability to produce RW agent material."[71] The program also was stripped of its mandate to produce radiological weapons for aircraft and guided missile delivery. Subsequent budget cuts further squeezed the program, and by 1956 the Army Chemical Corps' "Estimate of the CBR [Chemical, Biological, and Radiological] Situation" declared that "the sole United States ability in radiological warfare as presently defined is to produce contamination by the use of nuclear weapons."[72]

Correspondingly, by the mid-to-late 1950s, popular interest in RWs appeared to wane as well. Most news and fictional accounts about atomic weaponry and the effects of radiation came to focus predominantly on nuclear fission, the escalating U.S.-Soviet nuclear arms race, and the health effects of nuclear weapons tests. Pulp science fiction was not immune from this trend, which also was reflected in a surge of highly popular post-apocalyptic-themed novels and films such as *On the Beach*, *Alas Babylon*, *The Martian Chronicles*, and *A Canticle for Leibowitz*.[73] In short, just as science fiction foreshadowed U.S. government conceptions of atomic warfare, including radiological weapons, actual nuclear weapons developments shaped the contours of fiction and contributed to the diminished attention to RWs.

On the classified side, meanwhile, technocratic advocates of RWs were able to build a consensus among key military-technical stakeholders to pursue RWs, but they were stymied in their efforts to promote broader support for the new weapons technology among the military services, Congress, and the executive branch—the "promotion" phase in Evangelista's model of the U.S. weapons innovation process. They also failed to exploit external threats to justify the new weapon's adoption or to secure high-level endorsement for the novel RW technology. These failures resulted in the RW program losing out in the competition for both financial resources and attention within the military-industrial establishment. It is worth examining how competing military priorities and bureaucratic politics combined with technical obstacles to doom a program that had once enjoyed considerable support in some sectors of the military and scientific establishment and had been heralded in the popular press as foreshadowing "a way of waging *humane* warfare."[74]

The fate of the U.S. RW program turned in part on the decision to pursue a supply chain involving one specific radioisotope. When Hamilton first delineated his vision of radiological warfare in his 1946 memo, he described in lurid detail the dosages and effects of radiation poisoning, informed by his field of expertise as a radiobiologist. He neglected to mention what the source of the radiation might be. Thus, although he noted that the most appropriate isotopes for a weapon would be those "whose half-lives range from several weeks to the order of a year," he did not identify specific isotopes or explain how they would be produced.[75] The more cautious estimation of RWs in the Noyes Committee report of August 1948 is largely the result of a thorough inquiry into how the radioactive material would be generated. The nuclear engineers on the panel indicated that although nuclear reactors produced a multitude of radioactive isotopes as waste material, few possessed the required characteristics for an effective area-denial weapon: gamma-emitters with a half-life no shorter than several weeks and no longer than a year or so.[76] In fact, they identified only one fission product as being useful for RWs: zirconium-columbium.[77] Although this isotope was available in abundance in the nuclear waste generated by the plutonium production reactor at Hanford, Washington, extracting it was prohibitively difficult and expensive, and priority was given to employing plutonium separation for the production of material for nuclear explosives. Processing the nuclear waste would have required specialized facilities for dealing with dangerous levels of contamination and, as environmental surveys of the nuclear weapons program in the early Cold War era attest, the U.S. nuclear establishment of the time did not pay particular attention to the disposition of the waste produced by the program.[78]

An alternative means to obtain material for a radiological weapon was to irradiate an inert metal inside a nuclear reactor through neutron capture. The engineers on the Noyes Committee recommended irradiating tantalum to produce its radioactive isotope, tantalum-182. Although not available in quite the abundance of the zirconium-columbium extracted from nuclear waste, this material had substantial advantages: its half-life is about 114 days, about the perfect "goldilocks zone" for tactical area denial—not too long, not too short. Moreover, it did not require a heavy investment in specialized facilities. In principle, the Hanford plutonium reactor could have been used to irradiate the tantalum during its normal operation. For these reasons, all the prototype radiological weapons produced over the course of the program used tantalum-182 as their radioactive payload.

The material needs of the RW program conflicted, however, with the requirements of the rapidly expanding atomic weapons program. In 1948, the United States possessed only one nuclear reactor capable of large-scale isotope irradiation, the B reactor at the Hanford site. The Hanford pile was devoted to the production not only of plutonium-239, the fissile material for most of the nuclear weapons then being built, but also of polonium, a necessary component of the neutron initiators in early bombs. Because RW components are constantly decaying, they have a short shelf life. This means that maintaining stockpile equilibrium requires constant production of radioactive isotopes. With the Hanford pile running at full capacity to furnish the materials for the nuclear weapons program, it was not obvious how one could also sustain an RW arsenal.[79]

By early 1948, the primary U.S. advocates of radiological warfare realized that a meaningful RW program would require a devoted production infrastructure and could not indefinitely piggyback on the nuclear weapon production complex. In the first meeting of the ad hoc panel investigating RWs, Lawrence floated the idea of having reactors run in standby mode around the country in order to be ready for RW production at a moment of military necessity. He estimated that "twenty or thirty reactors would not be fantastic to contemplate."[80] Albert Holland at Oak Ridge issued a directive in 1949 that, in all future nuclear reactor construction, provisions must be made to include "space for irradiation of materials and sufficient excess reactivity to cover possible use of this space" to serve the RW program.[81] Yet, Lawrence's grand plan for a fleet of reactors devoted to RW-agent production never came to fruition, and there is no evidence that Holland's directive resulted in any reactor being redesigned to accommodate the RW program.

Nonetheless, sufficient material was accumulated to undertake dozens of field tests at the Dugway Proving Ground.[82] These tests focused on the potential of RWs for relatively short-term area-denial effects and were not designed to examine other possible uses of RWs.[83] Reports on the field tests do not provide a qualitative assessment of their success or failure. They do indicate, however, that most of the munition types functioned and that they dispersed radiation over a considerable area.[84] This modest achievement was nevertheless insufficient to persuade the Weapons System Evaluation Group to recommend continued funding for an active RW program. Although the factors responsible for this outcome are unclear, it is likely that, in addition to the issue of competing resources, two considerations played a significant role: (1) the lack of a compelling military rationale for RWs in an era dominated by nuclear arms and (2) bureaucratic politics.

The Demise of the U.S. Radiological Weapons Program

Military Rationale and Bureaucratic Politics

A number of U.S. military figures were intrigued by radiological weapons in the immediate postwar period, but none of them viewed RWs as essential to their service's military mission. General LeMay's early interest in the potential of RWs already has been noted, and General McCormack, the director of Military Applications of the AEC, encouraged investigation of a number of alternative ways to use RWs.[85] General Douglas MacArthur reportedly proposed creating a belt of radioactive cobalt dust "five miles deep and 100 miles wide" to cut off Chinese supply lines during the Korean War.[86] Although most proponents of RWs during this period viewed the weapons as best suited for purposes of area denial, some advocates envisioned their potential as strategic weapons. In June 1947, Colonel M. E. Barker, commandant at the Chemical Corps School, expressed special interest in toxic radioactive gas, which he believed might "be even more effective against strategic targets than atomic bombs."[87] At about the same time, one also could find arguments that RWs might be attractive as a "relatively benign form of warfare," the idea being that they could be used in dosages that disrupted an adversary's economy and spread fear without killing people.[88] This view is reflected in a 1949 article on RWs in the Department of the Army's monthly publication, *Officers' Call*, in which an entire section is devoted to RW as a humane weapon.[89] A darker variant of this view, articulated by Lawrence, suggested that because of the absence of a clear norm or taboo against their employment, RWs might be more usable than atomic bombs, especially with regard to first use.[90]

None of these arguments, however, generated strong support among key institutional players in the U.S. defense establishment, and by 1956, radiological weapons were no longer regarded by any of the military services as effective in fulfilling priority military missions. To some extent, this view of the diminished value of RWs was justified by technical considerations and relative cost effectiveness. The devaluation of RWs, however, also was affected by competing organizational interests and bureaucratic political infighting.

Consistent with the logic of bureaucratic politics, the fate of the RW program in the United States was intrinsically linked to competition with its primary competitors: nuclear and chemical weapons. To be sure, some Army officials regarded RWs as a possible complement to or even substitute for chemical weapons as a means to defend Europe from Soviet aggression, and Air Force figures such as LeMay were intrigued by the military applications of RWs in general. Neither the Air Force nor the Navy, however, was ever a strong institutional RW advocate. By the mid-1950s, both services were far more interested in securing "their fair share" of the rapidly growing defense budget for nuclear explosives of all shapes and sizes. For the Air Force, this initially meant nuclear gravity bombs and, subsequently, nuclear-tipped intercontinental ballistic missiles.[91] The Navy, for its part, was never invested in the concept of RWs but had established an office to develop nuclear weapons for deployment on surface ships, submarines, and naval-based aircraft only months after the end of World War II. More importantly, since the early 1950s, Admiral Hyman Rickover had focused naval efforts in the nuclear sector on designing, manufacturing, and deploying nuclear-powered submarines, the first of which was commissioned in 1954.

In terms of intranational bureaucratic political bargaining, RWs were always at a disadvantage in comparison to the sprawling and rapidly expanding nuclear weapons complex. As already noted, production of RW agents depended on the Hanford breeder reactor, whose chief mission was plutonium production for nuclear weapon pits.[92] The devastating effect of nuclear weapons also had been proven on the battlefield, and after the first Soviet nuclear test in 1949, arms-racing logic drove the quantitative and qualitative expansion of the nuclear arsenal at the expense of other systems.

RW development also was constrained ultimately by the more established chemical weapons program. The Army Chemical Corps, which initially embraced RWs as a means to restore funding and relevance during an institutional nadir immediately after World War II, benefited from the Department of Defense's reevaluation of the role of chemical and biological weapons. In June 1950, a committee tasked by the secretary of defense to undertake a full examination of chemical, biological, and radiological warfare returned a report recommending a significant upgrade and reinvestment in chemical weapons. Most importantly, the report urged the military to abandon its "for retaliation only" policy toward chemical weapons and to be prepared to employ chemical weapons immediately upon the onset of war.[93] The report included a brief analysis of the advantages and disadvantages of RWs and urged continued study to evaluate the feasibility and desirability of these weapons, but afforded RWs a much lower priority than chemical weapons and, to a lesser extent, biological weapons.[94] While the enhanced status of the ACC accelerated RW development by reauthorizing open-air testing of chemical (and radiological) munitions at Dugway Proving Ground, it also forced the RW program to compete simultaneously for funds and high-level attention with both the nuclear and chemical weapons programs—a competition that RW advocates were ill-prepared to wage and destined to lose.

An additional bureaucratic factor that may have vitiated against U.S. adoption of RWs as a weapons innovation is the military's dominant frame of reference and preference for kinetic warfare—what Frank Smith refers to as the "kinetic frame." According to this thesis, military bureaucracies have a preference for innovations that resemble traditional bullets and bombs.[95] Weapons that propagate radiation, an invisible and frequently misunderstood physical phenomenon, would be particularly disadvantaged by this bias in military thinking.

Normative Considerations

Conceivably, normative considerations also may have diminished bureaucratic support within the U.S. government for radiological weapons. RWs frequently were depicted as an analogue to or variant of chemical weapons by their proponents, and an aversion to chemical weapons could have made some policymakers less receptive to RWs. In any case, the potential pitfalls of conflating the two weapons categories were ignored by some of their military and scientific advocates. Hamilton, for instance, promoted the concept of RWs to U.S. military authorities as a superior chemical weapon with both potential tactical and strategic capabilities whose use could be as effective in making a city uninhabitable as those of an atomic bomb.[96] Although the Armed Forces Special Weapons Program steered research away from the strategic mission envisioned by Hamilton, the RW program after 1948 did focus its efforts on a device that resembled a chemical bomb in its design and attributes, and, as noted above, the U.S. Army Chemical Corps was tasked with its development and testing.

It would be reasonable to assume that a number of policymakers shared the view of AEC chairman Lilienthal that RWs were part of a category of weapons that were both undesirable and beyond the pale. After all, in 1948, the United Nations had already defined radiological weapons as a weapon of mass destruction in the context of developing disarmament and nonproliferation initiatives.[97] The issue of RWs also began to receive more attention in the public domain in both scientific publications and the mass media. Especially noteworthy was the 1948 book by Austrian physicist Hans Thirring in which he described the humanitarian horror of radiological weapons, or fine-grained "death sand," as he called it. Perhaps the most striking passage in his book refers to the potential of this fearsome new weapon to exterminate frontline soldiers "like vermin in a space that's being gassed with hydrogen cyanide"—a clear allusion to the Nazis' use of gas in the death camps.[98]

Although there exist hints of moral opposition to RWs sprinkled throughout the documentary history of the program, it is not apparent that the views of Thirring or like-minded scientists and bureaucrats inside or outside the U.S. government had much impact on building a norm against RW development or use. Instead, the preponderance of evidence suggests that RW proponents believed them to be a legitimate method of warfare whose development was justified by the actions of U.S. adversaries. This perspective is clearly articulated by General McCormack in the early period of the Cold War in a communication to Carroll Wilson, the first general manager of the

AEC. McCormack acknowledges that "the subject is not a pleasant one to contemplate, but it must be subjected to a critical examination in the United States, especially as regards the possibility of an enemy waging radiological war against us."[99]

Even Thirring's work, when popularized in the United States, was interpreted in a way that downplayed the ethical component. This is apparent in a 1950 article in the *Bulletin of the Atomic Scientists* by Louis Ridenour, who had been a special assistant to the U.S. secretary of the Air Force.[100] Ridenour accurately portrays the science behind Thirring's work but chooses not to mention the Austrian scientist's moral concerns. Instead, he observes that while the "novel thing" can be viewed "as a horrid and insidious weapon," it also "can be regarded as a remarkably humane one," because "it gives each member of the target population a choice of whether he will live or die."[101] Contrasting RWs to the horrific weapons of the last war, which deprived citizens of a choice in the matter of life or death, Ridenour even suggests that there is an excellent chance of survival for a person exposed to the radioactivity of this new weapon if the individual "flees at once with a folded, dampened handkerchief over his nose and mouth."

While some within government may have shared Ridenour's view, it did not sit well with one outside critic: novelist, poet, and essayist E. B. White. In his August 26, 1950, "Comment" for *The New Yorker*, White recalls a morning spent hanging a swing for a little girl before coming inside to read "an article on death dust, or radiological warfare, in the July *Bulletin of the Atomic Scientists*, Vol. VI, No. 7."[102] He writes that he "couldn't seem to separate the little girl from radiological warfare—she seemed to belong to it, although inhabiting another sphere."[103] He concludes by imagining her with other children riding the subway to its 242nd Street terminus, disembarking, and walking north—each with a handkerchief "properly moistened and folded neatly—the way it said in the story."[104]

Lack of Perceived Threat

At almost the same time that Ridenour's article appeared in print, a report by the secretary of defense's Ad Hoc Committee on Chemical, Biological and Radiological Warfare was released, recommending further research and development of RWs—in addition to an expansion of CW and BW capabilities.[105] This remarkable document, likely meant to steel U.S. officials' resolve to use any weapon necessary to defeat states that attempted to challenge the United States, repeated Lawrence's argument that "the target populace can detect the presence [of RW] and move out of the danger area." It uses this argument to question the relevance of the concept of "weapons of mass destruction" (introduced by the Commission for Conventional Armaments of the United Nations in 1948) when applied to RWs, and it advocates strongly for their continued development with intention to use whenever they would offer a military advantage. In short, the report of the secretary of defense's Ad Hoc Committee represents a stark repudiation of any emerging norm against the development, and even the use, of radiological weapons.

Had policymakers been aware of its magnitude, the Soviet RW program may have constituted an external threat to justify greater investment in the U.S. program. As it was, however, U.S. intelligence about Soviet RW activities was practically nonexistent and certainly was much less robust than the Kremlin's knowledge of U.S. RW developments. A Central Intelligence Agency intelligence memorandum from September 20, 1949, concluded that no foreign country was engaged in the production of radiological warfare agents;[106] a February 1950 CIA working paper likewise reported "no information on Soviet national policy with respect to the employment of radiological warfare materials either openly or subversively."[107] The same paper observes that the United States was unaware of any reports in the Soviet media about defensive measures having been undertaken specifically with respect to RWs.[108] Its conclusion underscores just how severely U.S. intelligence agencies underestimated Soviet RW pursuits:

> The USSR does not have available at the present time a sufficient quantity of radiological warfare materials to be useful in a military sense, but they do have the capability of disseminating small quantities of radioactive poisons within the U.S. through the employment of subversive individuals and organizations, if they should so desire.
>
> It is our opinion, however, that from a practical standpoint, as compared to BW and CW, the production of a significant quantity of RW materials requires an extensive plant installation and would interfere with atomic bomb production. In addition [RW materials][109] are dif-

ficult to handle and disseminate, and their use is relatively ineffective. For these reasons their employment by the USSR is considered to be unlikely.

The CIA assessment of Soviet RW capabilities, particularly the obstacles in their path, may well have been a product of "mirror-imaging," and the presumption that if Soviet Union embarked on an RW program, it would follow a course similar to the one pursued by the United States.[110]

TWO
The Soviet Union

Unbeknownst to many at the time and today, the Soviet Union actively pursued radiological weapons (RWs) for approximately ten years beginning in 1947. In contrast with the United States, however, RWs were not a regular feature of Soviet science fiction during the period in which this program was active. A notable exception is the 1953 propaganda film *Serebristaya pil'* (Silver dust), which depicted a new American military innovation—radioactive dust—that a former Nazi scientist and his henchmen planned to unleash on unsuspecting African American test subjects. Unlike similar depictions of RWs in U.S. popular culture, however, the film was produced in consultation with Soviet specialists who studied nuclear weapons effects and was screened for RW testers at Kapustin Yar as an example for them to follow in their work.

It is not wholly surprising that the Soviet defense establishment would use science fiction as a means to communicate the objectives of the Soviet RW program to its participants. Indeed, the documentary record shows that many Soviet defense officials and weapons designers were avid science fiction fans, and some perceived similarities between their work and themes depicted in books, on television, or in movies. In a 1961 meeting with Nikita

Khrushchev, for example, nuclear weapons designer and human rights advocate Andrei Sakharov described his work on "nuclear explosions to power spacecraft" as one of several "science fiction schemes" his department was pursuing. Soviet rocket engineer Academician Boris Chertok, meanwhile, has traced the origins of his career to the first film he ever saw in the theater: an adaptation of Aleksey Tolstoy's science fiction story *Aelita*.[1]

As Anindita Banerjee has found, science fiction's popularity in the USSR can be linked in part to its contributions to "intellectual debates about the best ways to engage with the new realities of the unfolding twentieth century."[2] Within the nuclear domain specifically, the genre served to elevate the prestige of nuclear physics in post–World War II Soviet society and to create what V. P. Vizgin refers to as the "cult of the atom."[3] In showing *Serebristaya pil'* to participants in the radiological weapons program, the Soviet defense establishment may have hoped that it would serve both of these purposes with respect to this new military innovation. If so, what explains the fact that Soviet radiological weapons failed to live up to their fictionalized potential?[4]

The Soviet Pursuit of Radiological Weapons

This chapter examines the history of the Soviet RW program and identifies the factors that influenced its rise and subsequent demise. It focuses especially on the role of perceived external threats in driving the USSR's initial interest in RWs and the subsequent technical and bureaucratic challenges its defense enterprise encountered in moving beyond the research and development phase of these efforts. Because of the high degree of secrecy and compartmentalization of the Soviet RW program, it is particularly challenging for contemporary scholars to knit together the various facets of these efforts. These challenges may explain in part why, with the exception of a few scattered references in the literature on the Soviet atomic weapons program, so little has been written on the USSR's RW pursuit.[5]

Despite this dearth of published material, it is nevertheless possible to reconstruct the basic outline of the Soviet RW program using primary source documents, including especially those from the Rosatom digital library. Recollections from program participants, a number of which have been catalogued by the Bellona Foundation, have also proven to be particularly useful in determining how the various components of this program fit together. In analyzing these materials, this chapter both draws from and contributes to the larger body of scholarship that examines Soviet military innovation. This literature includes earlier work by Andrew Aldrin, John Hines, Harley Balzer, and Peter Almquist, who offer insights into the role of individuals in driving the pursuit of new weapons systems and the influence of the irrationalities of the Soviet command economy on this process.[6] Particularly informative in this regard is Matthew Evangelista's 1988 comparison of U.S. and Soviet military innovation, which is one of the few systematic efforts to examine the life cycle of weapons research and development in the USSR.[7] Although this chapter does not seek to test the validity of Evangelista's findings, it determines that Evangelista's conclusions about the influence of security considerations, bureaucratic politics, and technological challenges on Soviet weapons innovation are largely borne out by the USSR's experience with RWs.

The Genesis of the Soviet Radiological Weapons Program

The documentary record shows that Soviet scientists were aware of the possible military applications of radioactive material by 1940.[8] In mid-October of that year, two doctors of physical mathematics—V. Maslov and V. Shpinel—submitted a proposal to the Bureau of Inventions of the People's Commissariat of the USSR on the "use of uranium as an explosive and poisoning substance."[9] Their proposal highlights the persistence of fission products, which the authors describe as "thousands of times stronger than the strongest poisons," leading them to wonder whether "the colossal explosive power or the poisoning properties" of uranium fission "is the most attractive from a military standpoint."[10] The authors also underscore the similarities between radiological and chemical weapons, noting that the effects of radioactive agents "do not manifest immediately, and in their character resemble mustard gas."[11]

Although Maslov and Shpinel's early interest in radiological weapons appears prescient today, their proposal gained no traction with Soviet defense officials at the time. Two reviewers from the Scientific Research Chemical Institute of the People's Commissariat for Defense dismissed it as unreasonable, unclear, and unfounded.[12] Vitaly Khlopin, the head of Leningrad's famed Radium Institute, felt the proposal "contain[ed] many fantasies" and appeared to have been written by people who "have never dealt with large amounts of radioactive material."[13] Without endorsement from the top, this initial attempt to innovate in the domain of "radioactive poisoning agents" went nowhere. This sequence of events supports Evangelista's thesis that the stifling of initiative marked the first stage of Soviet weapons innovation.[14]

Only after intelligence determined that other foreign governments were defending against the military use of radioactive material did high-level Soviet interest in the development of RWs take hold. This interest was apparent in a January 1943 report that alleged that "Americans are building sensitive Geiger-Muller contraptions, which they will mount on the roofs of city buildings in order to detect radioactive substances as soon as they are dropped."[15] "'They also intend to install portable measuring instruments for establishing the danger zone" the report continued. "The English are taking analogous measures."[16] The report foreshadows by over one year Operation Peppermint, the Allied effort to protect against the potential use of radioactive materials to seed the beaches at Normandy. As discussed in more detail below, it is almost certain that Moscow was aware of early U.S. and British radioactive detection preparations due to Alan Nunn May and possibly other Soviet agents.

Soviet decision-makers gained additional insights into foreign efforts regarding radiological weapons in January 1946 when Henry Smyth's report *Atomic Energy for Military Purposes* was translated into Russian and distributed among the Soviet defense establishment.[17] The document contains Smyth's findings about the potential utility of radioactive poisons and U.S. defensive research in this area. Eleven months later, the Soviet Council of Ministers issued Order No. 13789 authorizing a thematic list of scientific research work to be undertaken related to nuclear physics, including research on the "possibilities of protecting organisms from the poisoning effects of radioactive agents." This task was assigned to the Institute of Organic Chemistry of the Academy of Sciences of the Soviet Union, the Ministry of Chemical Industry, and the Chemical Institute of the Red Army, reinforcing the perceived overlap between radiological and chemical weapons within the Soviet defense establishment.[18]

Although the documentary record does not indicate precisely when Soviet RW research assumed an offensive dimension, this orientation was evident by 1947. A report from September of that year noted that the program of work at Laboratory B (part of the facility known today as Snezhinsk[19]) included developing methods for the use of fission products as combat poisoning substances, as well as defensive measures.[20] By the end of 1947, V. L. Vannikov, who served as deputy to the head of the Soviet secret police, Lavrenti Beria, in the Special Committee of the Atomic Project, was clearly contemplating specific military applications of radioactive products, too. He wrote to Joseph Stalin on December 17, 1947, that "radioactive materials, considering their resilience, can be used in times of war on a large scale as equipment for long- and short-effect artillery shells, for an air bomb, for long- and short-effect aviation and, finally, for sea mines and torpedoes, similarly to how they're used as poisonous material for chemical ammunition."[21]

It is unclear whether Vannikov reached this conclusion based on research conducted in Laboratory B or through knowledge of corresponding projects in the West. If the latter, he may have been informed by spies embedded in the U.S. and British atomic weapons programs. There is circumstantial evidence to suggest, for instance, that John Cairncross, the "fifth man" of the UK's "Cambridge Five," may have provided Moscow with insights about the military potential for RWs. Another possible source of information is Klaus Fuchs, whose signature is present on a June 1, 1949, document in the United Kingdom's National Archives on the tactical and strategic utility of RWs.[22] Fuchs passed to his Soviet contacts information relating to reactor design, isotope production, and radiation measurement during the final years of his career in espionage, from which Soviet scientists could have derived information relevant to the development of RWs.[23] Although it is possible that Fuchs also informed his Soviet handlers about British interest in these weapons, his final rendezvous with them took place in spring 1949, making it unlikely that he knowingly passed along information related to British or American RW pursuits.[24]

A more probable source of information is British atomic spy Alan Nunn May, a physicist who worked on the UK's Tube Alloys project. May shared atomic secrets with the Soviet Union from 1943 until his unmasking in 1946. In 1942, a year prior to being "activated" by his Soviet handler, he reportedly used his contacts within the Communist Party of Great Britain to relay the news of this new military threat to the Soviet Union.[25] On his deathbed, the former spy described having been asked to review an American document assessing Nazi plans to develop a radiological weapon (almost certainly the document referred to in the January 1943 report above).

An even more authoritative source of Soviet knowledge about offensive RWs, however, may have been the German and Austrian scientists who were "recruited" to work on the Soviet atomic program during this time.[26] Their link to the Soviet RW program is clear from a letter written by the chief of the 9th Directorate, Colonel General A. P. Zavenyagin, to Beria in January 1946.[27] Zavenyagin oversaw the program that recruited and supervised German scientists working on the Soviet atomic project during the postwar period.[28] His letter refers to a cache of German documents from 1944 that mention "the development of an atomic bomb and uranium warfare agents/poisons."[29] By 1946, large numbers of German scientists were working in the Soviet Union as part of its nuclear enterprise, including at Laboratory B, which, in September 1947, was tasked with developing defenses against and weapons based on radiological poisons.[30]

Development of the Soviet RW Program

Whatever the source of their knowledge, Soviet officials were acutely aware of the direction U.S. research on RWs was taking by April 1950. One document from this period identifies "radioactive O[travlyayiushchie] V[eshchestva]," or radioactive poisoning agents, as among the "new types of atomic weapon" under production in the United States.[31] A decision was made shortly thereafter to invest significant Soviet institutional resources in the development of RWs. These efforts persisted under strict secrecy until the late 1950s and involved numerous design bureaus, testing facilities, and scientific institutes within the sprawling Soviet defense complex.

It seems doubtful that Soviet policymakers appreciated the relatively small investment the United States was making in RWs because perceived foreign threats were a major driver behind the formal establishment of the Soviet RW program. Indeed, after two years of preliminary research, the Soviet pursuit of RWs moved from low-level efforts into what Evangelista characterizes as a phase of high-level, targeted response to weapons development abroad.[32] This transition involved the reallocation and redirection of existing resources toward research and development on RWs, including, significantly, within the Soviet Navy. On July 10, 1951, its 6th Directorate established two special scientific/research subdivisions devoted to conducting research on radiological weapons. These subdivisions, referred to as the 15th and 1st Programs,[33] were housed under research institutions NII-10 (Nauchno issledovatel'skiy khimicheskiy institut) and NII-17 (Nauchno issledovatel'skiy meditsinskiy institut).[34] Their base, a nineteenth-century explosives laboratory on Vasilyevsky Island in Leningrad, provided an inconspicuous location for this clandestine work.[35]

On paper, both the 1st and 15th Programs were responsible for researching the effects of nuclear weapons on naval equipment.[36] In practice, though, they weaponized radioactive waste so that it could be utilized in different warhead and bomb munitions. They also tested the effects of radioactive substances on humans and animals. Both the 1st and 15th Programs were initially headed by C. C. Zhikharev, a medical doctor, and then by G. A. Zadginedze and chemist Vasillii Vladimirovich Kesarev. The 1st Program was overseen by medical doctor Lev Aleksandrovich Pertsev.[37] Their plan of work was mapped out by specialists at the 1st Main Directorate of the Soviet Council of Ministers under V. L. Vannikov, whose leading role in promoting both defensive and offensive RW research speaks to the importance of high-level advocates in the weapons innovation process.[38]

Participants in the Soviet radiological weapons program claim that the plutonium production plant Mayak provided the radioactive solution with which the two naval programs worked.[39] The actual source of this material, however, was likely Laboratory B, which had been charged with weaponizing radiological poisons in 1947. The substance in question—referred to as Solution 904—was reportedly derived from spent fuel from which the plutonium had been extracted. Its radioactivity came primarily from high levels of zirconium-95 and niobium-95—the same isotopes recommended for use in the U.S. RW program. This solution was transported to Leningrad by train in 500-kilogram containers filled with thirty liters of atomic waste each.[40] Once specialists there had formulated it into the correct concentration for experimentation, the substance was referred to as "SK (or 'Spetskomitet') concentrate." When it had been mixed with a viscous substrate (resin, for example) to make it difficult for an adversary to remove, it was called "SK preparation."[41]

The Soviet Union tested the lethality of this substance in prototype weapons at four known locations during the mid-1950s. The Navy primarily carried out its RW experiments in the northwest archipelago of islands in Lake Ladoga—an area known as Object 230.[42] Although the experiences of different program participants do not always align perfectly, it is clear that the scale of testing at Object 230 was significant. These experiments included effects tests on animals aboard a captured German vessel moored near Makarinsaari Island and often resulted in the inadvertent exposure of test site personnel to SK in the process.[43]

Program participants contend that the frequency of these tests increased in August and September 1953, and new locations for testing also were reported during this period. For example, multiple sources note that testing initially began on the island of Makarinsaari, also known as Malyi (a code name utilized to keep its location secret), in 1953[44] and that these experiments continued into the spring of 1954. Tests of empty shells intended for chemical aerial bombs into which Solution 904 had been poured were conducted on the island of Heinsenmaa (also known as Suri) and on the ice in the water surrounding Object 230 during this time as well.[45] Similar tests also were carried out on the island of Mukerikku (code named Myuarka), part of the Valaam archipelago. Thirty-five full-scale models of special ammunitions filled with the radioactive substance referred to as "SK preparation" were detonated at this location.[46] Solid radioactive waste from the research conducted in Leningrad was then dumped at a base in Privetninskoe, located in the Vyburg Oblast' near St. Petersburg. This was reportedly also the site of additional tests focused on the effects of radioactive material on animals.[47]

According to several participants in the Soviet RW program, part of the testing overseen by the Navy included detonating radioisotopes aboard a captured German vessel known as *Kit*, which was moored just off Makarinsaari Island. The purpose of these tests was to determine the effects of SK on "experimental" animals.[48] In interviews, former program participants recall how they and their colleagues would paint the surfaces of the boat with radioactive mixtures to measure how quickly they evaporated and to derive other information about their utility in weapons. While the intended subjects of these tests were rabbits, dogs, and mice, the personnel who carried out the tests simultaneously exposed themselves to the effects of the radioactive solutions they were testing, to their significant detriment.[49]

Participants in the testing of RWs in and around Lake Ladoga recall that security for Object 230 and its surroundings was provided by Military Unit 99795. The patrolling ships belonged to a military division referred to as the 60th Detachment, which was based in the gulf of Rybnyj. These vessels were also used to transport the radioactive substances developed in Leningrad to the appropriate testing location in the archipelago. The liquid radioactive material was brought by car from Leningrad to the port of Rybnyi and then lifted by cranes into boats headed to the *Kit* or to the testing range. To protect workers from radiation, the radioactive material was stored in lead containers in the shape of a truncated cone approximately one meter in diameter, one meter high, and 20 centimeters thick, which were sealed with a lead plug. Each container weighed many hundreds of kilograms, and there were at least two major incidents in which the lead plug became dislodged, exposing workers to the highly radioactive material within.[50]

According to Vice Admiral E. A. Shitikov, these tests demonstrated that radiological material was not suitable or practical for creating weapons of use to the Navy.[51] His conclusion likely reflected findings that (1) the highly toxic nature of the radioactive material in the weapons made it difficult for personnel to work with, and (2) the material was not easy to disperse effectively over a large area. Additionally, Shitikov notes that it proved challenging to protect the crew from being irradiated by the weapons themselves during their transport. By way of illustration, he refers to an experiment in which personnel placed a radioactive cobalt bar shielded in a lead container in a specially-outfitted Tu-104 aircraft. The experiment showed that even very large and heavy protective shielding were ineffective.[52]

These incidents and others like them may have eventually contributed to Soviet Navy Commander-in-Chief S. G. Gorshkov's decision to stop work on radiological weapons issues in December 1956.[53] Nevertheless, the radioactive solutions developed and refined by the Navy at its facilities near Lake Ladoga continued to be tested in at least three other sites from approximately 1952 to 1957. Some of the more well-documented radiological weapons tests were carried out at Semipalatinsk Test Site, where the Soviet Union also tested nuclear weapons until 1989. A 2002 monograph published by the Russian Ministry of Atomic Energy indicates that RW tests were carried out at Sectors 4 and 4A of Semipalatinsk between 1954 and 1956.[54] Schema of the test site from this period show that these sectors were located northwest of the Experimental Field and even provide the coordinates where these activities took place.[55]

Vitol'd Vasilets, a retired Soviet Navy officer, reports that these tests involved prototype bombs containing radioactive material, which were referred to as "liquid air bombs," or "NAB" in Russian.[56] Personnel from the Leningrad-based radiological weapons research institutes recall that these cluster munitions were conceived of primarily as a means to attack enemy aircraft carriers at sea.[57] Vasilets indicates that a number of other research and design institutes in the Soviet defense enterprise were also engaged in these tests besides the Navy. A remote-controlled instrument for refueling the liquid air bombs, for instance, was developed by NIIChimMash, a research institution based near Zagorsk.[58] The liquid air bomb prototypes were developed by GSKB-47, a Moscow-based design bureau specializing in bomb development.[59] Experimental Design Bureau 240 (OKB 240) of the Ministry of Aviation Industry was responsible for retrofitting cluster bomb racks with a special internal fuselage for hanging nine liquid air bombs and filling them with liquid radioactive substances.[60] The bombs were then dropped from two Il-28 planes, which had been modified to accommodate this unusual cargo.

According to Vasilets, the planes also incorporated safety features designed to protect the crew in case of an emergency. Nevertheless, the tests at Semipalatinsk presented serious—often deadly—hazards to the personnel involved. One accident reportedly occurred when a plane transporting a prototype weapon from Zagorsk to Semipalatinsk unexpectedly lost pressure, causing radioactive material to spill out onto the pilots.[61] This weapon, developed for the Soviet Army in either 1951 or 1952, apparently derived its radioactivity from strontium-90 and was therefore exceptionally dangerous. Eventually, the liquid radioactive substances in the test munitions were replaced with a less reactive simulator, but not before this and other accidents caused countless injuries and even deaths.[62]

Personnel from the Leningrad-based radiological weapons research institutes also recall the development of these cluster munitions, noting that they were conceived of as a means to attack enemy aircraft carriers. According to their accounts, Major General Nikolai Ivanovich Pavlov, head of one of the main directorates of the Ministry of Medium Machine Building (or MinSredMash, the ministry responsible for the Soviet atomic energy program), oversaw this work. In their remembrances, program participants mention the development of highly viscous, "floating" radiological substances that could be blown on the water's surface by the wind either to the shore or to an enemy ship. This would ensure that the ship and territory were contaminated by difficult-to-remove material.[63]

Declassified documents from the Rosatom archive indicate that the radiological weapons tests conducted at Semipalatinsk involved V. P. Goncharov of Military Unit 51105, I. F. Volodin, V. V. Kosolov, V. A Logachev, and K. F. Uspenskij.[64] Goncharov's military unit is associated with the 12th Central Scientific Research Institute of the Ministry of Defense (TSNII12), which was located in Zagorsk-7. According to the Russian-born nuclear weapons expert Pavel Podvig, TSNII12 was responsible for organizing nuclear weapons effects tests,[65] and this work also appears to have fallen under the institute's jurisdiction with regard to the Soviet RW program. TSNII12 was tasked with finding a way to measure levels of radioactivity emitted by these weapons, work that became especially critical once the liquid radioactive substances in the munitions was replaced with a less reactive simulator.[66]

At the same time that the Soviet Union was testing radioactive liquid air bomb and cluster munition programs, it was also developing missile warheads containing radioactive material. This phase of the Soviet RW program appears to have been initiated in either 1952 or 1953 and may have continued until as late as 1957.[67] As Vasilets recalls, prototype warheads were initially flight-tested at the 71st Air Force Test Base near the Crimean village of Bagerove.[68] The base was established in August 1947 and was used for a variety of testing purposes associated with the aerial delivery of nuclear weapons and, apparently, also radioactive weapons. According to Vasilets, flight tests of warhead prototypes began here in the third quarter of 1953.[69] The warhead prototypes were developed and overseen by S. P. Korolev of the Central Design Bureau of Experimental Machine Building's Scientific Research Institute 88 (NII 88). Experimental Design Bureau 156 (subsequently known as the Topelov Design Bureau) oversaw the retrofitting of Tu-4s with two underwing pylons for bomb racks holding radiological warheads weighing up to 1,500 kilograms, which were used for testing purposes.[70] The flight tests were preceded by extensive preparatory work that was carried out by the 71st Air Force Test Site personnel. This work included the construction of a technological building for storage tanks for the liquid radioactive substances and the refueling of the test objects. Vasilets also notes that M. I. Voskoboinikov was present as one of the test coordinators. Voskoboinikov was, at this time, the director of NII 10 of the Soviet Navy—one of the institutions that housed Programs 1 and 15.[71]

At least three warhead models were subsequently tested on short- and medium-range missiles at Kapustin Yar, where their performance was generally disappointing. The two series of missile tests of radiological warheads conducted there were codenamed Geran' and Generator. The Geran' series entailed mounting warheads containing radiological material on R2 short-range ballistic missiles, but testing quickly showed that this particular warhead design was not effective in distributing radioactive material over a wide area.[72] The second series of tests—Generator—debuted two new designs: the first, a warhead filled with radiological material featuring a remote system or radio-controlled altimeter that would detonate a blast charge as it approached its target, and the second, a warhead filled with one hundred or more shells containing radiological material that would explode on impact with a target.[73] Some reports also suggest that work began on the development of the Generator-5 warhead in 1955. While virtually no information is available regarding this warhead, one source claims that at least three tests on an R-5 intermediate-range missile were carried out before the end of 1957.[74]

Perhaps more interesting than the warhead designs themselves, however, is the environment in which the tests took place. Boris Chertok provides a rare firsthand account of these tests in his memoir, *Rakety i lyudi* (*Rockets and People*).[75] It is here that he and his colleagues were shown the science fiction film *Serebristaya pil'* (Silver dust), described at the beginning of the chapter, as a way of briefing them on the Geran' warhead's intended effects. The film suggested that radiological weapons could fill an important gap in the Soviet weapons arsenal as a means to kill without fighting while preserving critical infrastructure. In reality, however, the tests in which Chertok took part demonstrated that these weapons were not ready for prime time.

During preparations for the first Geran' launch, for example, the warhead began to leak what appeared to be radioactive material. While the launch team ran for cover, the senior scientist in charge of testing climbed to the top of the rocket, ran his finger through the trickle of brown liquid, and then tasted it. Concluding (correctly) that the liquid was a simulant, he entreated the team to return to work. "It tastes like crap," he said, "but it's harmless."[76]

The Demise of the Soviet Radiological Weapons Program

The Soviet RW program did not end abruptly, but instead withered away over several years. Although the lack of publicly available documents makes it difficult to detail its demise, it is clear that the program never progressed to what Evangelista calls "mobilization" (an all-out effort to pursue innovation) or "mass production," the final two stages in his model of the typical Soviet weapons innovation process.[77] Several factors help to explain why these weapons never lived up to their promise.

Comparative Lack of Military Effectiveness

The demise of the Soviet pursuit of RWs was likely catalyzed by a revised assessment of their military effectiveness relative to other weapons. The Soviet Union conducted its first hydrogen bomb test in August 1953, and its growing arsenal of more lethal nuclear weapons undoubtedly reduced the appeal of primitive radiological dispersal devices. This finding aligns with the substitution-effect hypothesis proposed by Michael Horowitz and Neil Narang in their study of the relationship among weapons of mass destruction and the perceptions of CWs and BWs as "poor man's nuclear weapons." Although Horowitz and Narang do not address radiological weapons, they do find that nuclear, chemical, and biological weapons are typically pursued simultaneously only until a state has acquired a nuclear capability, at which point states are unlikely to continue their CW or BW programs.[78]

The shortcomings of RWs would have been especially apparent in comparison to chemical weapons, which were already part of the Soviet arsenal and served a similar battlefield purpose to that envisioned for RWs. Joachim Krause and Charles Mallory surmise that a major buildup of Soviet chemical weapons—including tube and rocket artillery, tactical missile warheads, air bombs, spray tanks, and hand grenades—was initiated in the late 1950s at almost the same time that support for the RW program was waning.[79] The perceived threat of a U.S. chemical weapons attack may have driven resources away from RW research, especially after the United States abandoned its no-first-use policy for CWs in 1956.[80] This decision likely increased the salience of the CW threat for Soviet decision-makers, given that the Soviet Chemical Troops doubled in size between 1954 and 1965.[81]

Lack of Organizational Slack

The lack of "organizational slack" within the Soviet Union's military establishment may also explain the demise of the Soviet RW program. Evangelista defines this concept as the extent to which an organization has access to uncommitted resources—a key facilitator of weapons innovation.[82] He finds that the Soviet military's emphasis on plan fulfillment left little organizational slack and increased reliance on tried-and-true weapons systems over new technology.[83] It is likely that Soviet military planners eventually decided to devote their finite resources to CW instead of radiological air bombs and cluster munitions, which bore a striking resemblance to Soviet chemical weapons but lacked their proven track record.

Changes in Perceived Threats

Just as the Soviet pursuit of radiological weapons was a response to the U.S. RW program, changes in perceived threats from foreign adversaries may have shifted Soviet defense priorities away from RWs, too. This appears to have been the case with respect to RW research and development within the Navy. By the time Admiral S. G. Gorshkov took over as its commander in chief in January 1956, the United States enjoyed a huge advantage over the Soviet Union in terms of its nuclear-powered fleet, and Gorshkov initiated a major effort to catch up. He would have had few reasons to squander limited resources on the unpromising RW program and, unsurprisingly, ended the Navy's pursuit of RWs in December 1956.[84]

Health and Safety Concerns

The issue of health effects and safety also probably figured into Soviet calculations, although one needs to exercise caution in this regard given a number of common but risky practices in the nuclear sector at that time (and subsequently). Still, the aforementioned accidents likely reduced the attractiveness of RWs for some branches of the military, especially given the overall lack of organizational slack. In his research for Bellona, for instance, Victor Tereshkin was told that the Soviet radiological weapons program ended because Andrei Tupelov, head of Experimental Design Bureau 156, determined that it was too dangerous to transfer RW munitions from one plane to another and discontinued the program.[85] As described previously, both the Army and Air Force experienced a variety of safety mishaps involving tests of RWs that reduced the attractiveness of the weapons for their branches of the military. There also was the challenge posed by the need to dispose of contaminated machinery and equipment. As late as 1958, for example, there are reports about the transportation to Novaya Zemlya of items contaminated by liquid radioactive substances at Semipalatinsk.[86] Additionally, in the winter of 1955–1956, one of the ships used for testing radioactive contaminates was sunk off the shore of Lake Ladoga after taking on water, which subsequently froze and tore open the vessel.[87] It took thirty-five years for it to be recovered, encased in plastic and towed 3,200 kilometers to Novaya Zemlya.[88] Although health and environmental issues probably played at best a secondary role in the overall Soviet decision to cease work on radiological weapons, there is little doubt that the RW program caused serious and long lasting environmental damage.

Changes in Leadership

Given that buy-in from high-level decision-makers was critical to initiating the Soviet radiological weapons program, it is reasonable to assume that their departure likewise contributed to its demise. By 1958, most of the original high-level RW advocates had passed from the scene. In addition to Stalin and Beria, who at a minimum must have blessed the pursuit of a novel weapon system, Zavenyagin died in 1957, and Vannikov stepped down in 1958. Although other senior advocates for RWs may have emerged, their voices are not apparent in the material available to us. Indeed, the extreme secrecy and siloed configuration of the Soviet weapons establishment may have constrained the emergence of other forceful proponents for RWs. This explanation is consistent with Evangelista's observation that the compartmentalized nature of Soviet military R & D erected major barriers to weapons innovation.

Looking to the Future

Whatever combination of factors explains the demise of the Soviet RW program, the weapons prototypes it generated often resembled something from the pages of *Astounding Science Fiction*. One example is a concept for a gigantic radiological weapon in the form of a ship encased in cobalt-59, which is described in a 2015 article in the Russian newspaper *Vzglyad*.[89] If a nuclear explosive were detonated within the ship, the article asserts, the cobalt shell would decay into cobalt-60.[90] The resulting highly radioactive material would then be spread across the harbor in which it was stationed, causing mass death and long-term area denial.[91]

Although the *Vzglyad* article attributes the idea for the radiological ship to Andrei Sakharov, the authors of this volume have found no evidence to suggest that a link to the famed weapons designer is anything more than fiction. While Sakharov did conceive of a huge torpedo as a means to deliver the Soviet Union's gigantic Tsar Bomba—detonated in October 1961 with a yield of approximately fifty megatons—the idea for a giant dirty bomb is more appropriately linked to Leo Szilard, the great Hungarian physicist who worked on the Manhattan Project and later opposed the use of nuclear weapons. Szilard worried that, if used in sufficient quantity, hydrogen bombs encased in shells of cobalt—so-called salted bombs—might produce so much radioactivity that they would extinguish life on earth.[92] These themes of nuclear annihilation are ones Szilard explored in his own postapocalyptic science fiction short stories, which he began writing in the late 1940s after the atomic bombings of Hiroshima and Nagasaki.[93]

Regardless of the role played by Sakharov in their development, salted bombs were almost certainly a familiar concept to Soviet military planners during the period in which the RW program was active. A 1958 issue of the Soviet periodical *Atomnaia Energiia* (Atomic energy) includes a summary of Edward Teller and Albert Latter's book *Our Nuclear Future: Facts, Dangers, and Opportunities*, which features a chapter on cobalt bombs.[94] One year later, in 1959, another book that addresses the topic of cobalt bombs was translated from Japanese into Russian and published in the Soviet Union. *Nuclear Weapons and Man*, written by radiologists Hajime Matsuda and Kashiba Hayashi in 1956, devotes a paragraph to cobalt bombs alongside a reference to radiological weapons and their utility.[95]

While there are no indications that the USSR ever pursued the concept of salted weapons as a potentially useful form of radiological weaponry, a supersized, nuclear-armed autonomous underwater vessel with RW-maximized capabilities now appears to have a new lease on life in Russia. Depending on the source, a new weapon, known variously as Kanyon, Ocean Multipurpose System Status-6, and Poseidon, is currently being prepared for testing in Russia.[96] It remains to be seen if the nuclear-powered unmanned underwater vehicle ultimately belongs more in the realm of science fiction or fact. When it comes to radiological weapons, however, the two categories are often not very far apart.

THREE

The United Kingdom

In the years immediately following the end of World War II, the United Kingdom faced an uncertain strategic future. It was worn down by nearly six years of war, in which the British Isles had been subjected to aerial bombardment, and the British overseas empire was on the verge of collapse due to anti-colonial forces and Japanese occupation. Meanwhile, the UK faced the prospect of a new European order dominated by an ascendant Soviet Union and uncertainty about the commitment of the United States to preventing Soviet dominance of Europe, at least until the founding of NATO in 1949. In this context, and despite severe resource constraints, the United Kingdom sought to develop an indigenous deterrent to ensure a seat at the table of great powers and the ability to pursue an independent foreign policy. Most of this effort was devoted to the pursuit of a nuclear weapons capability. However, Britain also explored other categories of nonconventional weapons, including radiological weapons.[1]

Until very recently, the British RW program was largely neglected by historians. Unlike the cases of the United States, the Soviet Union, Iraq, and Egypt, there is practically no mention about British RW activities by either scholars or journalists.[2] Although several of the authors refer to the

British RW program in their 2020 *International Security* article and provide a longer account in their 2019 report for the U.S. Air Force addressing the threat of state-level radiological weapons programs,[3] the first extended discussion of the British experience appears in William King's important 2021 essay in *War in History*.[4] This chapter expands upon our prior work, while taking careful note of King's analysis. Key documents, however, remain inaccessible, and some linked to the activities of Soviet spies within the British nuclear establishment appear to have been intentionally destroyed. As such, considerable speculation is necessary to fill the gaps in the still fragmentary record of the UK radiological weapons program.

External Threat Perceptions and RWs during World War II

There is little indication that the United Kingdom seriously considered pursuing radiological warfare during World War II. The UK's 1941 Report of the MAUD Committee, which studied the feasibility of the atomic bomb, did not consider the use of radiation as a weapon in the absence of a nuclear explosion. In fact, the MAUD Committee report influenced the United States to pursue the atomic bomb rather than radiological warfare. As discussed in chapter 1, prior to the MAUD report's assessment that enriching sufficient uranium for a nuclear bomb was feasible, "radioactive products" were considered to be a top priority for military applications of atomic research in the United States.

According to King, the Defense Services Panel established to review the recommendations of the MAUD Committee was critical of its narrow focus on the feasibility of an atomic bomb to the exclusion of other possible weapons applications of atomic energy, such as radioactive byproducts, and encouraged more research on the subject.[5] Significantly, this panel was chaired by Lord Maurice Hankey, whose personal secretary at the time was John Cairncross, later revealed to be the "fifth man" of the "Cambridge Five," who had been recruited as a Soviet spy by Guy Burgess. David Holloway suggests that information drawn from meetings of the Defense Services Panel, presumably including information suggesting weapons applications of atomic energy besides nuclear explosions, was transmitted to Moscow, "almost certainly" by John Cairncross.[6]

While Cairncross may have been the initial Soviet agent to provide Moscow with information about the possible limitations of the MAUD Committee report, it is was another Soviet atomic spy—Alan Nunn May— who likely alerted Moscow to U.S. interest in radiological weapons. Unlike Cairncross, who was a student of modern languages before joining the British Foreign Service, May was a gifted nuclear physicist and researcher at the Cavendish Laboratory in Cambridge before joining the Tube Alloys Project, the British effort to explore the possibility of making an atomic bomb. Among his tasks was to review a U.S. report in mid-1942 about work by German scientists on a possible radiological weapon.[7] In a deathbed confession, Nunn indicates that he passed along his findings to Moscow about plans for a Nazi "dirty bomb" but that the "Russians were not very impressed by this warning."[8] King reports that May also drew upon U.S. research for a report for British officials in August 1942 on the utility and limitations of RWs, one of the earliest British studies of its kind.[9]

Although both the UK and the United States harbored concerns at various points during the Second World War that Germany might use radioactive fission products for military purposes, the countries differed in their assessment of the form RWs might take and the target of their use. In one of the rare early accounts of U.S. and British activities related to RWs, the historian Barton Bernstein suggests that "in 1942 and early 1943, the U.S. focus was mostly on German use of radiological weapons—against troops, possibly British cities, or maybe even U.S. cities."[10] By the fall of 1943, the United States was quite confident that Germany would not employ a radiological weapon against the continental United States.[11] U.S. policymakers, however, continued to be concerned that Germany might try to use radioactive material in V-rocket warheads or as a means to deny the Allies landing beaches in the run-up to a D-Day invasion. British military officials at Supreme Allied Headquarters were informed of the U.S. defensive preparations and initiated a radiological defense mission in parallel to the U.S. Operation Peppermint.[12] Nevertheless, some accounts suggest that while Anglo-American cooperation persisted, the United States was more anxious about RWs than the UK was, in part due to the different experience of the two countries in terms of their exposure to both conventional explosives and mustard gas. As King puts it, "British officials viewed RW as just one more obstacle in the war and not as an exceptional or unique threat, in contrast to scientists and defense officials in the United States."[13] While this may well have been true, the difference in assessment also may have been the result of greater U.S. research on both the defensive and offensive facets of RWs and, in particular, the potential effects of radiation exposure.

The Impact of the Postwar Threat Environment

The British wartime program related to atomic weapons, like that of the United States, was motivated almost exclusively by international security considerations and the perceived need to produce a powerful new weapon with which to wage war against Nazi Germany.[14] There is evidence, however, that even during the war, this incentive was supplemented in the United Kingdom by an interest in the postwar security benefits of possessing atomic weaponry, as well as the commercial energy potential that might be a byproduct of atomic weapons research. The July 1941 report of the MAUD Committee, for example, tellingly observes: "Even if the war should end before the bombs are ready the effort would not be wasted . . . since no country would care to risk being caught without a weapon of such decisive possibilities."[15] Appendix X of the same report also discusses nuclear energy as a source of power and emphasizes the imperative for Great Britain to "take an active part in this [nuclear energy] research so that the British Empire cannot be excluded by default from future developments."[16] No such evidence exists that similar incentives were at work during the war with respect to radiological weapons.[17] In fact, based on U.S. information available to British defense officials at the end of the war, it was not at all clear that RWs offered much in the way of military advantages in comparison to existing weapons such as chemical weapons. This view was reinforced by the findings of one of the earliest postwar assessments of RWs, which concluded that the prospective weapon had serious limitations due to the rapid decay of the fissionable product and the requirement for heavy shielding of the material.[18] Interestingly, the problem of protecting the crew piloting an aircraft carrying "radioactive poisons" was anticipated in May's August 1942 report.[19]

In 1947, the UK Chiefs of Staff (COS) committee held a series of meetings in which it identified the Soviet Union as the chief postwar strategic threat to British interests.[20] In a May 1947 meeting, the COS issued a report on future defense policy in which it concluded that the USSR would likely develop a nuclear weapons capacity that could threaten the United Kingdom and would require an appropriate deterrent. While the committee's preferred deterrent was the atomic bomb, it hedged its recommendation by suggesting the deterrent need for possession of and the ability to use a more generic "weapon of mass destruction."[21] This reference to a wider body of nonconventional weapons would appear to include radiological weapons.

In April 1948, the COS met again to review a March 1948 report by a subcommittee of the Defense Research Policy Committee on the strategic aspects of atomic energy. The report had been prepared to inform military planners on the technical feasibility of a British nuclear weapon and how it might be integrated into the British arsenal. After over ninety brief bullet points breaking down the issues involved with the atom bomb, including the production of fissile material, the means of delivery, the necessary industrial capacity and facilities, effects of the weapon, and potential targets, the report discusses possible future types of bombs and military uses of radioactivity as a weapon.[22] This section briefly addresses the possibilities of boosted fission and hydrogen "super-bombs" before arriving at a page-long analysis of "radioactive poisons." As in the Soviet RW program (about which the UK appears to have been unaware) but in contrast to that pursued by the United States, the modality for the British RW program suggested in the report is "radioactive products of atomic piles [reactors] as contaminants or as a form of poison."[23] In other words, the idea was to exploit the radioactive byproducts of nuclear fission for use as a weapon.

The subcommittee discussed three possible uses for radiological warfare: contamination of the air in the manner of a gaseous chemical weapon, contamination of drinking water, and contamination of the ground for area denial. While contending that "much further study" was necessary, the subcommittee appears to have regarded the first and second methods as unfeasible and ineffective, respectively. It saw the most promise in the third option, area denial through ground contamination, and suggested that the products of a single reactor over the course of one month's operation could deliver a lethal dose of radioactivity to a sixty-square mile region.[24] This assessment of radioactive waste to deny the use of large areas echoes the rather optimistic proposal that Dr. Joseph Hamilton made in 1947 in support of the initiation of the U.S. radiological weapons program.

The Impact of Key Scientists

Despite the relatively low priority afforded to RWs at the March and April 1948 meetings, a few high-ranking scientists in the British military establishment began to explore possible ways that radioactive fission products might be weaponized and the problems that might arise in this effort. Among these scientists was Sir John Cockcroft, director of the Atomic Energy Research Establishment (AERE). He was a renowned physicist who had been instrumental in kick-starting the U.S. atom bomb project and was a promoter of U.S.-UK nuclear cooperation. Another was Dr. William G. Marley, a physicist who, like Cockcroft, had worked on the Manhattan Project in the United States on the implosion bomb. Dr. Marley was head of the Health Physics Division at the AERE and became the chief authority on RWs within British military-scientific circles.

A number of British scientists spent the remainder of 1948 making inquiries about various aspects of RWs. One of these inquiries survives in the documentary record, although it is unclear whether it was specifically about RWs: the Chemical Defense Research Department was consulted about "radioactive dusts and mists," terms often used to describe notional radiological weapons.[25] The response, however, presumes that these "radioactive dusts and mists" would be the result of an atomic explosion. Whether the response indicates confusion as to the nature of RWs or an answer to a question about the related but distinct phenomenon of radioactive fallout is uncertain. Interestingly, in light of his emergence as the leading British authority on RWs, Dr. William G. Marley is copied on the letter.

These preliminary investigations led to a more full-fledged British RW developmental effort in early 1949. One can trace this progression to a meeting on January 21, 1949, attended by six military scientists at the Shell Mex House on the Strand in London. John Cockcroft, then in the United States and having witnessed the advances made by the U.S. RW program and also based on "some experimental work at Edgewood Arsenal," urged Dr. F. G. Wilkins, the principal director of Scientific Research (Defense) to convene the meeting for the purpose of discussing "the toxic effects of radio-active dusts." These effects, Cockcroft concluded, were "about as effective as mustard gas."[26] In advance of the meeting, Wilkins wrote to Dr. Marley to seek his input regarding the "maximum weight of material which can be included in one bomb [involving fission products] and the area of ground which it should contaminate."[27]

As before and in contrast to the prevailing concept of RWs in the United States, RW agents in the British perspective were expected to be byproducts from atomic piles. Because of this assumption, the participants at the Shell Mex House meeting identified the chief problems with RWs as being the extraction and preparation of the bombs, and particularly shielding the bomb bay to protect air crews during bombing runs. As British ballistic missile technology was not yet advanced enough to deliver a warhead with an acceptable degree of accuracy, the UK was reliant on gravity bombs. Also, in contrast to the U.S. RW program, the one conceived by the UK was based on the premise that it would be easier to disperse radiation evenly using a single concentrated bomb as opposed to sub-munitions. The meeting concluded with the action item that Dr. Marley would provide more exact figures on fission products and then consult with chemical bomb-makers to inform an assessment of RW systems. Meeting participants were admonished to keep the information as compartmentalized as possible and not to discuss it beyond a few designated individuals.[28]

Soon after the meeting, Dr. Marley produced the more in-depth analysis on the generation, storage, and processing of nuclear waste for RWs, building largely on information that had been collected since the April 1948 COS meeting.[29] In it, he briefly considers irradiation of inert metals in reactor cores, the sort of RW agent then being pursued in the United States, but he ultimately recommends use of fission products from nuclear waste for reasons of economy. Marley's analysis did not advance thinking about RWs significantly except for its more thorough accounting of the amount of fission products produced by a reactor and their suitability for weaponization. However, the analysis appears to have been regarded in the UK as the closest thing to an authoritative text on RWs and was referred to occasionally when the possibility of RWs was raised in different quarters in the ensuing years.

Significantly, when Marley proceeded to seek input on the means of weaponizing RWs, he did not follow the information security guidance set down at the conclusion of the January 1949 meeting. On May 31 and June 2 of that year, he consulted with two scientific advisers to the Air Ministry regarding shielding and storage problems onboard bombers, within the purview of the action item in the January meeting. In addition, on June 1, he consulted with the head of the Theoretical Physics Division, the brilliant thirty-seven-year-old physicist Klaus Fuchs, who, from the early 1940s until his arrest in February 1950, had been a Soviet spy.[30] During his career in the United States, Canada, and the United Kingdom, Fuchs passed along invaluable information to his Soviet handlers, including technical information on uranium enrichment and hydrogen bomb design. At the time of his interaction with Marley in spring 1949, he was still a senior and well-regarded scientist at the Atomic Energy Research Establishment. It is unclear why Marley consulted with Fuchs, and we do not know the precise nature of Marley's inquiry. Fuchs's response is a rather banal observation that radiological warfare could have both strategic and tactical applications. We therefore cannot discern if Fuchs was intrigued or unimpressed by the British pursuit of RWs, nor do we know if he passed the information along to Soviet intelligence.

While this determination cannot be made based on the available record, including extended interviews with Fuchs after his arrest for spying that were conducted by MI5 interrogator William Skardon and Dr. Michael Perrin, a specialist on the German atomic research program, it is noteworthy that many of Fuchs's papers from his time in the AERE were confiscated and destroyed on the order of Sir William Penney, who led the British nuclear weapons program.[31] The motivations for Penney's action have yet to be adequately explained, although they may be due as much to the sensitive information that Fuchs provided to Penney about the U.S. pursuit of a hydrogen bomb as to information that he may have passed on to his Soviet handlers.[32] What is known is that the revelations of various Soviet atomic spies operating in the United Kingdom doomed British efforts to restore the wartime collaboration on atomic weapons with the United States, which the political and scientific leadership of the United Kingdom had sought. Indeed, even prior to Fuchs's confession, it appears that senior British atomic energy officials were reluctant to disclose their suspicions for fear of the damage they might do to Anglo-American relations.[33]

RWs in the Shadow of the Atomic Bomb

The documentary trail of British radiological pursuits grows cold for most of the period between spring 1949 and summer 1952. As best we can discern, Marley was mostly engaged in radiological civil defense projects, means to add shielding to protect air crews, and the testing of protective clothing against radiation.[34] While it is conceivable that work on RWs continued without his direct engagement, it is likely that British efforts in the nuclear realm in this period were almost entirely directed at building and testing an atomic bomb as soon as possible.[35] Consistent with this thesis is the correspondence in time between the likely hiatus in work on RWs and the decline of the UK's biological weapons program.[36]

The subject of radiological weapons resurfaces again at a meeting of the Chiefs of Staff Committee on June 6, 1951, during which attention was directed at a report of the Defense Research Policy Committee that addressed the operational implications of atomic energy for military purposes. Although much of the report was focused on the production, delivery, and effects of various types of explosions, Section 13 deals with radiological warfare. Limited to one page—just slightly less than that devoted in Section 14 to the hydrogen bomb—the report notes, among other points:

- It is possible in principle to contaminate an area of a few square miles with radioactive products from a pile to such an extent that it would be impossible for personnel to stay more than a few hours in the area without receiving radiological injury which would make them ill within a week.... Radioactive products might therefore be used to force the evacuation of a strictly limited area which it was particularly undesirable to destroy by conventional armaments....[37]

- A contamination of five million curies of fission products per square mile would deliver a fatal dose to a human being in about 24 hours....[38]

- The fission products accumulated in the course of one, three and five years operation of the U.K. piles would amount to about 20, 40 and 50 million curies respectively....[39]

- The delivery of these radioactive products would be extremely difficult, although war-time experience suggests that sources of 10,000 curies could be suitably handled. The fission products would probably be associated with about 1,000 lbs. of liquid and personnel exposed for any period of a few hours would have to be protected from the radiation by a shield of about four inches of lead, weighing several tons. . . ."[40]

- It would be possible in principle to produce radioactive products other than fission products which would have a shorter life and which would therefore produce higher degrees of contamination for a shorter time. This would require the construction of special piles operating at high power. . . . Radioactive materials, including fission products could also be used, *possibly surreptitiously*, at lower concentrations, over a correspondingly wider area of strategic importance to induce radiation sickness, and for this purpose they might be introduced into water supplies. . . ."[41]

The section concludes with the telling observation that "the use of radioactive materials as neutralizing agents must be compared with the use of chemical warfare agents. It seems probable that the latter would be simpler to handle and would be less costly."[42]

There is no indication in this authoritative report or in any other government document with which we are familiar to suggest that the UK conducted—or seriously contemplated conducting—any actual tests involving the dispersal of radiological agents as RWs. Given the concern expressed about aircraft crew safety and the tonnage associated with protective lead shielding, we are inclined to dismiss as fictional one magazine account from 1952 sensationally titled "Our Silent Mystery Weapon: Death Sand." Written by the American newspaperman and biographer J. Alvin Kugelmass, the article asserts that in July (presumably 1951), a British plane "dropped five tons of atomic sand in a classified area. Chances are that this was done in Australia."[43] Much greater chances are that nothing of the sort ever occurred, as no explanation is provided by the author about how tons of radiological material were transported to Australia for this purpose or why UK defense officials would expose a crew to the grave radiation risks with which they were very familiar.[44]

As best we can ascertain, the next serious discussion of RWs in the British high command occurred in August 1952, shortly before the UK exploded an atomic bomb in Western Australia and became the third member of the nuclear weapons club. The results of the discussion took the form of a brief memo by unknown officials in the Air Ministry, examining the advantages and disadvantages of RWs.[45] The memo is peculiar for a number of reasons, including the lack of references to prior studies by the UK on the subject and the discussants' apparent unfamiliarity with the topic under consideration. One has the impression that participants in the meeting were recounting—and sometimes misremembering—secondhand accounts of talking points. The report observes that all potential advantages of RWs are counterbalanced by equivalent disadvantages or are dependent upon economic benefits in comparison to other weapons (implied to be CWs), which do not exist. The report concludes that there is no requirement at present for a radiological weapon for the Royal Air Force. It further notes, however, that research in RW design, particularly for guided missiles, "should be closely watched so that advantage could be taken of any developments which might lead to economy of effort."[46]

In subsequent months, there was a flurry of brief communiqués between RAF officers seeking answers about RWs. The tenor of these letters is mostly dismissive of the concept of these weapons. One officer, for example, in describing how much radiological material he thought would be necessary to stop an advancing army, concluded "it would be difficult to imagine them being in the same fit state if the material had been mustard."[47]

A final tranche of documents after this apparent end to the UK's pursuit of radiological weapons provides an intriguing coda to the program. The first is a memo to the AERE director in March 1953 on "weapons and equipment suitable for the dispersion of active material in the form of particulate dust." The document states that the work that had recently been done on biological cluster or "child" bombs would seem to be applicable. Perhaps reflecting a more rigorous information security culture than prevailed in 1949, the document does not state directly that it is referring to RWs. However, a handwritten note by Dr. Marley to the director confirms that this is indeed the matter at hand: "This is the note from Porton received in response to our enquiries on attainable performance. I shall use these figs in consultation with Tait; ideas on radiological weapons."[48] While there is not a clear follow-up to this line of inquiry, it would seem that Dr. Marley had not yet quite given up on RWs.

For all practical purposes, however, by the end of 1953 the British RW program had ceased to exist. This outcome was formalized in the October

1953 determination by the British Chiefs of Staff Committee that "no effort should be devoted in this country to the development of weapons of radiological warfare."[49] It was reaffirmed by the Defense Research Policy Committee in April 1955, fittingly with the endorsement of Sir John Cockcroft, who had presided over the Atomic Energy Research Establishment at the time of the RW program's launch.[50]

Nevertheless, a 1956 document by Air Force Major Janisch suggests that RWs may have had an afterlife in the British military or clandestine services. The report describes the pursuit of a ghastly sabotage weapon consisting of micron-sized quantities of strontium-89 designed to "cause serious incapacitation or death to limited numbers of VIPs at any one time."[51] Although this is an entirely different sort of radiological weapon than the area denial gamma-emitters envisaged in the late '40s and early '50s, who should be copied on the memo but Dr. Marley. It may be that, after years of research into the applications of radiation for the British military, RWs finally found their home as a tool of sabotage and assassination in the British clandestine services—a twist worthy of an Ian Fleming novel.

The British Case in Comparative Perspective

As this chapter demonstrates, it is possible to trace the basic outlines of the British RW program, to identify with fair confidence key turning points in the country's assessment of RWs, and to make educated guesses about the principal drivers of and constraints on the emergence, evolution, and ultimate abandonment of what would have been a weapons system innovation. Much, however, remains unknown and unknowable in the absence of greater access to archival documents and closer scrutiny of the historical record. While not a substitute for such information, comparing the British experience with RWs with that of the few other countries known to have pursued them may afford a better appreciation of its contours. Additional insights may be gleaned by examining the post–Second World War evolution of two other nonconventional weapons programs in the United Kingdom about which more has been written—those involving biological and chemical weapons.

One potentially fruitful area of comparison has to do with the role played by international security considerations. As noted in this book's introduction, the dominant explanation for military innovation among international relations scholars is perceived threats from adversaries. It also is often assumed that states will emulate one another's military innovations in an action-reaction fashion, which relies heavily on military technical intelligence.[52]

There is little doubt that perceived threats from adversaries contributed to initial interest in radiological weapons in the United Kingdom, as they did in the United States, the Soviet Union, Egypt, and Iraq. In the U.S. and British cases, that threat emanated from Nazi Germany and was related to the fear that Hitler's scientists might be ahead of the Allies in exploiting atomic energy for military purposes, including the dispersal of radioactive material in the form of dust or liquid particles. There was a perceived need, therefore, to study the military uses of radiological weapons and possible defenses against them. As such, most of the limited research on RWs in the U.S. and the UK during the war was defense oriented, notwithstanding the fact that the perceived dangers of German radiological warfare diminished as more information became available about the state of Nazi Germany's nuclear program. In other words, although an external threat contributed to initial U.S. and British interest in RWs, the threat was far more influential in driving Anglo-American collaboration in the urgent development of an atomic bomb.

If the threat of German radiological warfare—reinforced by U.S. fears—provided an international security rationale for early British RW research activities, the emergence of the Soviet Union as a Cold War adversary served as a new external justification for the continued exploration of the military potential of radioactive fission products. Especially prior to the United Kingdom's first nuclear weapons test in October 1952, RWs probably were regarded by British defense officials as having the potential to contribute, albeit in a very limited fashion, to British deterrence policy, along with more well-established nonconventional armaments involving chemical and biological weapons.

Although British RW research activities were hampered during this period by the reluctance of the U.S. to share its nuclear secrets, a small cadre of defense scientists and officials engaged in the British atomic weapons program—including at least two Soviet atomic spies—were aware generally of U.S. RW research. Ironically, however, there is no indication that the UK was any better informed of Soviet work related to radiological weapons than the U.S. In fact, we are unaware of any British knowledge of or particular interest in Soviet RW activities. It would appear, therefore, that if any action-reaction or diffusion of innovation dynamic with respect to RWs were in effect, it probably involved U.S.-U.K. interactions rather than ones between the UK and the Soviet Union. If so, the interactions were unidirectional, as there is little evidence to suggest that the U.S. intelligence community was aware of the United Kingdom's exploration of RWs, and it is far from certain that it would have cared had it been so informed.[53]

Moreover, although the U.S. was determined to prevent the transfer of any information about nuclear weapons to its close wartime ally after the passage of the 1946 Atomic Energy Act, RWs fell into an ambiguous category—neither exactly nuclear nor chemical weapons.[54] We know, for example, that in advance of U.S.-U.K. meetings on CWs in 1948, U.S. Army Chemical Corps Chief of Research and Engineering William Creasy argued that items such as protective equipment "which have radiological warfare aspects" should be appropriate for discussion, but it is unclear if they or other RW-related items were discussed in the meeting.[55] It is noteworthy, however, that the British delegation to the joint CW meetings in September and October 1948 was headed by Dr. F. J. Wilkins, director of scientific research at the UK Ministry of Supply. As mentioned above, after Wilkins returned to England following the meetings, he jump-started the UK's exploration of RWs with a request to William Marley to conduct an initial investigation about two technical issues related to the use of fission products in a bomb and to arrange a meeting in January 1949 to discuss the issue.[56]

A major criticism of external security-oriented explanations of foreign policy decisions in general and weapons innovations in particular is their tendency to discount the impact of domestic factors, including bureaucratic politics, organizational processes, and individual actors. This explanatory shortcoming is apparent in both the initial rise and subsequent demise of the U.S. RW program, whose history was closely linked to competition with two other nonconventional weapons programs—nuclear and chemical. In the immediate postwar period, RWs were seen by some senior military figures as a potential complement to or even substitute for chemical weapons as a means of area denial for Soviet military operations in Europe and Chinese aggression in Asia.[57] Early on, the military services and even the Joint Chiefs of Staff took active interest in the subject of radioactive warfare and endorsed research in the field,[58] leading subsequently to the design, construction, and testing of RWs under the auspices of the Army Chemical Corps. This enthusiasm, however, never generated sufficiently broad or sustained support among any of the military services, Congress, or the executive branch to withstand bureaucratic competition with nuclear (or chemical) weapons in a resource-constrained environment. Although the role of domestic, bureaucratic drivers of radiological weapons is more difficult to determine in the Soviet case, the technical shortcomings of RWs as battlefield weapons are likely to have been recognized in Moscow by the late 1950s and even earlier by the Soviet Navy. This downgrading of Soviet research and development in RWs corresponded in time with major investments in nuclear weapons and the means for their delivery, as well as a significant buildup of Soviet chemical arms.[59]

In contrast to the U.S. and Soviet experiences with RWs, there is no evidence that any of the British military services or political leaders ever regarded RWs as a viable competitor with or major supplement to other nonconventional weapons. This assessment is in marked contrast to biological weapons, which, for a period of time in the early postwar period, were seen by the Chiefs of Staff as on par with nuclear weapons as a peacetime deterrent.[60] Also striking is the contrast between the manner in which very senior British officials, including prime ministers, were directly engaged in debates over the role of chemical weapons in British defense and deterrence during much of the postwar period and not engaged, as best we can tell, on the subject of RWs.[61]

Another category of explanations for military innovation highlights the role played by science and technology as catalysts for new weapons systems and portrays scientists as "technological entrepreneurs." In the U.S. experience, scientists such as Robert Oppenheimer, Enrico Fermi, and Ernest Lawrence (and at a much lower but still influential level, Joseph Hamilton and Robert Stone) were forceful proponents of RW research and development. While we are unable to identify comparable scientists who served as RW change agents in the Soviet Union, a similar advocacy function was performed by V. L. Vannikov, deputy to Soviet secret police chief Lavrenti Beria in the Special Committee of the Atomic Project. There was no similar technological entrepreneur in the UK—be it among scientists, defense officials, or political leaders. In fact, the only individual who is closely associated with RWs over the lifespan of the British R & D program is William Marley, whose persona is difficult to determine based on available sources. On the one hand, as William King suggests, he generally may have been a dispassionate civil servant and cautious bureaucrat rather than an ardent RW supporter in the vein of Joseph Hamilton. However, on occasion, he resembled Dr. Hamilton in the bland understatement with which he wrote about the gruesome effects of radiation on the human body. In "Preliminary Note on Military Uses of Radioactive Materials Derived from Nuclear Reactors" in 1949, he impassively noted, after several pages dealing with the potential effects of air contamination by means of RWs, that many survivors of the attack would fall ill and die of bone cancer in subsequent years, which "would probably prove to be a serious political embarrassment."[62] Later in the same memo, he similarly observed that exposure though contamination of very small quantities in drinking water could, over time, have carcinogenic effects that "might prove to be a considerable political disadvantage."[63] In other words, while King may be correct in crediting Marley's bureaucratic longevity to his cautious managerial skills, the tenacity with which he pursued RWs could also reflect a less-than-objective assessment of the weapon's costs and benefits. In either case, ultimately, he was not a successful technological entrepreneur.

Just as science and technology can serve as catalysts for new weapons systems such as RWs, they also can impose major impediments to weapons innovation. In the case of RWs, these obstacles included the need for radioactive isotopes with an appropriate half-life of about one hundred days (neither too long or too short to perform battlefield area denial tasks),[64] cost-effective means to extract the radioactive isotopes from nuclear waste or to irradiate an inert metal inside a nuclear reactor, and requirements for shielding the highly radioactive payload from personnel who were responsible for its handling and delivery. Although there were technical solutions to each of these problems and different states pursued different approaches, in each instance the solutions were perceived as not cost effective or otherwise realistic. In the U.S. case, for example, even the most ardent supporters of radiological weapons recognized that a substantial RW program involving the irradiation of tantalum would require a costly production infrastructure that was independent of the rapidly expanding nuclear weapons program. While the Soviet Union adopted a different RW production mode involving the extraction of radioisotopes from the operation of a plutonium reactor, defense decision-makers in Moscow also ultimately concluded that the costs of the new weapons system exceeded its military benefits.

For its part, the UK—apparently for economic reasons—chose to produce radioactive isotopes in a fashion similar to that employed by the Soviet Union rather than following the U.S. approach involving the irradiation of inert metals in a reactor core. It remains unclear from the available historical record if this initial decision was ever revisited based on knowledge of the burgeoning U.S. program. What is clear, as William King points out, is that the output of radioactive material from the Windscale (Sellafield) plutonium reactor, which fueled both the British RW and early nuclear weapons programs, was inadequate to the task. According to the "top secret" Chiefs of Staff note "Radiological Warfare" of October 26, 1953, the amount of radioactive material that could be produced for purposes of RWs was insufficient "to contaminate more than a very small area."[65] Although in principle this supply bottleneck might have been overcome by investing in dedicated RW production facilities, the funds were not available at a time when the overriding defense priority was production of nuclear weapons.

Unlike the U.S., Soviet, and Iraqi RW programs, British pursuit of radiological weapons never advanced beyond the exploratory phase and stopped short of testing. One possible explanation for this variation in state behavior could be cross-national differences in the normative considerations on the part of defense scientists, senior military officials, and political leaders, perhaps influenced by domestic public opinion. It is conceivable but not demonstrable with available evidence, for example, that, as the issue of RWs began to receive more attention in the media in the United States (including in popular culture such as the comic strip *Li'l Abner*), it may have complicated efforts to build bureaucratic support for radiological warfare within the government. More likely, the rise of popular concerns about radioactive contamination from atmospheric testing in the mid-1950s contributed to difficulty in promoting RWs on the part of scientists, defense officials, and—to the extent they were involved—politicians. Obviously, these constraints were far more likely to be a factor in the more open U.S. and British societies. While we are unable to provide any direct linkages between public angst about radioactive poisons and decisions regarding their development, production, and abandonment, it would be surprising if policymakers were indifferent to such considerations.[66] That was certainly the case in the UK with regard to decision-making involving chemical weapons.[67] Moreover, while King may overstate the degree to which prominent British scientists as a group were more instrumental than their American counterparts in dismissing the merits of RWs, there is merit to his finding that British defense officials were disinclined to override their prevailing skepticism.[68]

The Bottom Line

Unlike the U.S. and Soviet programs (and the Iraqi program, as will be detailed in chapter 5), British pursuit of radiological weapons never moved beyond the exploratory phase. One can attribute this outcome to a combination of factors, including technical impediments, resource constraints, normative considerations, limited military effectiveness, and the absence of strong advocacy among the scientific, military, and political communities. Moreover, whatever initial appeal RWs held as a prospective weapons innovation, it was soon eclipsed by far more lethal nuclear weapons. In this respect, the British experience with RWs resembles that of other countries, which simultaneously pursued nuclear, chemical, biological, and radiological weapons but then discontinued most forms of nonconventional weapons in favor of nuclear arms.[69]

FOUR

Egypt

"A Radiological Arms Race in the Middle East?" "Poor Man's Nuclear Warfare?" "The Problem of a Garbage Bomb." Thus read headlines in the spring and fall of 1963, covering the complex web of Israeli allegations, U.S. intelligence assessments, and Austrian, German, and Swiss police and court records regarding Egypt's purported efforts to develop a radiological weapon.[1] In the early 1960s, Gamal Abdel Nasser's Egypt sought to develop nonconventional weapons and means for their delivery, recruiting a cadre of expatriate German scientists, engineers, and military personnel for that effort. Against the backdrop of Arab-Israeli animosity and Egypt's quest for leadership in the Arab world, which principally defined Egyptian perceptions of its security environment, it appears that Cairo's military innovators also explored a radiological weapons (RWs) capability.

In contrast to the other case studies presented in this volume, much of the evidence regarding the Egyptian RW effort remains circumstantial and rests to a large degree on Israeli claims and the testimony of Austrian scientist Otto Joklik, an enigmatic, self-proclaimed arms merchant, former military officer in the German army and likely Israeli intelligence asset. Joklik, who was arrested in Basel in March 1963 and put on trial on charges of coercion, testified to the Swiss police that he conducted work on Egypt's nonconventional weapons programs between the spring and fall of 1962. According to Joklik's testimony, Project Ibis—run by the Egyptian air force and involving Joklik as lead scientist—foresaw the development of artillery shells filled with various radioactive isotopes to be used by a special Egyptian independent artillery regiment. From radiological artillery shells, the project was envisaged to expand into radiological aerial bombs and warheads for Egypt's inchoate missile force.[2]

An account of the events that led to Joklik's court testimony might easily be mistaken for a convoluted spy movie: To thwart the broader efforts of German scientists in Egypt, Israel's national intelligence agency, the Mossad, had undertaken Operation Damocles, a campaign of intimidation, sabotage, and even assassination to dissuade German scientists and technicians from offering their services to the Egyptian military.[3] The campaign had one unforeseen additional consequence: it induced Otto Joklik, who was intermittently working in Cairo, to defect to Israel.[4] When Joklik was flown to Israel and interrogated, Mossad chief Isser Harel and Foreign Minister Golda Meir considered Joklik's claims regarding Project Ibis credible. However, Shimon Peres, the deputy defense minister and confidant to Prime Minister David Ben-Gurion, was skeptical and instructed officials from the Israeli Science Liaison Bureau (Lakam, Israel's scientific intelligence organization) to conduct an independent interrogation.[5] These officials, who possessed specialized knowledge of nuclear science and CW/BW weapons, determined that Joklik's technological credentials were thin and his claims suspicious. Nonetheless, Foreign Minister Meir raised the issue of Egyptian radiological warfare with President Kennedy during a meeting in Palm Beach in December 1962.[6] The split in the Israeli government over this issue initially festered outside public view until events in March 1963 brought international attention to Joklik and the affair of the German scientists in Egypt.

Despite the reservations that many Israeli officials had about Joklik, Isser Harel believed he would be useful as an agent to dissuade other German scientists from working with the Egyptians. He arranged for a Mossad agent who went by the alias Joseph Ben-Gal to be Joklik's handler. The two spent the early months of 1963 approaching German scientists and engineers who had been in contact with the Egyptians and coercing them into forswearing any assistance to Egypt. In March, Joklik and Ben-Gal arranged a meeting in a hotel in Basel, Switzerland with Heidi Goercke, whose father was one of the German rocket engineers working in Egypt. At the meeting, Joklik and Ben-Gal threatened Goercke and her family with "serious consequences" if her father did not return from Egypt. Unknown to Joklik and Ben-Gal, Ms. Goercke had arranged for the police to have the meeting under surveillance, and after the meeting, the two agents were arrested and charged with attempted coercion and illegal activities on behalf of a foreign government.[7] Both agents were found guilty, sentenced to two months in prison and finally expelled from Switzerland. Joklik and Ben-Gal's trial attracted global media attention, and the Egyptian experimentation with RWs featured prominently in Joklik's defense, generating a wealth of commentary that is cited in this chapter.

When we situate Egypt's pursuit of RWs on a continuum of activities of military innovation—which ranges from intent, procurement of expertise and needed materials, and experimentation to testing, production, and deployment—it appears that its RW effort was the most rudimentary and the most short-lived among the state-level programs examined in this volume. Unlike Iraq's RW program, which proceeded to the testing stage and is examined in the next chapter, the Egyptian effort never advanced beyond the exploratory phase. Joklik claims that, at the time of his departure from Egypt in the summer of 1962, cobalt-60 and other material worth 500,000 marks had been acquired from West Germany, Canada, and India for Project Ibis, and first tests with radiological shells were planned to be conducted by the air force.[8] Yet, since Joklik decided not to return to Egypt, a battery of tests allegedly scheduled for September 1962 probably never occurred.

Although Israel, for whom Joklik appears to have begun working as an intelligence asset in late 1962, actively raised concerns about Egypt's purported RW effort through 1963, it admitted by November of that year that Cairo probably had shelved its plan for radiological warfare.[9] Much of the available evidence, media outcry, and diplomatic fallout about the rudimentary Egyptian pursuit of radiological devices thus falls into the 1962–1963 timeframe, approximately a decade after the conclusion of the British foray into RWs and not long after the demise of the Soviet RW program. Besides its premature abandonment due to the departure of its lead scientist, what sets Egypt's pursuit of RWs further apart from the other case studies examined is that it materialized almost exclusively with foreign assistance, appears to have owed its existence to an individual technological entrepreneur, did not cease due to the conclusion of a successful nuclear weapons program, and appears to have been the only effort to focus on the longer-lived isotopes of cobalt-60 and strontium-90.

This chapter provides a detailed account of the highly obscure and short-lived Egyptian experimentation with RWs—the genesis of Egypt's interest, its drivers, the obstacles Egypt would have encountered if it had proceeded from experimentation to testing and deployment, and the intra-Israeli and international disagreements it generated—situating it in the context of Egypt's foreign and security policy under President Gamal Abdel Nasser. It analyzes the relationship between Egypt's flirtation with RWs and the country's pursuit of ballistic missiles and other nonconventional weapons while also highlighting similarities and discrepancies with the British, Soviet, and U.S. programs.

The analysis will specifically address the following questions: Did Egypt express an interest in RWs in the early 1960s, and if so, why, and how serious was that interest? What international security imperatives drove the Egyptian interest? What military objectives did Egypt anticipate could usefully be served by RWs in the context of its regional confrontation with Israel and quest for leadership in the Arab world? What role did the RW effort play within Egypt's overall search for unconventional weapons? To what degree was the RW project the result of an indigenous Egyptian interest or an idea promoted by the "imported" German scientists? To what extent did considerations of status and prestige motivate President Nasser's quest for advanced missiles and nonconventional weapons, including RWs? To what extent did technical difficulties, bureaucratic political determinants, expectations of international opprobrium over Egypt's pursuit of nonconventional weapons, or other factors hinder the Egyptian effort? Why was Egypt's experimentation with RWs so short-lived, failing to proceed to the testing stage? And why did it become a source of irritation in Israel's relations with Austria, Germany, Switzerland, and the United States?

The chapter will first analyze the drivers behind Egypt's interest in RWs, situating it in the context of Cairo's broader foreign and security policy in the late 1950s and early 1960s. It will show that RWs were likely viewed as a possible, albeit relatively minor, tool among a range of options to both match and deter Israel, especially amid reports of progress in the latter's nuclear program following the revelation of the Dimona nuclear reactor in the Negev desert in December 1960. Further, the Egyptian leadership viewed advances in nonconventional weapons and missiles generally—including, apparently, in obtaining an RW option—as conducive to Egypt's claim to leadership in the Arab world at a time when the demise of the short-lived United Arab Republic (UAR) had dealt a serious blow to the country's pan-Arab prestige. However, there is no evidence linking Joklik's experimentation with RWs to specific approaches to deterrence or operational concepts entertained by the Egyptian military establishment. This chapter shows that there is no indication that Egypt—unlike Iraq—pursued RWs for deployment as area-denial weapons in a land war, whether on the Sinai Peninsula or in the type of military campaign that would see Egypt stand accused of chemical weapons (CWs) use in Yemen from 1963. In addition, the chapter shows that Otto Joklik's ability to pursue a radiological device for Egypt is partially explained by bureaucratic political determinants. Egypt during the early 1960s—a time when the young republic actively involved German scientists in support of its missile and nonconventional weapons programs—provided a welcome institutional context for scientific entrepreneurs to pursue novel efforts and for "dreamers or exploiters" to "convince their bosses to back some scheme."[10]

Having probed the drivers, the chapter will turn to inhibitors to Egypt's pursuit of RWs, returning to the causal relevance of bureaucratic political determinants to its short-lived nature. The analysis will show that the RW effort—much like the pursuit of other nonconventional weapons—was never sufficiently prioritized by the Egyptian government and was eventually undermined by the departure of its lead scientist, Otto Joklik. The chapter then analyzes the technical challenges related to both the use of cobalt-60 and weaponization, concluding that these challenges were overwhelming and were unlikely to have been overcome had Egypt's RW effort advanced beyond the exploratory stage. The chapter closes by investigating why the Egyptian flirtation with RWs caused irritation in Israel's relations with Austria, Germany, Switzerland, and the United States, while also being a source of Israeli inter-agency friction.

Issues attendant to Egypt's radiological experimentation—President Nasser's ballistic missile program, Israel's campaign against the German scientists in Egypt, the Swiss trial of Otto Joklik and his Israeli handler Josef Ben-Gal, and resultant diplomatic tensions between Israel and several countries—generated a wealth of primary and secondary source material in German, Hebrew, Arabic, and English. It was therefore possible to study, for the purpose of this chapter, Israeli allegations regarding Egypt's pursuit of nonconventional weapons, relevant U.S. intelligence assessments, and hundreds of Austrian, German, and Swiss police and court records relating to Joklik, the most prominent figure in Egypt's pursuit of RWs. To compensate for the lack of Egyptian archival material relevant to this case study, the authors also depended on contemporaneous media accounts, Department of State memos of meetings with Egyptian and Israeli principal actors, as well as Mohamed Hussein Heikal's (President Nasser's de facto spokesperson) accounts, which were helpful in contextualizing Egypt's external threat perceptions at the time. Still, much of the evidence regarding the Egyptian experimentation with RWs remains circumstantial and rests to a large degree on difficult-to-verify Israeli claims and the testimony of Otto Joklik.[11]

Drivers of Egypt's Interest in RW

Perceived International Security Imperatives

Egypt's pursuit of nonconventional weapons and means for their delivery in the early 1960s materialized against the backdrop of a fluid regional and international security landscape. At the time, the country's threat perceptions were shaped by crystallizing American Cold War strategies, local pressures for self-determination across the Middle East, Soviet plans for expansion, the remnants of British and French colonialism in the region, and the apparently intractable Arab-Israeli conflict.[12] Following the 1952 Free Officers' coup in Egypt and Gamal Abdel Nasser's ascendancy to power, the revolution he led aspired to eradicate imperialism; abolish feudalism, monopolies and capitalist control; create a strong national army; and support social justice and a democratic society.[13] Amid a sustained focus on molding Egypt internally, Nasser did not immediately see Israel as a threat, though his emerging ambition to become the vanguard of the Arab world required maintaining a state of belligerency with the Jewish state.[14] Egypt's claim to pan-Arab leadership, meanwhile, was sustained by Nasser's conviction that the country's unique geography and historical legacy enhanced its ability to influence Africa and the Muslim and the Arab worlds.[15] Yet, in the period prior to the 1956 Suez crisis, Israel was not a priority for the young Egyptian republic, due in part to the preoccupation of the Free Officers with domestic issues and the priority they ascribed to eliciting Great Britain's withdrawal from Suez.[16]

From the mid-1950s, the nascent Cold War standoff between the United States and the USSR increasingly shaped regional alliance politics and, concomitantly, Egyptian threat perceptions. Following the 1955 creation of the Baghdad Pact, whose regional members included Iraq, Turkey, Iran, and Pakistan, Egypt announced its intention to procure arms from Czechoslovakia. While the United States initially remained committed to financing Egypt's Aswan High Dam in order to prevent Cairo from drifting further into the Soviet orbit, Nasser's May 1956 decision to recognize Communist China unnerved Washington. It ended a period that Nasser-confidant Mohamed Heikal characterizes as one of "seduction" in U.S.-Egyptian relations during which Washington sought to "woo" Nasser.[17] The ensuing 1956 Suez crisis heralded a new chapter in Egyptian history, resulting in Nasser's strengthened international position, the United States replacing Britain and France as the key external actor in the Middle East, and Egypt moving closer to the USSR.[18]

Against the backdrop of this fluid regional landscape, U.S. policy vis-à-vis Egypt evolved. Under the Eisenhower administration, any attempts to "seduce" Egypt gave way to the Omega Plan, a covert operation to coerce and isolate Egypt, which was driven by the realization that Nasser could not be instrumentalized for realizing U.S. Cold War objectives.[19] Since the Nasserist regime embraced nonalignment and also led the nationalists' opposition to the conservative monarchies in the Middle East, its foreign policy orientation proved increasingly incompatible with the United States' attempt to incorporate the conservative forces of the Arab world into its global alliance network. Heikal characterizes U.S. policy vis-à-vis Egypt during the second half of the 1950s as one of initial "punishment" followed by "containment."[20]

When John F. Kennedy replaced Eisenhower in the White House in January 1961, Nasser was determined to explore a qualitatively different relationship with the United States. The Egyptian president admired Kennedy and was impressed with his inauguration speech, yet also felt some doubt as to his counterpart's foreign policy intentions. As chronicled by Heikal, the two men exchanged personal letters—aimed at strengthening bilateral relations—with astonishing regularity, with Kennedy in a May 1961 correspondence offering Egypt aid in return for the latter loosening its ties with the USSR. Nasser's response, following intensive internal Egyptian deliberations, suggested that he "did not take Kennedy's overtures seriously."[21] His reply also conveyed his views on U.S. policy in the Middle East candidly: he labeled the Balfour Declaration a fraud, accused the United States of setting itself against law and justice, and lamented the undue influence of American Jews on U.S. policy.[22]

The Kennedy-Nasser exchanges were indicative of a U.S.-Egyptian relationship that was highly ambivalent, plotting a graph that was "sometimes up" but "often down."[23] Egyptian uncertainties, generated by such ambivalence, were amplified by growing concerns about Israel. In December 1960, Israel had officially acknowledged the construction of a nuclear reactor for civilian purposes near Dimona in the Negev desert. The announcement immediately raised suspicions regarding Israeli intentions in the Arab world and prompted Egyptian officials, who were meeting with their State Department counterparts the day after the announcement, to manifest "almost an hysterical attitude concerning Israel's atomic capabilities."[24] The breakup of the UAR—a state established only in 1958 at the height of pan-Arabism—in late 1961 following a coup in Syria further complicated Egyptian threat perceptions. Heikal recalls that the UAR's collapse "tormented" Nasser, and when the latter heard rumors of CIA involvement in Syria's turmoil, "he was both hurt and puzzled," becoming increasingly suspicious of Kennedy's true intentions.[25]

Meanwhile, Egyptian-Soviet relations were in flux during the period investigated in this chapter. Ever since Stalin's death in 1953, the USSR had embarked on a more aggressive policy in the Third World and paid closer attention to the national liberation movements, including Egypt.[26] The country's size, strategic value, and anti-imperialist bearing, as well as its influence in Africa, the Arab world, and the nonaligned movement, made Egypt the natural entry point for Soviet involvement in the Middle East.[27]

Egypt quickly became the hub of Soviet interests in the region. Nasser, in facilitating the creation of Soviet links to emerging allies such as Syria and Yemen, became a central "consultant to the Soviet Union on Arab affairs, an instructor for the newly initiated in the labyrinth of Oriental politics."[28] While Egypt was central to Soviet policy toward Yemen—which was managed out of Cairo—the reverse became true with Soviet support for Nasser amid the Yemen civil war: in 1962, first secretary of the Communist Party Nikita Khrushchev authorized the dispatch of Soviet planes and pilots to help Egypt's campaign.[29] As Jesse Ferris argues, the consequences of that campaign—a suspension of U.S. aid to Egypt, which exacerbated the burden wartime expenditures placed on the economy—drove Egypt yet more deeply into the Soviet sphere.[30]

Volatile U.S.-Egyptian relations, growing concerns over Israel's military potential following the revelation of the Dimona nuclear reactor, the breakup of the UAR, and Egypt's growing centrality to the USSR combined to shape Egypt's complex and fluid threat perceptions in 1960 and 1961. These form the backdrop for understanding Egypt's missile and nonconventional weapons efforts, including the exploration of a radiological device.

"Weapons of Terror" to Match and Deter Israel's Nuclear Pursuit

The circumstantial evidence surrounding Egypt's rudimentary exploration of a radiological device suggests that Cairo was attracted to the idea of such a weapon in its quest for an array of options to deter Israel and match the latter's efforts to employ nuclear energy for military purposes. Catching up with Israel acquired particular urgency after the revelation of the Dimona reactor in December 1960, though Egyptian intelligence had harbored suspicions over the purpose of the site for years. In this context, it appears that the precise prospective military application of a radiological weapon in Egypt's arsenal was left underspecified, with different options floated according to Joklik's deposition. Project Ibis, the Austrian scientist claimed, involved the development of artillery shells filled with various radioactive isotopes to be used by a special independent artillery regiment. Artillery shells may well have marked the first stage of the effort given the shortcomings of Egypt's air force at the time. Subsequently, the project was envisaged to expand into radiological aerial bombs and warheads for Egypt's inchoate missile force.

Whether in the form of artillery shells or as warheads for Egyptian missiles, radiological devices were meant to serve, according to Joklik, as "weapons of terror" aimed at holding Israeli cities at risk.[31] Beyond such general ideas about RWs being suited for "terrorizing," however, it is unclear whether and how such weapons were ever considered by the military establishment as part of a coherent and thought-through approach to deterrence or in pursuit of area denial.

Radiological Warheads for Egypt's Missiles

Between the Suez Crisis of 1956 and the Arab-Israeli Six-Day War of 1967, Egypt pursued the development of a ballistic missile program. To achieve this aim, it employed a large cadre of German (and Austrian) scientists and technicians from 1959 to 1960—much as the Soviet Union had recruited German scientists to work on its atomic program earlier. U.S. intelligence analysts considered the military value of these Egyptian missiles "trifling" and unlikely to represent a threat to Israel,[32] but the Israeli government and public were concerned. In July 1962, Egypt announced that it had successfully test-fired four missiles from the Jabal Hamzah launch facility: Two al-Zafir (Victor) missiles with a projected range of 370 kilometers and two al-Kahir (Conqueror) missiles with a projected range of 600 kilometers.[33] Israel was presumably the intended target of these weapons, which Nasser unsubtly boasted could reach locations as far away as "just south of Beirut."[34]

The clearest indication that Egyptian scientific entrepreneurs and military strategists were interested in the possibility of equipping the country's planned missile fleet with radiological warheads comes from Joklik's depositions. In his testimony to Swiss police on March 5, 1963, he claimed that Wolfgang Pilz, a German scientist instrumental to the Egyptian missile program, had requested payloads with radioisotopes for missiles that could carry a payload of up to 1000 kilograms. The missiles, according to Pilz's purported request, should be equipped with "automatic loading systems" so that the loading of a "ready-to-launch missile with cobalt-60 or strontium-90 could occur just before launch" and "reproduce the radiation effectiveness and destructive impact of an atomic weapon through pressure and heat."[35] In another deposition, Joklik testified under oath that the German scientists in Cairo wanted to use radiological substances in Egypt's ballistic missile warheads to "poison Israel's atmosphere."[36] The insinuation that Egypt had considered radiological warheads for its missiles also came from Nasser himself, who conceded at a June 1963 meeting with John McCloy, President Kennedy's special envoy to the Middle East, that he had sought, unsuccessfully, "to find something more powerful than TNT" for his missiles but "could not find anything between TNT and a nuclear warhead."[37]

Israeli reactions to Joklik's claims suggest that the RW-missile nexus was taken seriously and caused considerable alarm among some Israeli government constituencies.[38] Isser Harel, chief of the Mossad at the time of Joklik's defection from Cairo, warned of Egypt's attempt at building "atom bombs ... death rays" and of German scientists assisting in the development of a cobalt warhead for surface-to-surface missiles that would scatter radioactive particles over large areas.[39] Moshe Dayan similarly published an article in *Ma'ariv* in spring 1963 that established a link between missiles and nuclear weapons that would try and destroy Israel: "Egypt's nuclear weapons need not be sophisticated either," Dayan noted. Even "primitive" nukes (he presumable meant radiological weapons) would allow Cairo to join what he called the "anteroom of the nuclear club."[40] The prospect that Egypt could fill its missiles with radiological substances was also raised by Israeli foreign minister Golda Meir in her interactions with President Kennedy.[41] Fears of a nexus between Egypt's ballistic missiles and weapons of mass destruction drove Israel's strong response to the Joklik testimonies, which materialized in a continuation of intimidation and assassinations of German scientists, and diplomatic outreach to West Germany, the United States, and other relevant countries.

Matching Israel after the Revelation of Dimona

Egypt's perceived deteriorating position compared to Israel's following the late 1960 revelation of the Dimona reactor principally drove Cairo's quest for options, including missiles, to match Israeli military innovations. Though the Israelis claimed publicly that Dimona was intended exclusively for civilian purposes, and President Kennedy sought to assure President Nasser in writing that Israel was not developing nuclear weapons, Egyptian intelligence had obtained confirmation of an Israeli nuclear weapons program.[42] In years prior, Dimona had become a major focus of Egyptian intelligence-gathering efforts.[43] Yet, it was not just apprehensions about the purpose of Dimona that spurred Egyptian efforts in the missile domain. By July 1961, Israel had also tested an unguided rocket (Shavit II), and although Cairo had probably known about the impending test, Egyptian general Mahmoud Khalil subsequently summoned the German scientists, insisting they work faster, "otherwise Egypt was going to be left behind."[44]

The contention that Egypt presumably decided both to accelerate its missile program and to start experimenting on a radiological device as a result of Israeli technological strides at Dimona and elsewhere is borne out by the sequence of events. By early 1962, Egypt's first missiles had entered the prototype test phase, and on July 21 of that year, Egypt announced that it had successfully test-fired four missiles. Around the same time, Otto Joklik claims to have been based in Cairo, experimenting with cobalt and strontium. It is thus conceivable that a select number of German scientists and their Egyptian patrons hoped for Egypt to obtain an option to equip its missiles with radiological payloads as one of several options to respond to Israel's forays into military applications of nuclear energy. The recollections of White House senior aide Robert Komer, who was dispatched to Cairo by Kennedy to probe Egypt's willingness to enter into an arms control initiative—including the nuclear dimension and missiles—in early 1963 appears to confirm this assessment.[45] Though Komer conversed with Nasser on Egypt's missile program only after Joklik's short-lived experimentation on an RW had concluded, he recalls Nasser emphasizing that Egyptian "reactions" were provoked by Israeli "actions," and though Nasser did not deny researching a radiological bomb, he insisted that Israel was planning to use "radiological products" in missile warheads.[46] Komer concluded from these exchanges in spring 1963 that Egypt was intent on "moving into military applications of nuclear energy because it was convinced that the Israelis were doing so."[47]

The importance of Dimona in spurring Egypt's missile efforts and radiological experimentation inevitably evokes the question as to whether the Nasserist regime might have viewed a radiological device as either a substitute for or a complement to a nuclear weapon. Indeed, conflation of Egypt's efforts toward a "nuclear" versus a "radiological" weapons capability was widespread at the time, both in media coverage as well as official correspondence on the German scientist affair. For instance, when raising the issue with U.S. officials in 1963, Israeli foreign minister Golda Meir frequently evoked a prospective Egyptian "nuclear" threat when referring to Otto Joklik's efforts to procure cobalt-60.[48]

However, there is no evidence that Egypt pursued a serious nuclear weapons program in response to the revelation of Dimona. Gamal Abdel Nasser had founded the Egyptian Atomic Energy Commission in 1955, with Ibrahim Hilmy Abdel Rahman, its first secretary general, presiding over nuclear developments, including the pursuit of several bilateral cooperation agreements, until 1958. Under a bilateral reactor deal, the USSR supplied Egypt with a small 2 MWt light-water research reactor, which went online in July 1961.[49] After the revelation of Dimona, according to James Walsh, Egypt expanded its nuclear program, increasing investment and research into nuclear technologies between 1960 and 1967. Notwithstanding such investment and President Nasser's occasional rhetorical indications of proliferation intent, however, there does not appear to ever have been a clear top-level political commitment to a domestic program to build nuclear weapons.[50] As Hassan Elbahtimy notes, Egypt might have held plans for nuclear expansion at the time, but they never materialized.[51] Avner Cohen, in his work on Israel's nuclear weapons program, echoes this assessment and more generally shows that Egypt's reaction to Dimona and to Israel's evolving nuclear opacity were "not the product of a well thought-out strategy."[52] Though Nasser had reacted harshly to the public revelation of Dimona, prompting efforts by the Kennedy administration over subsequent months to reassure Cairo over the benign nature of Israeli activities, he never attempted to match Israel's efforts in the nuclear realm. Cohen contends that this was the case because Egypt was developing other unconventional weapons, chiefly missiles, of its own, did not consider Dimona an immediate military threat, and moreover attributed secondary importance to the Arab-Israeli conflict, keen to "keep it in the icebox."[53]

In their contributions to the scholarly debate on Egypt's nuclear probes, Maria Rost Rublee and Walsh further show that the non-committal nature of Egypt's nuclear program was unlikely driven by a lack of resources, given how Egypt fared economically compared to other countries seeking to acquire a nuclear weapon and considering that Nasser spent enormous funds on other military pet projects at the time.[54] But precisely because Egypt appears to have pursued several projects—a small nuclear program but also missiles and other nonconventional weapons—any individual effort might have been perceived as dispensable. Indeed, Rublee's account of why Egypt chose nuclear forbearance in the 1960s argues that an alternative form of WMD—in Egypt's case, chemical weapons—can undercut the need for a nuclear weapons program. Though CWs are often called the "poor man's WMD," Rublee contends, Egypt might still have considered them as helping it match Israel's WMD capabilities. The presence of an alternative form of WMD may have helped assuage both Cairo's security concerns and psychological needs, convincing Nasser that Egypt would not be "left without any defense" against a WMD attack and in fact could launch one of its own.[55]

Given the lack of primary source evidence, it is impossible to establish conclusively whether Egyptian officials under Nasser deliberately opted for a fluid approach to deterrence—pursuing a range of options in response to Israeli nuclear advances—as opposed to a like-for-like approach to developing retaliatory capability. Since Joklik's exploration of RWs coincided with Egypt's forays into missiles and other unconventional weapons, however, it is conceivable that such weapons were viewed as one potential component of a fluid approach.

Deterrence: Compensating for a Weak Air Force after 1956

In addition to catching up with Israel and its assumed advances at Dimona and other military innovations, Egypt also appears to have hoped to compensate for its weak air force. The fact that Project Ibis initially foresaw the development of artillery shells filled with radioactive isotopes followed by radiological aerial bombs and warheads for missiles suggests concerns about the performance of the Egyptian air force. After the 1956 Suez War, Walsh argues, Egypt's ballistic missiles "became a natural response to increased Israeli air and air defense capabilities which blunted the effectiveness of Cairo's bomber force." From Egypt's perspective, "its inability to hold Israeli urban areas at risk denied it a crucial deterrent against another 1956-style attack."[56] This inability was rooted in the range and type of Egyptian aircraft, to which Israeli population centers remained effectively out of reach.

Some scholars characterize the Egyptian interest in missiles as having been generated well before the Suez Crisis, with Owen Sirrs showing that, after its 1948 defeat against Israel, Cairo professed an appetite for artillery rockets, which later morphed into an interest in ballistic missiles to offset Israel's qualitative military edge.[57] In addition, Sirrs contends that the 1956 war was likely important for Nasser's interest in long-range rocketry. During that crisis, Egypt found itself outmaneuvered by Israel and "lost numerous aircraft both on the ground and in the air."[58]

In response, Egypt's efforts to upgrade its capabilities and enhance operational performance proceeded painstakingly slowly. Military strategist Anthony Cordesman shows that by the time of the 1967 war, Egypt's air force remained largely reliant on mass, ground-controlled intercepts and ground-based surface-to-air missiles rather than on a modern concept of air operations.[59] If it wanted to preserve a credible deterrent, Cairo appears to have concluded after 1956 that it would need to remedy its existing air power limitations, acquire a means to strike Israel with an assured-penetration weapon, and offset the inability of its bombers to penetrate Israeli air defense.[60] Missiles represented an adequate tool toward that end.

Radiological Weapons for Area-Denial Purposes?

While there is no evidence that Egyptian military strategists held clear views on the role of RWs in an overall deterrence approach, it also remains unknown whether such weapons were tied to a specific operational mission—such as area denial—thought of in advance. While Iraqi plans for an RW stipulated a wide array of Iranian targets for area denial, including industrial centers, airports, railroad stations, fortified defense areas where the enemy is holding firm, bridges and troop crossings, Egyptian geography and vulnerabilities vis-à-vis Israel would have made area denial a less attractive military proposition for Cairo. Cordesman notes the Egyptian military's long-standing challenges in dealing with the geography of the Sinai, a largely rugged and barren terrain that causes difficulty in moving and sustaining forces and increases their vulnerability to air attack. The Sinai is vast, which makes the idea of area denial in the classic sense problematic.[61] Once Egypt moved into the Sinai, Cordesman notes, it would be exposed to an Israeli attack in far more depth than a Syrian force advancing into the Golan Heights. Compounding such vulnerabilities, Egypt's border with Israel is far from most Israeli population centers, and the Negev desert gives Israel strategic depth. "The Sinai is an exposed killing ground where land forces are exposed and/or must move through narrow predictable routes," Cordesman concludes, and the Egyptian air force is not strong and effective enough to provide survivable air cover.[62] Analyzing the technical specificities of Egypt's rudimentary experimentation with RWs in 1964 in *The New Scientist*, Leonard Beaton concurred that the quantities of cobalt that Joklik claimed to have procured for his experimentation could "presumably be used only on specific points of importance and not to deny access to a belt of land." The idea that "they were being packed into artillery shells also suggests strictly local uses."[63]

While an area-denial role would thus have made little sense for Egyptian RWs from a geographical and operational point of view, it also appears that the Egyptian RW effort was, in any event, not tied to specific operational concepts. An "area denial" mission would suggest an operational concept evolving from the moment of conception of the project, whereas Project Ibis developed opportunistically and chaotically, driven largely by an individual technological entrepreneur: Otto Joklik.

From 1963, however, Egypt purportedly did use an unconventional weapon for area-denial purposes. Starting in July of that year, Egypt is alleged to have deployed mustard bombs in support of South Yemen against royalist troops in North Yemen.[64] The use of phosgene and mustard aerial bombs against the Yemeni tribesmen is said to have been the first known use of chemical weapons in the Middle East.[65] Egyptian bombers were the primary delivery method for dispersing the aerial bombs filled with chemical agents.[66] Egypt presumably considered CWs an effective weapon against the tribesmen hiding in caves without adequate defensive equipment and additionally expected that Yemen might be a good testing ground for such weapons.[67] Analysts have nonetheless noted that Egypt had no strategic plan for the use of CWs (at least none that is known of from declassified sources) and that its forces might simply have wanted to take advantage of a weapon in their arsenal against which their enemy had no protection.[68] Further, initial Egyptian chemical devices were reported to be "home-made, amateurish, relatively ineffective," and their initial use before 1965 was limited, possibly because Nasser feared President Kennedy's reaction and because "experimental use . . . on a limited scale could allow the shortcomings of Egyptian aerial delivery and dispersal systems to be analyzed so that more effective chemical bombs could be developed for later use."[69]

Iraq in the 1980s—a case discussed in the next chapter—sought to complement its employment of CWs against Iran with an additional option to obtain an advantage over Iran. As a result, Iraq ended up experimenting with and testing radiological weapons. The contention that Egypt might similarly have wanted to complement its nascent use of CWs in Yemen with radiological devices, however, is not borne out by either the sequence of events or the available evidence. Yemen's civil war began with a coup in September 1962, which Egypt was reportedly involved in planning. However, Cairo likely did not anticipate that the guerrilla tactics of the resisting tribesmen would be effective and had not planned for the need to increase its military presence.[70] Its use of chemical weapons in Yemen did not start until July 1963, one year after Otto Joklik's short-lived experimentation with RWs had ended. Egypt's unexpected need for nonconventional weapons in the deteriorating Yemeni campaign thus cannot explain Egypt's initial interest in RWs, which predated the Yemen war.

That said, although Joklik never indicated in his depositions a potential area-denial application of RWs—whether against Israel or other enemies—he appears to have made a curious reference to area denial as late as 1964. The *Guardian* newspaper ran a front-page story titled "Nasser's Nuclear Breakthrough" in that year, which reported as exclusive news what had been revealed during the Joklik and Ben-Gal trial a year before.[71] The *Guardian*'s special correspondent in Frankfurt relayed, among other details, the story of Project Ibis from "informants connected with the work." The familiar revelations were joined by new allegations, including Egyptian plans to bribe British air force officers to deliver nuclear weapons to Egypt and to use agents or saboteurs to plant radiological materials in foreign cities. These explosive allegations caused such a tumult that the *Guardian* dispatched its science correspondent to vet the source for the original story, after which the newspaper ran an article-length retraction.[72] This retraction reveals that the informant for the original story was almost certainly Otto Joklik.[73] Under the more skeptical questioning of the science correspondent, the source (presumed Joklik) abandoned claims of a fearful strategic weapon capable of massive societal disruption and instead described the cobalt weapon as tactical, as a means of contaminating battlefields and delaying advancing armies.[74]

Besides this brief, belated, and ultimately unconfirmed statement by Otto Joklik, there is no evidence that Egypt intended to deploy radiological devices as area-denial weapons.

Nonconventional Weapons as a Source of Status and Prestige

It appears that Cairo anticipated that the development of missiles and unconventional weapons would afford it gains in status in the region. Accounts of Egypt's nuclear program in the early 1960s indicate a broader desire by Cairo not merely to deter Israel but to "match" it, with Nasser refusing to accept "being second rate" in the nuclear realm.[75] Heikal recalls the attendant deliberations amid the launch of the 1955 Atomic Energy Establishment, with Nasser himself declaring: "We missed out in the steam age, and also in the electricity age, but we ought not allow ourselves under any circumstances to be left behind in the atomic age."[76] Considerations of prestige are also considered to be among the principal drivers of Egypt's ballistic missile program in the early 1960s, alongside Nasser's quest for regional leadership and the perceived need to field a response to increased Israeli air and air defense capabilities.[77] Responding to efforts by the Kennedy administration to get Nasser to support a regional arms control initiative, Cairo appeared unenthusiastic, given the perceived implications for Egyptian sovereignty, and argued that there was nothing to inspect regarding nuclear matters. In that context, Nasser also reportedly argued that his country's missile effort was more for building up national morale and prestige than for military purposes.[78] The UAR's breakup in September 1961, caused by Syria's departure after a military coup, "deeply dispirited Nasser" and was perceived in Cairo as a significant blow to Egypt's status as pan-Arab leader.[79]

It is conceivable that this development further spurred Egyptian ambitions to compensate for this loss in prestige with nonconventional weapons and advanced missiles. While these factors cannot alone account for Egypt's rudimentary experimentation with RWs, and while there are no unclassified statements by Egyptian officials serving as proof that RWs specifically would have afforded Cairo prestige, considerations of status appear to have been an important contextual factor accounting for Nasser's pursuit of nonconventional weapons and missiles.

The Taboo against Nonconventional Weapons in the Post-World War II Middle East

Since Egypt was the first state in the Middle East to have reportedly used CWs in combat, as well as to have flirted with the option of developing a radiological weapon, it is difficult to probe whether perceptions of a taboo against the employment of such weapons played into the calculations of Egyptian decision-makers. Egypt's experimentation with RWs occurred more than two decades before Saddam Hussein used chemical devices in the context of the Iran-Iraq war. The question as to whether and to what extent international norms against WMD would resonate in the Middle East was largely uncharted territory in the early 1960s. Against that backdrop, the evidence that President Nasser cared about or anticipated negative international reactions to his pursuit of nonconventional weapons is mixed.

On the one hand, several of his statements betray his bewilderment at international opprobrium over the German scientists' activities in Egypt. Once Israel started to raise "a great international fuss" over the scientists in the spring of 1963, Mohamed Heikal recalls, Nasser told the U.S. ambassador in Cairo: "The Russians have German scientists working for them. You have them working for you. So why shouldn't they work for Egypt?"[80] Yet, the evidence for dismissing the constructivist factor in an account of Egypt's RWs is not unequivocal. After all, Otto Joklik, the chief scientist behind Egypt's radiological experimentation, claimed that his premature departure from Cairo was driven by a mix of security concerns and moral qualms with the work he was being asked to conduct. Whether such qualms extended to his Egyptian hosts is uncertain. James Walsh notes that, in both 1962 and 1963, Nasser responded to requests by U.S. president Kennedy that Egypt remain non-nuclear with the pledge that "he would never bring nuclear terror to the Middle East."[81] Further, in the context of its chemical warfare in Yemen from 1963 until 1967, Egypt was not indifferent to international reactions either.[82] Nasser denied Egypt's use of chemical agents, betraying some level of concern over international condemnation, even though the reaction remained relatively muted.[83] Such concern, however, appears to have fluctuated over the course of the Yemeni campaign. It abated from 1966, when Nasser became increasingly exasperated with the military situation in Yemen as well as less interested in Western public opinion following Kennedy's assassination.[84]

In sum, the degree to which a purported taboo against RWs resonated among key Egyptian decision-makers is probably negligible and in any case unknown from the available evidence. Normative considerations related to Egypt's pursuit or battlefield deployment of nonconventional weapons can serve as proximate indicators, yet evidence is ambivalent at best.

Bureaucratic Political Determinants and Insufficient Political Prioritization

As shown above, the Egyptian flirtation with a radiological weapon was likely enabled by the perceived need for a range of options to respond to Israeli military innovations and encouraged by anticipated gains in prestige afforded by the possession of advanced missiles and nonconventional weapons. Perhaps most importantly, however, the nature of Egypt's military-industrial enterprise at the time facilitated Otto Joklik's short-lived exploration of RWs in that it created conditions in which an individual scientific entrepreneur could apparently pursue a "special project."

Joklik claims that Project Ibis was run by the Egyptian air force and that he was personally subordinated to air force commander Mohamed Sedky Mahmoud. The technical and financial implementation of the project was run by General Mahmoud Khalil, who reported directly to President Nasser. The existence of Project Ibis was otherwise tightly compartmentalized. According to Joklik's claims, only he, President Nasser, Field Marshal Abd al-Hakim Amer, Commander Mohamed Sedky Mahmoud, General Mahmoud Khalil, Brigadier General Selim Taher, Colonel Elsayed Nadim, and five officers subordinate to Joklik and tasked with implementation knew of it.[85] It is impossible to know from available sources, however, to what degree Nasser was informed about the radiological weapons effort and took an active interest in it. And while Nasser's rivalry and fraught relationship with Abd al-Hakim Amer—who was highly influential with the military— has been widely assessed, it is unclear whether and how that relationship impacted the prospects for Joklik's work.[86]

Project Ibis appears to have developed in parallel with state structures as a "special project," and the individual "entrepreneur" driving it—Otto Joklik—is key to understanding its fate. Indeed, considering the available evidence, neither can it be excluded that Project Ibis was independently initiated and executed by Joklik nor that his claimed place in the Egyptian chain of command (and Nasser's knowledge of his activities) was merely self-serving grandiosity. The extent to which Joklik's activities enjoyed even tacit Egyptian support or were subject to even minimal deliberation by Egyptian decision-makers might never be known.

What made such autonomy by a scientific entrepreneur possible? It appears that Egypt in the early 1960s provided a welcoming context for different actors (domestic and foreign) to put forward ideas for new weapons programs. Egypt's military innovators were receptive to the pursuit of all types of weapons, rather than specializing in any area, which resulted in a wide variety of projects that lacked urgency and prioritization. Egypt's nuclear weapons program is a case in point. As noted, Egypt's most intensive efforts to acquire such weapons (or at a minimum the capability to produce them) began in 1960 and were accompanied by increased investment and research into nuclear technologies.[87] At the same time, Egypt's leadership never allocated the financial resources and political capital necessary for the success of a nuclear weapons program.[88] There appears to have been neither a written plan nor a formal cost-benefit analysis for nuclear weapons development.[89] Meanwhile, military innovation was being pursued in other directions. In need of an organization to administer the ballistic missile and aircraft development programs, President Nasser created the Egyptian General Aero Organization in 1960.[90] There was also a special projects group in the military under General Khalil, which was allotted a large budget to explore acquisition and development of "exotic weapons."[91] As Andrew Rathmell notes in his review of Egypt's military-industrial complex during that period, relying largely on European technology and German scientists, Egypt in the early 1960s "aimed to produce all types of weapons rather than specializing in any area . . . [and] this resulted in a wide variety of projects."[92]

In this context, it is entirely conceivable that the modest experimentation with radiological weapons was indicative of a broader Egyptian approach to pursue military innovation into multiple directions, yet without committing serious resources or following through on any given one of them. One Egyptian source, when asked by James Walsh about Nasser's pursuit of radiological weapons, responded that "naturally," Egypt had looked at a "trash bomb" at that time. He explained that "in every military there are dreamers or exploiters" who, per Walsh, "convince their bosses to back some scheme."[93]

Was this conducive environment for "dreamers and exploiters" a result of weak state capacity—as in the case of Iraq? As will be shown in the next chapter, Saddam's regime did not systematically vet projects in terms of their scientific or technological merit, and it also failed to monitor or follow up on many of these projects because it lacked the know-how and institutional resources. As a result, especially during the Iran-Iraq war, Iraqi scientists operated with unlimited budgets and weak oversight, their leaders stuck with their technological preferences while discarding alternatives, and scientists got away with not delivering results despite ample funding—all while Saddam did not interfere. This bureaucratic-institutional backdrop facilitated the pursuit of radiological weapons up to the testing stage, notwithstanding the unpromising nature of the effort.

In Egypt's case, the similarly enabling context for creative entrepreneurs, such as Joklik, to pursue military pet projects is not so much explained by weak state capacity as it is by political prioritization. Egypt was not a weak authoritarian state in the early 1960s to the extent that Iraq was during the 1980s. Indeed, there is evidence that President Nasser tightly controlled the country's CW program himself.[94] The lack of systematic pursuit of nuclear weapons and a radiological capability appears to have been rooted in insufficient prioritization of any given effort at pursuing nonconventional weapons.

The personalities of specific "dreamers and exploiters" likely also mattered. Otto Joklik, whose biography suggests a penchant for boasting and exaggeration, appears to have encountered a welcoming context for experimenting with radiological substances when he arrived in Cairo in 1962. Born in 1921 in Bohemia and Austrian by nationality, Joklik had served as an officer in the German army in WWII before working in the chemical industry and studying nuclear science. Joklik obtained sketchy academic credentials and published papers of dubious scientific merit along the way.[95] Documents from the Swiss attorney general from March 1963 suggest that Joklik had filed a patent at the Swiss patent office in Bern describing a machine capable of producing cobalt bombs under the name KOBALTRON.[96] He also came to be involved in illicit activities, including the selling of restricted information and the unauthorized transfer of controlled technologies. He founded two shell companies, the Transcontinental Atomic Company and Transcontinental Oil Company, both of which existed only as post office boxes in Liechtenstein.[97] Later, in 1973, years after his experience in Egypt and brief international prominence, Joklik was involved in a scheme to illicitly resell controlled computer and laser parts from the United States to the Soviet Union.[98] His proclivity for fabrication and bravado, which comes through clearly in his depositions, possibly aided him in convincing his Egyptian hosts that it was worth running some experiments with cobalt-60.

Joklik could also easily "bandwagon" with the existing work on missiles, which was being conducted by German scientists in Egypt in 1962. His depositions claim that Project Ibis had been encouraged by Professor Wolfgang Pilz, who was interested in payloads with radioisotopes for missiles.[99] Pilz, alongside Eugen Sänger and Paul Görcke, held a key managerial position within the emerging Egyptian missile program. Considering that Egypt's foray into ballistic missile development was progressing at high speed during the 1960–1962 period[100] and that the Egyptians most likely intended to eventually tip their missiles with unconventional warheads, it is conceivable that the momentum on the missile front additionally fueled interest in scientific entrepreneurs like Joklik.

Finally, there is the question as to whether Joklik's rudimentary experimentation with RWs benefited managerially from Egypt's other nonconventional weapons efforts. In the United States, proponents of RWs had found an enthusiastic partner in the Army Chemical Corps. And as will be shown in the chapter on Iraq, the government's interest in an RW capability likely originated among Iraq's CW weaponeers, who then approached the Iraqi Atomic Energy Commission with a request for irradiated materials. There is no indication that Egypt's experimentation with radiological weapons was similarly stimulated by or benefited from the expertise of Egypt's CW enterprise. Egypt's integrated CW and BW project, which commenced in the early 1960s and was code-named Izlis, was implemented in a military-civilian consortium located in Abu-Zaʿabal.[101] There is no open-source evidence of overlap in the military or administrative dimensions of the RW and CW efforts.

Inhibitors to Egypt's RW Effort

Bureaucratic Political Determinants Revisited

Why was Egypt's flirtation with RWs so short-lived, failing to proceed from nascent experimentation to the testing stage? Were the obstacles confronted by Egypt a matter of bureaucratic politics, technical challenges, or a shortage of economic and other organizational resources? As will be shown in the chapter on Iraq, weak state capacity amplified the technical obstacles encountered in Saddam's pursuit of a radiological weapon. In the case of Egypt, the demise of the project came with its abrupt halt in the fall of 1962, after only a few months of experimentation, and was, first and foremost, due to its chief scientist—Otto Joklik—deciding to abandon the effort.

Though it was Joklik's decision—driven by a combination of security, financial, and allegedly moral considerations—that ended Egypt's radiological exploration prematurely, the unpromising prospects of the RW effort were still bound up with broader bureaucratic-institutional factors. While Egypt cannot be classified as a weak authoritarian state in the early 1960s, some of the hallmarks of weak state capacity—a proliferation of military projects with insufficient high-level attention, expertise, and adequate resources devoted to them—were nonetheless present and can account for the timing of the demise of Joklik's venture. According to Stephen A. Cook, civil-military relations in Egypt during the 1960s are incorrectly characterized as merely transactional, since the military establishment trusted the president as the steward of the state and political development.[102] In that context, the president maintained a perspective that tracked closely with that of his uniformed colleagues, and while the executive may have briefed the parliament on questions related to armament procurement and allocations, the parliamentarians were not culturally inclined to question the military.[103] Yet, even though President Nasser was aligned with the military and personally spearheaded efforts to develop an indigenous manufacturing base for Egypt's military-industrial complex from the 1950s, it appears that there was insufficient high-level intervention from the presidency to sustain the country's efforts on nonconventional weapons in particular.[104]

As noted, Egypt's leadership never allocated the financial resources and political capital necessary for the success of a nuclear weapons program. Given the far fewer resources devoted to experimentation with a radiological device—which was essentially conducted by one individual—it is likely that radiological weapons were similarly viewed as one option but never a priority. The fact that Joklik's endeavors, unlike those of Iraq's radiological weaponeers, did not substantially benefit from direct interaction with the Egyptian missile or chemical weapons programs further reinforced their short-lived and uncommitted nature.[105]

The lack of seriousness in the Egyptian state's pursuit of a radiological device was further amplified by the poor quality of military entrepreneurs involved in the effort. Joklik's credentials were considered dubious by both Israeli and U.S. intelligence. More generally, the German scientists making their way to Cairo in the late 1950s and early 1960s were considered "mediocre,"[106] "fourth-tier experts,"[107] with "the great majority" not being "important."[108] Though Egypt had a number of good nuclear scientists,[109] Sirrs argues that the paucity of trained Egyptian engineering talent proved to be a formidable obstacle throughout the missile project and a challenge that was never adequately resolved.[110] Indeed, Joklik himself claimed in his deposition that, subsequent to his departure from Egypt, local personnel would have been incapable of staging the planned tests with radiological shells or of operating his hot cell laboratory without him.[111] Since Joklik was prone to exaggeration and inflation of his skills, it is impossible to gauge the accuracy of this claim.

To the extent that Egypt was interested in pursuing a radiological weapon in the early 1960s, that effort was never sufficiently prioritized by the Egyptian system and was eventually undermined by the withdrawal of German technical support. In that regard, the radiological venture appears to have fallen victim to the same fate as other Egyptian military innovation efforts of the 1950s and 1960s, which "were entirely dependent upon German expertise and collapsed as a result of the withdrawal of these personnel."[112] Insufficient high-level attention for any specific nonconventional weapons program thus appears to account for both Joklik's ability to pursue experimentation on a radiological device in the first place (as argued in the previous section), as well as for the effort's short shelf life.

Technical Constraints: Cobalt-60 and Challenges with Weaponization

Though Cairo's flirtation with a radiological device was ended prematurely by the departure of Otto Joklik, technical obstacles would have likely obstructed any further progress beyond the testing stage. The first such obstacle related to the irradiated warhead. Egypt's probing of a radiological device is the only known effort by state actors that focused on the weaponization of the longer-lived isotopes of cobalt-60 and strontium-90 (half-lives of about five and twenty-eight years, respectively). According to Joklik's deposition, at the time of his departure from Egypt, radiological material worth 500,000 deutschemarks had been acquired from West Germany, Canada, and India between April and August 1962. Joklik's defense team substantiated these claims by producing photostatic copies of written offers of large quantities and some actual deliveries of radioactive cobalt-60 obtained for medical experiments.[113] Already by July 1962, Joklik claimed that the Egyptian air force had managed to acquire all material necessary for first tests, which would have included shells filled with cobalt-60, strontium-90, and cesium-137, as well as several other isotopes.[114]

During the Basel trial, Joklik and Ben-Gal's defense featured a Swiss expert, Professor Walter Minder, who presented alarmist assessments of the damage that could be wrought by radiological devices containing cobalt-60. Hired to reinforce the defendants' claims that their actions—attempted coercion and illegal activities on behalf of a foreign government—were aimed at thwarting a murderous Egyptian plan, Minder testified that the amounts of cobalt referred to in the documentation presented by the defense could contaminate the atmosphere above Israel for "five years," with "50 times the maximum genetically tolerable amount."[115] Inflating the damage the acquired amount of cobalt-60 could cause was in the interest of Joklik, who contended that he had progressively realized that the Egyptian plan greatly exceeded its defense needs and posed a deadly threat to Israel.[116] Joklik's claims were picked up and amplified by the sensationalist press coverage of the Basel trial, which included assertions that the material purchased for Project Ibis was "three times the amount needed to destroy Israel's entire population and render the country uninhabitable for five years."[117] Fears generated by such reporting were likely reinforced by a persistent conflation of Egypt's purported quest for a radiological and nuclear weapons capability.[118]

After the drama surrounding the Basel trial had somewhat subsided, a 1964 article in *The New Scientist*, reviewing Egypt's purported plans to deploy a radiological device using cobalt-60 against Israel, cautioned that "large quantities" of the material "would be needed to have an effect" over a sizeable area "because of its short half-life of 5 years."[119] The article suggested that one would need one ton of cobalt-60—"4,000 times as much as the unnamed German source believed was being sought by the Egyptians from Canada"—to contaminate an area of one square mile.[120] It concluded that Egypt would have an incentive to buy radiological materials only if it planned to use them imminently (or had an immediate purpose) as they otherwise would decay—and even if it did use the cobalt-60 immediately, the material could be used to target only a specific location and would prove unsuitable for area-denial purposes.

Such shortcomings of the irradiated source would likely have been compounded by challenges with weaponization had Joklik pursued his radiological experimentation further. According to Joklik, Project Ibis was envisaged to expand from radiological artillery shells into radiological aerial bombs and warheads for Egypt's domestic missile force. The *New Scientist* article detailed anticipated challenges in identifying appropriate delivery systems for the cobalt-60, citing loading, handling, and fabricating problems, since "armourers . . . would have to deal with radiological weapons while they were radiating at their maximum intensity."[121]

Any attempts to field radiological charges in warheads on missiles would have faced considerable obstacles. Despite Nasser's frequent boasts about the al-Zafir and al-Kahir missiles, none actually reached operational service because of insurmountable guidance system difficulties.[122] Owen Sirrs, who concedes that "the Egyptians most likely intended to tip their surface-to-surface missiles with unconventional warheads," argues that Cairo would have had to overcome material and technical difficulties to succeed in delivering chemical weapons by missiles, including specialized reentry vehicles, a release mechanism, and preferably cluster munitions. It is plausible to suggest that attempts to deliver radiological warheads by missiles would have faced similar, if not greater difficulties. After all, Egypt's experimentation with CWs proceeded with greater success and at greater speed since it managed to fill bombs and artillery shells with phosgene and mustard agents for delivery by bombers in the Yemen civil war.[123]

In sum, had Project Ibis advanced beyond basic experimentation, it would have likely proven extraordinarily difficult to combine sufficient quantities of the chosen radioactive charges with practicable delivery systems.

International Fallout from the Joklik Affair

Even though the Egyptian radiological weapons effort was aborted at the experimentation stage and would have likely faced considerable hurdles if pursued further, Otto Joklik's activities received considerable attention in the international media and stirred controversies between various governments.[124] They also amplified splits within the Israeli leadership—splits whose root causes, however, went far beyond disagreements over how to deal with purported unconventional threats emanating from Egypt but included divergent views on Israel's relations with Germany and rivalries over who would lead Israel after Ben-Gurion, as well as personal tensions. The concluding section summarizes why Joklik made such headlines in 1962–1963 and why specific constituencies—particularly in the Israeli government—had an interest in inflating Egypt's purported radiological weapons threat.

Israeli and U.S. Reactions

As noted in the introduction, Joklik and Ben-Gal's Swiss trial attracted global media attention, and the Egyptian experimentation with RWs featured prominently in Joklik's defense. Joklik argued that his criminal activity was justified to prevent Egypt from obtaining weapons with genocidal implications. These claims were widely reported in the global press, particularly in Israel, where the German scientists' affair dominated the front page of the *Jerusalem Post* for weeks. Politicians and parties left, right, and center denounced the activities of the German scientists, as well as the government of West Germany for allowing its citizens to take part in Egypt's WMD development.[125] Many invoked the memory of the Holocaust, accusing Egypt and the German scientists of seeking to "continue Hitler's uncompleted campaign to wipe out the Jewish people."[126]

In contrast, the response of the U.S. intelligence community was muted. A brief National Intelligence Estimate summary from January 1963, after Foreign Minister Meir's revelation of the Egyptian exploration of RWs to Kennedy, made no mention of RWs but concluded that "no Arab state will be able to develop a nuclear weapon capacity for years to come."[127] A Special National Intelligence Estimate titled "The Advanced Weapons Programs of the UAR and Israel," released on May 8, concluded that neither Egypt nor Israel "can produce radiological warfare weapons."[128] Some insight into the reasoning behind this assessment can be gleaned from a brief, heavily redacted memorandum from Ray Cline, deputy director of Intelligence, to John McCone, director of Central Intelligence. This memo characterizes the insinuations of Egypt's development of chemical, biological and radiological weapons as "Israeli propaganda" that Israel itself does not believe.[129] Cline notes that he received this information from a redacted individual, presumably Israeli. This suggests that a member of the Joklik-skeptic camp in the Israeli government reached out to U.S. intelligence regarding the Egyptian pursuit of an RW. A series of talking points prepared by Robert Komer, who was dispatched to probe Egypt's willingness to enter into an arms control initiative in early 1963, are equally indicative of a dismissive U.S. attitude, in that they characterized radiological weapons as "not a realistic threat," adding in one instance that the United States even omitted RWs from present U.S. disarmament proposals at the Conference on Disarmament in Geneva.[130] What remains unclear from such documents is whether the Kennedy administration did not believe either Israel or Egypt to be pursuing RWs at the time or whether it had principally concluded, based on its own experience, that such efforts would never succeed.

Intra-Israeli Disagreements

In his trial, Joklik claimed that Israel did not know about Project Ibis prior to his defection.[131] Indeed, it appears that Israeli intelligence was not principally focused upon the prospect of Egypt developing unconventional warheads until the fall of 1962, even though Egypt had already tested ballistic missiles by that time. Why, then, did Isser Harel and Golda Meir pay considerable attention to Joklik's claims regarding a purported Egyptian radiological weapons threat and engage in efforts to get the United States and other governments to act upon them?

First, it is conceivable that the radiological warfare scare during World War II resonated among select Israeli officials. As discussed in chapters 1 and 3, during the Allied invasion of Normandy in 1944, the U.S. military—and to a lesser extent its British counterpart—were concerned that Germany might try to use radioactive material in V-rocket warheads or as a means to deny the Allies landing beaches in the run-up to a D-Day invasion.[132] Since some of the German scientists supporting Cairo's missile program from the 1950s had been previously involved in the Third Reich's V-2 program,[133] it is conceivable that Otto Joklik's radiological weapons–related claims registered with particular concern among Israeli officials.

Second, personalities again appeared to have mattered. Isser Harel was especially sensitive to allegations concerning the German scientists' nefarious intentions vis-à-vis the State of Israel. In the wake of the capture of Adolf Eichmann in Argentina in May 1960, Harel's views had reportedly "undergone profound changes," and he adopted the perspective that Germany was Israel's "worst enemy" and "staunchly [believing that] Germany was supporting its scientists in Egypt."[134] Having asked Prime Minister Ben Gurion to call Chancellor Adenauer to intervene and having been refused, Harel started his own anti-German campaign toward Egypt, commencing in September 1962.[135] In cabinet meetings on the German scientist affair broadly and Joklik especially, Harel "came with an agenda"—according to Meir Amit, who headed IDF intelligence and was more circumspect regarding Joklik's claims.[136] Since Harel, who had a penchant for assuming the worst regarding the German scientists' activities in Egypt, headed the Mossad until his resignation in 1963, he was in a powerful position to amplify concerns about a purported radiological weapons program.[137]

Finally, some Israeli officials might have calculated that to speak loudly about an Egyptian radiological weapons threat would be conducive to diverting nascent international opprobrium over Israel's own nuclear program while also justifying Israeli requests for further U.S. military assistance. After Egypt's missile test in the summer of 1962, Israel requested additional

U.S. weaponry and managed to convince the Kennedy administration to deliver Hawk surface-to-air missiles, which Washington had previously withheld. As Sirrs notes, "along with radiological weapons and chemical munitions, ballistic missiles were invoked in a veritable revolving door of threats that underpinned Israel's requests for arms and security guarantees" from the United States. In addition, such threats also sought more generally to neutralize any U.S. rapprochement with Egypt under President Kennedy.[138] Against the backdrop of growing U.S. suspicions that Israel itself was intent on developing a nuclear weapon, U.S. efforts at drawing Egypt and Israel into an arms control initiative, and Israel's desire to receive more weapons from Washington, it would have appeared logical for Israeli officials to inflate Egypt's rudimentary exploration of radiological weapons.[139]

The Egyptian Case in Comparative Perspective

This chapter demonstrates that Egypt's short-lived and murky experimentation with RWs represented a special project that was likely initiated and executed by a technical entrepreneur in parallel to state structures. It was enabled by Egypt's desire to develop a range of options to match and deter Israel following the 1960 revelation of the Dimona reactor. In line with Soviet experiences with military innovation, as per Evangelista, perceptions of external threat were thus prominent at the time of Egypt's RW experimentation, though there is no evidence linking Joklik's work to specific approaches to deterrence or operational concepts entertained by the Egyptian military establishment.

Moral concerns failed to inhibit Egypt's pursuit of nonconventional weapons broadly, though the chief scientist leading Egypt's radiological experimentation maintained that he specifically abandoned work on this subject due to impossible-to-verify ethical qualms. In addition, insufficient high-level attention to and political prioritization of Egypt's several nonconventional weapons efforts facilitated Otto Joklik's short-lived entrepreneurial pursuits in the radiological realm. With regard to Evangelista's hypotheses, Egypt's experience with RWs more closely resembled the U.S. pattern, in which a push for new weapons technology arises from below (i.e., from scientists and the military officials with whom they interact), than the Soviet model, in which directives typically come from above in response to technological developments abroad. Given the inchoate nature of the Egyptian RW effort, as well as the lack of empirical evidence, it is impossible to answer whether, as in the case of U.S. military innovation, bureaucratic consensus building and policy advocacy preceded a formal decision for radiological research and development in Egypt or whether Joklik's experience more closely resembled the post-adoption "mobilization"/implementation phase characteristic of the Soviet weapons innovation process. In all likelihood, there was neither any meaningful bureaucratic consensus-building predating the effort nor any mobilization once it was underway.

The analysis further examined the obstacles Egypt would have confronted in developing RWs beyond the experimentation stage. These include technical challenges related to the irradiated material and weaponization, impediments that would have likely been insurmountable notwithstanding unsubstantiated hysterical claims advanced during Joklik's court trial regarding the purported damage that could be wrought by the cobalt-60 he had sought to procure. Finally, the chapter turned to an exploration of the international fallout from the Joklik affair, suggesting that constituencies within the Israeli government had historical reasons to be highly alarmed by Joklik's activities and stood to gain politically from inflating their significance.

The Egyptian experience with RWs points to a number of interesting parallels and differences with the U.S., Soviet and British programs. Similar to the United Kingdom's efforts, Egypt's pursuit of radiological weapons never moved beyond the exploratory phase, and considerable speculation is necessary to fill the gaps in its fragmentary record. While similarly driven by perceived threats from external adversaries, the Egyptian RW effort— unlike the U.S., Soviet, and British programs—does not appear to have sought to emulate or respond to other states' forays into radiological warfare in the action-reaction pattern observed in the previous chapters. Instead, Egypt decided to respond to Israel's advances involving the military applications of nuclear energy with a *variety* of efforts; radiological experimentation was merely one of them. There is little indication that the Egyptian radiological weaponeers—unlike their American and British predecessors—thought specifically about area denial applications of RWs. Rather, the available evidence indicates that Egypt coveted a radiological capability to match and deter Israeli military innovations, including in the nuclear realm, without specifying the concrete military applications for such a capability.

While the United States and Great Britain discontinued their RW programs largely in favor of nuclear arms, the Egyptian effort did not fall victim to a "substitution effect" in a similar fashion; rather, it was abandoned due to insufficient high-level interest throughout, which was amplified by its chief weaponeer—Otto Joklik—fleeing the country just a few months after having commenced his work. Indeed, like the British and Soviet programs, the Egyptian effort suffered from a lack of high-level advocacy and involvement of scientific entrepreneurs to sustain momentum. While the roles of different scientific entrepreneurs and consensus building lent themselves to a rich analysis of the "technocratic initiative" phase of RW innovation in the U.S. and, to a lesser extent, the British and Soviet cases, there is a paucity of similar data on the Egyptian case—with the exception of information on Otto Joklik as chief and likely singular RW weaponeer. Indeed, since the Egyptian effort was so short-lived and inchoate, it never benefited—as did the Soviet program—from a high-level targeted response, which would have entailed the redirection of existing resources toward research and development on RWs. What is perhaps most interesting about the inchoate Egyptian RW effort—and what sets it further apart from those of the other states examined—is that it was almost entirely dependent on assistance by German scientists, though they may have contributed indirectly to the Soviet RW program as well.

FIVE
Iraq

"On 29 August 1995, a biological inspection team (UNSCOM 125) was given a brief account by the Iraqi authorities of an experiment in the radiological weapons field conducted at the end of 1987 by the Al-Muthanna State Establishment." Thus reads an excerpt from the tenth United Nations Special Commission (UNSCOM) executive chairman's report to the United Nations Security Council from 17 December 1995.[1] It marks the first mention of Iraq's attempt to develop radiological weapons (RWs) in an official document related to the international inspection regime, which was tasked with uncovering Iraq's weapons of mass destruction (WMD) programs in the wake of the 1991 Gulf War, pursuant to UN Security Council Resolution 687.[2]

In 1987, as Iraq was waging a war of attrition against Iran and considering possibilities for crippling enemy forces, its Military Industrialization Corporation (MIC) worked with its Nuclear Research Centre to explore radiological weapons, predominantly as a means of area denial. As detailed in a secret Iraqi progress report from 1988, which was later provided to the UN, the metal used for the RWs was mostly zirconium-95 irradiated in the IRT-5000 research reactor at the Al-Tuwaitha site, and three prototype bombs were produced and exploded at various test sites at ground level and dropped from an aircraft in late 1987.[3] Al-Tuwaitha, located eighteen kilometers southeast of Baghdad, was the main site for the Iraqi nuclear program and housed the Osiraq reactor bombed by Israel in 1981.

In light of the unconvincing performance of the devices during testing—radiation readings on the ground were rather low, and the weapon's radioactive charges lost strength quickly, among other problems[4]—Iraq decided to shelve the effort and never produced an RW for deployment. In the early 1990s, the International Atomic Energy Agency (IAEA) Action Team and UNSCOM, mandated to probe Iraq's WMD programs, commenced their efforts inside Iraq. At that time, concerns with Iraq's nuclear and chemical weapons programs were so extensive in scope—and nothing was known about Iraq's ultimately unsuccessful foray into the RW domain—that the RW experimentation and tests received no attention. It was not until the latter half of the 1990s that the Iraqi government decided to confess to its RW effort, prompting the inspectors' engagement with the file. Yet, when the *New York Times* reported on the story in early 2001, amid ongoing pressure on Iraq given enduring concerns about its WMD, the Iraqi government publicly acknowledged its earlier intent to develop an RW for "defensive" purposes "at the height" of the Iran-Iraq war and its experimentation toward that end, but it denied that it had ever moved to the testing stage—in contrast to what Iraqi authorities had reported to UNSCOM inspectors in late 1995.[5]

This chapter provides the most detailed account to date of the little-known and short-lived Iraqi RW program—its inception, drivers, obstacles, and aftermath—situating it in the context of Iraq's war with Iran and pursuit of other WMD while also highlighting similarities and discrepancies with the U.S., Soviet, British and Egyptian RW programs. It specifically addresses the following questions: Why did Iraq express an interest in RWs in the 1980s, experiment with and even test such weapons, but conclude that their production and deployment were not worthwhile? What military objectives did Iraq anticipate could usefully be served by RWs in the context of the Iran-Iraq war and potentially beyond? Did considerations related to status and prestige play a role in driving the Iraqi effort? To what extent did technical difficulties, bureaucratic political determinants, shortages of economic or other organizational resources, or the resonance of a taboo against the use of RWs hinder the Iraqi effort? And why is the effort generally treated as a footnote, whether in declassified intelligence reports, the memoirs of scientists involved in Iraq's nuclear program, or scholarly accounts written on Iraq's WMD programs?

First, this chapter will analyze the drivers behind Iraq's RW program—namely, the perceived Iraqi military requirements during the Iran-Iraq war. It will show that Iraq pursued RWs as area-denial weapons against Iran after the 1986 defeat at al-Faw—though such weapons had been considered in Iraqi doctrinal publications earlier—and that the inception of the program likely occurred sometime between 1986 and 1987.[6] The chapter will then probe the causal relevance of normative considerations among senior Iraqi leadership, concluding that Baghdad likely expected little international condemnation for a prospective RW deployment against Iran. Further, the chapter shows that the evolution of the RW effort—both the fact that it managed to take off in the first place, as well as its abrupt demise—can be partially explained by bureaucratic political determinants. Iraq during the 1980s provided a welcome institutional context for scientific entrepreneurs to pursue novel weapons efforts, while the nature of the Saddam regime also mitigated against an honest, bottom-up reporting of anticipated failure in such pursuits. The fact that Hussein Kamel, Saddam's son-in-law and head of the MIC, assumed in 1987 leadership of the Iraqi Atomic Energy Commission (IAEC)—which was headquartered at Al-Tuwaitha and would collaborate with the MIC on the RWs—also temporarily sustained the RW effort, since it was of personal interest to him.

Having probed the drivers, the chapter turns to inhibitors of Iraq's pursuit of RWs, returning to the causal relevance of bureaucratic political determinants for the program's failure. The analysis will show that the RW program's awkward position at the nexus of Iraq's nuclear weapons and chemical weapons programs limited interest in the effort by Iraq's most talented nuclear scientists, and other bureaucratic factors mitigated against more favorable outcomes in the program. The chapter then proceeds to analyze the technical challenges confronted by Iraqi scientists, related to both the irradiated material and its weaponization, concluding that those would not likely have been overcome even in a more conducive institutional context.

Next, the chapter investigates why so little became known about the Iraqi

RW effort during the international inspection regime of the 1990s. It appears that Iraqi deception and obstruction of inspections, the absence of foreign intelligence alerting outsiders to the RW program prior to the Gulf War, and a lack of physical evidence at Al-Tuwaitha and the RW test sites explain why UNSCOM and IAEA inspectors did not take a greater interest in the file. Moreover, the inspectors' acute concerns with Iraq's other WMD programs and capabilities constrained the available bandwidth and resources to pursue other, more obscure avenues of investigation. Without the Iraqi government's proactive admission of the RW effort, apparently prompted by Hussein Kamel's defection to Jordan in 1995, it is therefore conceivable that Saddam's radiological weapons would have remained an untold part of Iraq's WMD saga to this day. The chapter closes by reflecting on the similarities and differences between the Iraqi RW program and U.S., Soviet, British and Egyptian pursuits of a radiological warfare capability—which preceded Baghdad's efforts by several decades.

Drivers of Iraq's Radiological Weapons

International Security Imperatives: The Iran-Iraq War

Saddam's decision to invade Iran in 1980 was marked by hubris and characterized by a set of flawed assumptions. Though Iraq had significantly expanded its armed forces in the wake of the Arab defeat in the 1973 Arab-Israeli War, driven by the prospect of further Kurdish revolt, perceived threats from Israel and Iran, and a substantial increase in Iraqi revenues after the 1973 oil embargo,[7] Baghdad's blueprint for invasion in 1980 was poorly conceived and inadequately prepared.[8] There was little detailed Iraqi planning, and initial airstrikes by the Iraqi air force suffered from inadequate intelligence preparation. Further, Iraq was generally "overconfident"[9] and operated under the false assumption that the Iranian people would welcome the invasion—which followed on the heels of the Islamic Revolution—and allow for a swift Iraqi victory. Though Iraq's initial invasion of Khuzestan Province benefited from Iraqi numerical superiority, it moved at a snail's pace given problems with tactical doctrine, inadequate intelligence gathering, insufficient training, and poor coordination between the infantry and armor, among other reasons.[10] Iranian counteroffensives through 1981 and 1982 eventually yielded to a long period of stalemate, which lasted from 1982 until 1986. As Ibrahim Al-Marashi and Sammy Salama note, the Iraqi military was tasked during that time with maintaining a defensive war that would inflict enough casualties on enemy forces and destroy its economic structure to force Iran to accept a ceasefire—yet "this was precisely the kind of war that was ultimately to the advantage of Iran due to its larger population base."[11]

Iraq's exploration of RWs needs to be understood in the context of the war's trajectory in 1986 and 1987, following years of stalemate. In February 1986, Iran's success in crossing the Shatt al-Arab river and taking the Al-Faw peninsula—even though the Iraqis, as military historian Kenneth Pollack notes, "threw everything they had at the Iranians"[12]—constituted a major crisis for Saddam and his entourage, as Hussein Kamel would later emphasize in discussing use of chemical weapons (CWs) at the time.[13] The perceived urgency to respond to Iranian advances was very high. According to Pollack, after the defeat at Al-Faw, which resulted in 8,000–10,000 Iraqi casualties, Saddam concluded that "the only way to end the war was to actually defeat the Iranian army on the ground."[14] The Al-Faw debacle ushered in a period in which the Iraqi generals were given greater autonomy, while the MIC engaged in increased activity, acquisitions, and experiments. According to Al-Marashi, there was a "window in which one could get away with things."[15]

While the 1988 Iraqi progress report on the RW effort does not specify the exact point in time at which the idea of pursuing RWs was conceived, it appears likely that preliminary thinking on such a weapons capability was done as early as 1986 on the heels of the Al-Faw debacle, if not before. Indeed, Iraqi doctrinal publications had highlighted the operational use of weapons of mass destruction, including those of a radiological nature, at least by 1984.[16] Khidhir Hamza, the nuclear scientist who claimed to be one of the founders of Iraq's nuclear weapons program but whose credibility as a source has since been disputed, alleges that he was called by Hussein Kamel for a meeting to discuss the idea of pursuing RWs in July 1987.[17] The Iraqi progress report also situates all experimentation and testing in 1987. However, the trajectory of the war itself suggests that the decisive impetus for exploring nonconventional weapons—in addition to CWs, which had already been used from 1983—for battlefield use against the Islamic Republic might well have been generated by the defeat at Al-Faw. Preliminary thinking might have been done by scientific entrepreneurs in years prior, ideas might then have percolated through the system, and, by mid-1987, Hussein Kamel and his entourage decided to test prototype weapons.

In fact, by early 1987, when Iraq successfully defended Al-Basra against the Iranians in Operation Karbala V and turned to preparing to recapture all Iranian-held Iraqi territory, the drive to explore nonconventional weapons for defensive purposes appears to have somewhat receded in urgency, compared to 1986.[18] That said, it might have been difficult to halt an idea already in circulation for institutional-bureaucratic reasons that will be addressed in detail below. Further, although chemical weapons were used extensively during this period both out of perceived military necessity and given what former Iraqi Republican Guard general Ra'ad Hamdani called "unbearable losses," there was a recognition on the Iraqi side of their limited combat effectiveness and the danger their use posed to Iraqi troops.[19] This recognition—and the fact that, even though the Iranians had failed to take Al-Basra, they managed to inflict heavy casualties on Iraq—might have additionally created an appetite for sustaining the pursuit of alternative nonconventional weapons, including RWs. Such weapons promised to enable the Iraqi air force—which had failed miserably during the protracted war to prevent Iran from taking Iraqi territory—to deliver more "bang for the buck" compared with conventional weapons.

Area Denial against Iranian Human-Wave Attacks

The Iraqi RW progress report of 1988 details an interest in using irradiated zirconium as charges in aerial bombs with a view to "contaminating the areas in which these bombs are used through spreading radioactive material in a wide pattern in the air."[20] The purpose of "contaminating areas" is then defined with greater specificity in the report, which lists prospective targets for a classic area-denial strategy—including areas where troops are expected to be massed—but also industrial centers, airports, railroad stations, fortified defense areas where the enemy is holding firm, and bridges and troop crossings, among other areas.[21] The Iraqi focus on aerial bombs stands in contrast to the Egyptian experience, which had envisioned artillery shells filled with radioactive isotopes initially and warheads for Egypt's inchoate missile force at a later stage. The Iraqi RW progress report does not provide detailed operational considerations as a justification for the choice of aerial bombs.[22] Since Iraq was producing aerial chemical bombs (known as Muthanna-4) at the time, and since they were reportedly modified for the RW effort, it is conceivable that the country simply hoped to accrue ancillary benefits from a weapons effort already well underway.

Area-denial weapons are commonly understood as being intended to prevent an adversary from occupying or traversing an area of land, although the contamination does not have to be entirely effective as long as it is sufficient to severely restrict, slow down, or endanger the opponent. Modern types of area-denial weapons include land mines; improvised explosive devices; and chemical, biological, radiological, nuclear, and high yield explosives (CBRNe), if the CBRNe agent is sufficiently long-lasting. Recent U.S. military field manuals discuss the radiological hazard risks posed by radiological dispersal devices (RDDs) to U.S. troops when employed for anti-access or area-denial purposes in extensive detail. RDDs are assessed as being capable of achieving "area denial if delivered in high concentrations; otherwise, they have a disruptive effect and are employed at locations that support the synchronization of other threat assets."[23] Though the U.S. Department of Defense concludes that "such weapons would produce far less immediate damage than devices that result in nuclear detonations, radiological weapons have enormous potential for intimidation.... Although incapable of causing tens of thousands of casualties, a radiological device, in addition to possibly killing or injuring any people who came into contact with it could be used to render symbolic targets or significant areas and infrastructure uninhabitable and unusable without protective clothing."[24]

The Iraqi progress report and related documentation provided to UNSCOM on the RW effort clearly indicate that Iraq hoped the radiological device would serve area-denial purposes by combining the effectiveness of conventional aerial munitions with the spreading of radioactive materials. It was hoped that the radiation effect would extend through inhalation exposure from the irradiated materials floating in the air.[25] Considering the desperation generated by the defeat at Al-Faw, which—as al-Marashi has described—nurtured a desire to "pursue anything to get an advantage over the Iranian numerical superiority,"[26] it appears conceivable that individuals familiar with Iraq's CW program asked what other agents capable of producing a lingering hazard and thus impeding Iranian military operations could be explored, turning to the IAEC for consultation. That said, it appears that chemical weapons were considered suitable not merely for area denial but also more offensive military purposes during the Iran-Iraq war. According to General Hamdani, the primary rationale behind using CWs was, among others, to attack the Iranian reserves "in depth" so that Iraqi forces "could fight more freely."[27] Considering that the prospective "target areas" listed in the Iraqi RW progress report included industrial centers and railroad stations—that is, not classic area-denial targets—it is at least conceivable that Iraq similarly considered RWs not exclusively for area denial but also for other purposes. Khidhir Hamza's contention that Hussein Kamel personally became "obsessed" with the idea of irradiating the Iraq-Iran border to create a "buffer zone" against Iran's human-wave attacks, however, suggests that area denial was the primary intended application of the weapons.[28]

Considering Iran's overwhelming numerical superiority on the battlefield, the Iraqis viewed nonconventional weapons as force multipliers.[29] Considerations of numerical imbalance were compounded by geography: in the Al-Faw area, for instance, Iraq felt compelled to turn to nonconventional weapons like CWs, according to Hamdani, "since the land comprises soft soil and marshes, which rendered (their) artillery and air-delivered weapons useless and prevented the effective employment of armor."[30] The Iraqis' desire to complement their nonconventional arsenal with RWs—to pursue anything to get an advantage over the Iranians—stands in contrast to U.S. and Soviet operational concepts related to RWs. As noted in chapters 1 and 2, the pursuit not just of atomic but also chemical weapons diminished the perceived need for RWs and eventually inhibited their pursuit. There is no indication that Iraq pursued RWs for purposes other than area denial and immediate military utility against Iran.

Normative Considerations: Perceptions of Near-Immunity during the 1980s

As noted in chapter 1, there is an assumption in the primary source literature, articulated by Ernest Lawrence, that because of the absence of a clear norm or taboo against their employment, RWs might be considered more usable than nuclear weapons, especially with regard to first use. Furthermore, in the U.S. context, RWs were frequently depicted as analogues to or variants of CWs by their proponents, though the potential pitfalls of conflating the two weapons categories were ignored by some of their military and scientific advocates.

In the case of Iraq, an overall sense of impunity with regard to employing nonconventional weapons vis-à-vis Iran prevailed during the 1980s. Considering that Iraq used mustard gas and tabun extensively, even early on in the Iran-Iraq war,[31] it appears plausible that military planners would likely have felt few qualms about complementing chemical attacks against the enemy with the use of radiological devices. International perceptions of the Islamic Republic of Iran fueled an Iraqi sense of impunity. As Woods, Murray, and Holaday note in their history of the Iran-Iraq war, "the fact that the international community made virtually no protest against the use of chemical weapons by the Iraqis underlines how much of a pariah state Iran had become by the mid-1980s."[32] The extent of Iran's political isolation was also reflected in the support major countries provided to Iraq's war effort, with the U.S. offering space-based military intelligence, several Western European states exporting military technology, the Soviet Union delivering military equipment, especially large quantities of short-range Scud missiles, and the Arab states mobilizing financial support in the form of a large solidarity fund to help stabilize Iraq's economy and strengthen its military capability.[33] In short, though the Reagan administration publicly condemned Iraq's use of CWs, according to Al-Marashi, "U.S. defense officials were assisting Iraq at the time and did not oppose their use against Iran, indicating to Saddam that these weapons could be deployed with little international opposition."[34]

Perhaps Iraq's sense of impunity about the use of nonconventional weapons was not total, however. Iraqi military and official documents, for instance, routinely referred to CWs euphemistically as "special weapons," avoiding direct reference to their chemical nature, which suggests a certain awareness of international norms against the use of such weapons.[35] At the same time, while there might have been an uneasiness about widely publicizing the use of nonconventional weapons, the fact that Saddam's regime even experimented with biological weapons in the 1980s—considered "perhaps the most insidious and feared of all weapons,"[36] according to Amy Smithson—suggests that Iraqi leaders held few moral qualms regarding the use of such weapons. This assessment does not apply unequivocally, however, to some of Iraq's senior scientists, who might have felt inclined to support the nuclear weapons program as a deterrent against Israel but were concerned that developing nonconventional weapons for battlefield use was something "a scientist should not do," according to former Iraqi nuclear scientist Hussain al-Shahristani.[37] Indeed, while scholars, including Kenneth Pollack, have recognized considerations regarding status and prestige as a driver behind Iraq's nonconventional weapons, arguing that "Saddam's standing among the Sunni elites who constituted his power base was linked to a great extent to his having made Iraq a regional power—which the elite saw as a product of Iraq's unconventional arsenal,"[38] such considerations are usually linked more to Iraq's pursuit of a nuclear weapon than to its CBW efforts.

A reluctance among former Iraqi military and scientists to speak about the WMD programs post facto was perhaps partially rooted in a fear of being implicated in and internationally prosecuted for these efforts, even after 2003. Such apprehensions were sometimes compounded by a sense of indignation about the perceived hypocrisy of major powers—especially the UN Security Council Permanent Five—who have their own nuclear arsenals, yet have consistently criticized Iraq's pursuit of WMD, all while Israel pursued its own policy of nuclear opacity with impunity.[39]

Bureaucratic Political Determinants

As shown above, the Iraqi quest for RWs was likely spurred by a perceived military need at an inflection point during the Iran-Iraq war, while normative considerations failed to mitigate against the effort. In addition, bureaucratic political determinants facilitated the RW pursuit from inception to experimentation and testing.

Målfrid Braut-Hegghammer's account of Iraq's nuclear weapons makes a compelling argument about state capacity as an intervening variable in explaining the success of a country's NW program.[40] She defines state capacity as being reflected in the professionalism of a state bureaucracy, specifically its ability to carry out specialized functions and its independence from state elites and the political leadership. In weak authoritarian states like Saddam's Iraq in which the leader—intent on "coup-proofing" the state—proliferates and fragments state institutions, the result is a lack of strong institutional mechanisms that can serve to vet and assess the performance of specialized activities, such as WMD programs.

In the case of Iraq's WMD programs, Braut-Hegghammer argues, the Iraqi regime did not systematically vet projects in terms of their scientific or technological merit, and it also failed to monitor or follow up on many of these projects because it lacked the know-how and institutional resources. As a result, especially during the Iran-Iraq war, scientists operated with unlimited budgets and weak oversight, their leadership stuck with their technological preferences while discarding alternatives, and scientists got away with not delivering results despite ample funding—all without interference from Saddam. Braut-Hegghammer notes that this pattern applied to the pursuit of nonconventional weapons during the Iran-Iraq war generally. According to an Iraqi official interviewed by UN inspectors, whom she cites, "anyone who came to us with an idea of a weapon, we would study and try to develop. The fact is that during the war, it was masses of people attacking Iraq. . . . Any idea that was presented to us to find a solution to this problem on our border with Iran . . . was welcomed."[41] This recalls the Egyptian experience with RWs in the early 1960s, which similarly benefited from an availability of organizational resources that allowed scientific entrepreneurs to pursue novel efforts and "dreamers or exploiters" to "convince their bosses to back some scheme."[42]

While Braut-Hegghammer builds her argument mainly on an examination of Iraq's nuclear weapon program, her insights regarding the causal relevance of state capacity help explain the inception and progression through experimentation and testing of the country's RW program. Indeed, sources familiar with Iraq's WMD programs consider it conceivable that technical entrepreneurs, benefiting from the context of weak state capacity, presented the idea for an RW to the management of the IAEC, which then took it up with Hussein Kamel.[43] Others contend that the idea more likely originated among Iraq's CW weaponeers, who then approached the IAEC with a request for irradiated material.[44] Be that as it may, in a state characterized by weak institutional capacity and poor oversight but which led a proclaimed struggle for survival against a mortal enemy neighbor, many "crackpot ideas" for new weapons systems gained traction at a lower level; "once Kamel liked an idea, it would be difficult to pooh-pooh it"—according to a former IAEA inspector—considering his status as Saddam's son-in-law and head of MIC.⁴⁵ While some Iraqi scientists involved might have realized the low probability of success of the RW program early on, a fear of refusing Kamel or of telling the truth likely mitigated against open criticism. Meanwhile, Kamel's reputation as a "military man" was poor, and he likely did not understand the limited military utility of the weapon under development. According to Kevin Woods, the Iraqi MIC led by him "often overpromised, underdelivered, and consulted insufficiently with the end user—the military."⁴⁶ Individual and institutional advocacy was important in driving the U.S. and Soviet RW programs, but its influence was most pronounced in the Iraqi case, given the key position occupied by Kamel.

The fact that Hussein Kamel, already heading the Iraqi MIC, took the helm of the IAEC in early 1987 likely further sustained momentum on the Iraqi RW effort, notwithstanding the resentment vis-à-vis the MIC felt among the nuclear scientists at Al-Tuwaitha: As al-Marashi notes, the nuclear scientists considered the MIC to be "ignorant folks from Tikrit," telling them what to do.⁴⁷ After Jafar Dhia Jafar retreated from his administrative duties at the top of the IAEC, Kamel moved in on the nuclear program, considering the organization a "juicy target" and seizing command of its weaponization program in April.⁴⁸ Kamel's "pairing of incessant demands for immediate results with a great willingness to countenance sudden shifts over to dramatically different technical solutions" likely provided a context conducive to the sustained pursuit of the RW effort up to the testing stage.⁴⁹ Since the weaponization dimension of the RW program was pursued at the MIC's Al-Muthanna and Al-Qa'Qaa' complex,⁵⁰ which were already under Kamel's control, his usurpation of the IAEC, which was responsible for conducting work on the irradiated material to be used in the RW, likely facilitated rather than inhibited the survival of the effort up until the testing stage. The fact that Al-Muthanna hosted the CW program and was well-funded—given the perceived success of the chemical weapons enterprise—probably also aided the RW effort. In this regard, the Iraqi case differs from the U.S. and Soviet experiences, in which RW programs competed with the CW enterprises for both financial resources and attention within the military-industrial establishments.

Inhibitors to Iraq's Radiological Weapons Effort

Iraq's 1988 progress report on its experimentation with and testing of RWs sheds light on some of the challenges it confronted. Radiation readings taken after tests on the ground were low, and it was noted that the radioactive charges lost strength quickly. While doubting the device's prospective military utility, the report also laments that the work had to be done in strict secrecy since an alert enemy might come to realize that the exploding bombs packed a lingering punch, which could allow it to develop defensive precautions in the future. Compounding the obstacles Iraq confronted in producing an irradiated material that would not lose potency quickly through radioactive decay, the report's final pages detail challenges regarding weaponization.[51] Iraq's prototype RW aerial bomb, the Qa'Qaa'-28, was unsophisticated relative to the radiological munitions tested by the United States and Soviet Union in the 1950s, especially due to its heavy weight.

Bureaucratic Political Determinants Revisited

Weak state capacity and its implications for military innovation might, again, be of partial explanatory value. The lack of vetting or horizontal communication between staffers from physics, chemistry, and engineering—all hallmarks of Iraq's scientific enterprise under Saddam[52]—likely mitigated against more effective collaboration in steering the RW effort in a more fruitful direction. The siloed configuration of the weapons establishment—which in the Soviet case apparently constrained the emergence of forceful proponents for RWs—in the Iraqi case produced the additional disadvantage of impeding a meaningful peer review of the country's radiological program. Although the WMD programs for battlefield use—that is, CW and BW—enjoyed extraordinary autonomy and resources, the majority of decisions regarding technical priorities and resource utilization were delegated to program managers with limited oversight and auditing authority. A similar pattern likely characterized the RW program as well.

Unlike its CBW programs—and in contrast to the Egyptian exploration of RWs, which developed in parallel to state structures as a "special project"—the Iraqi RW effort involved scientists from different organizations and with different expertise. The key personnel engaged in designing sources, zirconium-95 might have appeared as the "easiest option" to Iraq's weaponeers, assuming they wanted to develop a weapon for regular military use (as opposed to a one-off or a terror-inducing RW that would have required much higher radioactive content).[61] Considering that Iraq hoped to use RWs to complement its use of CWs for area denial—presumably for the purposes of being able to counterattack across the same terrain, as opposed to rendering it difficult to traverse for a period of years—zirconium-95 might have appeared to be a suitable source of radiation.

When considering further that zirconium was already used in Iraq's incendiary bombs and therefore added "nothing new to 'the line of work,'"[62] an unwillingness to devote greater resources and expertise to the RW project may have prevented Iraq from experimenting with other sources of radiation and testing a more effective bomb. This finding would somewhat qualify the earlier claim that there was an abundance of funding and resources for Iraq's nonconventional weapons programs during the 1980s. Finally, it appears likely that Iraqi scientists and weaponeers had no knowledge of the U.S. and Soviet experimentation with zirconium in the context of their RW programs (and there is no evidence that Iraq knew that Otto Joklik had conducted rudimentary work on RWs for Egypt). Since these programs were highly secretive, there was little opportunity for Iraq to learn from other actors' challenges in radiological weapons innovation. It is also conceivable that the status of Iraq's nuclear program at the time constrained the availability of other materials in sufficient quantity for the RW effort. If so, this would mirror the supply bottleneck at play in the UK's experience with RWs, in which the output of radioactive material from the Windscale (Sellafield) plutonium reactor, which fueled both the British RW and early nuclear weapons programs, was inadequate to the task.

The second technical obstacle encountered by Iraq in its RW program concerned weaponization. When the Iraqis briefed a biological inspection team (UNSCOM 125) on their RW tests in August 1995, they claimed that they had exploded the Qa'Qaa'-28 (also referred to as the Nasser 28 bomb)—each weighing about 1,400 kilograms because of extensive shielding but containing only 0.5 to 1 kilogram of irradiated zirconium oxide—at a chemical weapons test site.[63] Later in December 1995, however, the Iraqis admitted that an alternative RW bomb design had been explored, as well. Some of

Iraq's LD-250 aerial chemical bombs (known as Muthanna-4)—whose production is mentioned in Iraq's full, final, and complete disclosures (FFCD) on its chemical weapons program—were reportedly modified for the RW effort. The Muthanna-4, according to the Iraqis, weighed only about 400 kilograms, meaning that more weapons could be carried by one aircraft.[64] Indeed, Iraq's chemical FFCD states that "in anticipation for an order for the field evaluation of what was called a radiation weapon . . . 100 pieces of Muthanna-4 aerial bombs were produced, 75 of which were sent to al-Qa'Qaa' for completion."[65] While the remaining twenty-five bombs at Al-Muthanna—those not sent to al-Qa'Qaa'—were destroyed unilaterally by Iraq in the summer of 1991, the fate of the seventy-five bombs remains unclear.[66]

Regarding the Qa'Qaa'-28 bombs tested in 1987, the Iraqi progress report itself is candid in its assessment, referring to an "opinion" of the Air Force Command that recommends studying "the possibilities of lessening the total weight of the bomb."[67] The 1,400 kilogram al-Qa'Qaa' bomb offered inefficient "bang for the buck," undermining the military effectiveness that nonconventional charges were meant to promise to a country with weak air power.[68] Although the more promising Muthanna-4 was not tested, it is noteworthy that the R-400, which would become a mainstay of the Iraqi chemical and (especially) biological arsenal, began testing shortly thereafter—a possible imprint of the abortive RW program on Iraq's broader WMD portfolio.

Was the ineffectiveness of the Iraqi al-Qa'Qaa' bomb ultimately more a result of bureaucratic political determinants or challenges related to the irradiated material and weaponization? The available evidence suggests that Iraq ultimately discarded its RWs for the same reason that nations with more advanced WMD programs, like the Soviet Union and United States, did so: their impracticability and unwieldiness, rooted in the difficulty of combining sufficient quantities of radioactive charges characterized by appropriate half-lives with practicable delivery systems that can be deployed without causing harm to a country's own troops. Hussein Shahristani aptly observes in this context that "when physics dictate reality, no amount of expertise can overcome the obstacles."[69]

Aborting the RW Program amid Reluctance to Report Failure

If Shahristani is correct, then why is it that the Iraqi progress report exaggerates the results achieved, advances conflicting claims about the device's purported effectiveness,[70] and misstates and neglects information related to the irradiated material, all while referring to an "acceptable congruence between the theoretical calculations and the actual results" during testing?[71] Weak state capacity might again explain why the report was not more forthcoming in acknowledging shortcomings: because scientists feared being truthful regarding such failure on the one hand and because they could get away with distorting reality on the other. As Braut-Hegghammer notes, since micromanagement in personalist regimes with weak state capacity is costly, especially when it comes to technical projects that require expertise, a situation emerges that "makes it possible for scientists to exaggerate their progress."[72] At the same time, she argues, such exaggeration is also driven by fear: "to protect themselves from the eyes of the leadership, scientists may inflate the numbers of ongoing projects or may constantly change the design of their organizations," since "institutions can blame each other for mistakes."[73]

Given the low quantities of irradiated material available to the Iraqis, a former IAEA inspector notes that "a rational program might have recognized that it should be terminated right away from the outset when they ran the numbers, but it might have been difficult to report that conclusion up the chain without having gone through the motions of some effort."[74] This argument is especially pertinent when considering how important Saddam considered progress in acquiring nonconventional weapons, including for his own legacy. As one expert on Iraq's WMD programs notes, "feeding the myth of a lingering viable unconventional weapons capability in Iraq was . . . important to regime survival, internally and externally."[75] Especially in the "pressure-cooker atmosphere" that prevailed under Hussein Kamel, who was in charge of both the MIC and IAEC by the time Iraq explored RWs, an "overpromising" of results in scientific pursuits was standard practice.[76]

The International Community and Iraq's RWs

UN Security Council Resolution 687, adopted on April 3, 1991, on the heels of the Gulf War, outlined the conditions for a ceasefire between Iraq and the coalition and ordered the lifting of economic sanctions on Iraq in exchange for the elimination of Iraq's WMD and related capabilities. With the resolution, the Security Council also established a subsidiary organ, the UN Special Commission (UNSCOM), "to implement the non-nuclear provisions of the resolution and to assist the International Atomic Energy Agency in the nuclear areas." UNSCOM's mandate contained immediate on-site inspections of Iraq's biological and chemical weapons and related capabilities and of prohibited missiles, while the IAEA director general subsequently established an action team for the nuclear dimension.[77] The inspection regimes of UNSCOM and the IAEA Action Team have been extensively covered in the scholarly literature, including their mandate, composition, relationship with international capitals, operational difficulties, budgetary constraints, and instances of competition, among other aspects.[78] Since, according to a senior inspector involved at the time, the inspectors arrived in Iraq feeling that "they could do anything,"[79] this chapter closes by asking why they paid so little attention initially to Iraq's aborted RW effort.

Iraqi Obstruction, Foreign Intelligence Failures, and Long-Gone Traces

Iraq's engagement with the international inspectors in the early 1990s was broadly characterized by attempts at obstruction and concealment. Numerous reports from the IAEA director general and the UNSCOM executive chairman to the UN Security Council from that period contain references to Iraqi decisions "not to provide key procurement information" or "confiscate documents ... despite strong protests" by the inspectors, with UNSCOM personnel frequently sensing a "fluctuation of the rules" for how Iraqis were to comport themselves with the inspectors.[80] Rolf Ekéus, UNSCOM's first executive chairman, sums up the prevailing sentiment by suggesting that "each new year presented its share of challenges to the inspectors"— from threats against UNSCOM's aerial surveillance via denying access to UNSCOM inspectors to Saddam demanding the immediate halt to all inspection activities in 1994 and 1995.[81] Saddam's deception and concealment strategy was especially acute in the context of Iraq's BW program, with the Iraqi leader perhaps anticipating that UNSCOM would remain short-lived and understaffed, while suffering from a lack of reliable intelligence on Iraq's nonconventional weapons.[82] Amy Smithson notes in her account of the dismantlement of Iraq's BW program that European diplomats were "entertained" by the level of dishonesty in Iraq's initial declarations to UNSCOM, which "revealed "just how tall an order it would be to meet the deadlines to render harmless or destroy Iraq's weaponry."[83] Overall, she notes that Iraq's concealment and obstruction strategy entailed such diverse elements as the moving around of critical documents, the blocking of access to inspectors, the elaboration of cover stories, the sanitization and destruction of infrastructure, and the intimidation of inspectors, as well as snooping on UNSCOM.[84] The Iraqis' engagement with the IAEA Action Team inspectors was little different. Overall, there was a tendency to disclose only what had already been discovered: According to Gudrun Harrer, "When Iraq was caught red-handed, it came forward with new information, later denying that it had produced this information under pressure."[85]

Against this backdrop, it did not help the inspectors that the United States intelligence community (or other foreign intelligence, for that matter) appears to not have been aware of the Iraqi RW effort prior to the Gulf War. The U.S. General Accounting Office conducted a review of prewar intelligence assessments and found that only one raised the possibility that Iraq could construct such a device. Furthermore, this assessment "judged that the probability of this happening was negligible."[86] Declassified U.S. intelligence assessments of Iraq's national security goals, ballistic missile developments, or the pre-1991 status of its WMD programs omit references to the short-lived RW effort.[87] Assuming their duties in Iraq with no indication that the country had experimented with and tested RWs, the inspectors were finally impeded by the fact that the RW experiments would, in any case, have been untraceable by the early 1990s. Since the Iraqis had irradiated zirconium oxide targets in the RW experiments at Al Tuwaitha, "the timing would have been such that any trace of radioactive zirconium and hafnium isotopes would have been long gone" when the inspectors visited, according to a former IAEA inspector.[88] The same problem applied to the RW test site: when visited by UN inspectors with radiation monitors, the reported level of radioactivity was so low that it was difficult to obtain a reading.[89]

The International Inspectors

While it would have been a veritable uphill battle for international inspectors to probe Iraq's RW effort in the early 1990s given Iraqi obstruction, lack of relevant intelligence, and the dearth of physical evidence available, UNSCOM and the IAEA Action Team also had other priorities. Their concerns with Iraq's nuclear weapon, chemical weapon, missile, and eventually biological weapon programs were extensive. By August 1995, when the Iraqis had admitted to parts of their BW program, it was regarded, according to Amy Smithson, "as the most alarming and elusive of all of the weapons of mass destruction endeavors undertaken by Iraq."[90] What is more, prior to this, there was acute concern over Iraq's CW agents, like VX, compounded by apprehension that the nuclear weapons (NW) program might have made serious progress, which likely explains why no attention was being paid to RWs.[91] The dismantlement of Iraq's CWs proved especially challenging—according to former UNSCOM director Rolf Ekéus, it was a "difficult, dangerous, and time-consuming task for UNSCOM not only to account for but to eliminate the stored quantities of precursor agents."[92]

Indeed, because they were preoccupied with addressing the mammoth challenge of Iraq's CWs in the first half of the 1990s, the inspectors were left with scant time to survey all of Al-Muthanna and investigate anything unusual. According to UNSCOM inspector Rod Barton, "At that time, no one at a senior level was really interested in trying to dig out a covert biological weapons program."[93] Given the limited bandwidth inspectors had for investigating additional threats, it comes as no surprise that no efforts were made to probe experimentation with RWs that no foreign intelligence agency had detected and that the Iraqis had no intention of exposing. The scope of the investigation challenge in Iraq combined with Baghdad's concealment strategies to pose a formidable challenge. "Given the size of what we conducted in Iraq," notes Gustavo Zlauvinen, who served as chief of staff to the UNSCOM executive chairman from 1995, "it was almost impossible to find out things held clandestinely. You had to be lucky to find evidence of something you didn't know existed."[94]

Even if there had been an effort to probe Iraq's RW program, it might have been unclear under whose authority and mandate the investigation would have fallen: UNSCOM, which had the overall authority to designate locations for inspection and covered Iraq's CW program, or the IAEA Action Team, which would have theoretically been responsible for probing Iraq's undeclared Zr-95 irradiation activities. The Iraqi government's own process for informing on its RWs, once a decision to that end had been taken in 1995, reinforces the impression of confusion: The BW inspectors were reportedly the first to be briefed in August 1995, followed by both the IAEA Action Team and CW inspectors in December,[95] before written information was provided in Iraq's draft chemical FFCD in early 1996 and later complemented by data in the nuclear FFCD provided to the IAEA. It is therefore not inconceivable that the occasional competition and uneasy working relationship between the two organizations might have complicated an investigation into Iraq's RWs had there been more intelligence and bandwidth available.[96]

Why Iraq Revealed Its RW Program

Given the above, it is likely that the international community would never have learned of Iraq's RW effort had Hussein Kamel's defection to Jordan in 1995 not spurred a decision at the highest level of the Iraqi government to come clean on additional dimensions of the country's WMD programs. Kamel's defection was preceded by a "rocky road of cooperation" between Iraq and UNSCOM, with Iraqi warnings culminating in an ultimatum, stated early in August 1995, that all "cooperation would cease if, by 31 August 1995, no progress was made in the Security Council in the direction of easing or lifting the sanctions and the oil embargo."[97] The decision by Hussein Kamel to flee to Jordan on August 7, however, completely "changed the game."[98] Iraq withdrew its ultimatum, and Deputy Prime Minister Tariq Aziz announced Iraq's new policy of complete cooperation and transparency with UNSCOM and the IAEA, without any time limits.[99] Letters were sent to both the UNSCOM executive chairman and IAEA director general alleging that Hussein Kamel "had been responsible for hiding important information on Iraq's prohibited programmes from the Commission and IAEA by ordering the Iraqi technical personnel not to disclose such information and also not to inform Mr. Tariq Aziz . . . of these instructions."[100] In response to these fast-paced developments, both the UNSCOM executive chairman and the IAEA director general headed back to Baghdad. UNSCOM was subsequently able to bring under its control a massive amount of documentation and material directly linked to proscribed programs, which had been hidden inside Iraq since the autumn of 1991 before being turned over at the "chicken farm" at Haidar on August 20, 1995.[101]

It is in this context that the Iraqi government appears to have taken the conscious decision to inform inspectors of its RW effort for the first time, alongside further disclosures about other prohibited programs. Since Hussein Kamel knew more than any other regime member, Saddam included, about the details of Iraq's former WMD programs, his defection put the regime under immense pressure.[102] It is likely that senior leaders in Baghdad decided that they should try to "beat Kamel to the punch," disclosing hitherto concealed aspects of the WMD programs and thereby trying to control the narrative before Kamel could be interviewed by inspectors in Jordan.[103] In that context, the Iraqis' decision to share details on the RW effort specifically might have been prompted by the perceived need to reconcile outstanding UNSCOM queries regarding inconsistencies and discrepancies in Iraq's CW declarations provided up until that time, including ones on munitions (some of which, as noted earlier, were modified as part of the RW effort).[104] Though the Kamel defection ushered in an unprecedented level of Iraqi cooperation in the latter half of 1995, causing Baghdad to reveal its pursuit of RWs, UNSCOM continued to bemoan the unknown fate and location of certain documents, including some in possession of the MIC and the Iraqi Ministry of Defense.[105] Regarding the RW file specifically, Zlauvinen notes that the evidence shared by the Iraqis was "taken seriously" by the inspectors, who asked Baghdad for further information in several meetings. Since Iraq did not come forward with additional insights and it would take a considerable amount of time to sift through the "chicken farm" documents in their entirety, it was decided that Iraq's RW file should not be closed but "kept dormant" until such time as further information would enable further investigation.[106]

The Iraqi Case in Comparative Perspective

This chapter showed that Iraq's relatively short-lived and unsuccessful pursuit of RWs—from experimentation to testing but stopping short of production and deployment—was driven by the narrow requirement of exploring capabilities predominantly for area denial during a critical stage of the Iran-Iraq war. With regard to Evangelista's hypotheses, perceptions of external threat were thus salient to Iraqi military innovation in the radiological realm from the outset, much like the Soviet case. Although military requirements constituted the primary driver, the pursuit of RWs was also likely sustained by the specificities of Iraq's bureaucratic-institutional landscape during the 1980s. Indeed, Iraq's experience with RW innovation resembles the U.S. pattern in which a push for new weapons technology arises from below (i.e., from scientists and the military officials with whom they interact) more than the Soviet model in which directives typically come from above in response to technological developments abroad. In Iraq's case, while it is not possible to situate the origin of the idea for developing RWs with precision, it appears that it originated either with technical entrepreneurs or CW weaponeers, who then approached IAEC management and Hussein Kamel. That said, unlike in the U.S. case, there is insufficient evidence to conclusively establish whether bureaucratic consensus building and policy advocacy preceded a formal decision in Iraq to pursue RW experimentation and testing.

The analysis further examined the obstacles Iraq confronted in developing RWs, arguing that the technical challenges related to the irradiated material and weaponization were of primary importance for failure, while institutional factors—chiefly the program's awkward position at the nexus of various WMD programs—might have additionally mitigated against more fruitful outcomes. Finally, the chapter turned to an exploration of the international community's limited investigation into Iraq's RWs, showing that a lack of foreign intelligence and on-site evidence, Iraqi concealment and obstruction, the negligibility of the RW program in scope and achievements, and the prioritization of Iraq's NW and CBW programs combined to impede the UNSCOM and IAEA inspectors in engaging with the RW dossier.

The circumstances surrounding the Iraqi government's decision to admit to its pursuit of RWs in 1995 and 1996 might never be fully known in the open source, but it appears that Hussein Kamel's 1995 defection to Jordan generated a desire in Baghdad to "beat the defector to the punch" and control the narrative about future WMD-related revelations. Kamel's defection set in motion a chain of events that allowed international inspectors to piece together the story of Iraq's RWs. At the end of the day, however, that story is usually brushed aside by practitioners and scientists with the argument that, in the case of Iraq's RWs, "absence of evidence is evidence of absence":[107] the reason not more is known about the program is that there simply is not more to say. Iraq's exploration of RWs was short-lived, ineffective, and no weapon was ever deployed—so goes the consensus among all sources interviewed for this research. This explains why international inspectors and scientists have treated the program as a footnote in their accounts of Iraq's WMD programs, which have otherwise received unprecedented international attention and scholarly treatment.

Though Iraq's pursuit of RWs appears inconspicuous when examined in the context of its other WMD programs, an analysis of its rise and demise yields important insights about the reasons weak authoritarian regimes might turn to this type of nonconventional weaponry in the face of external threats and the obstacles they will have to overcome to complete the weapons innovation process. A comparison of Iraq's pursuit of RWs with the much earlier efforts by the United States, the Soviet Union, the United Kingdom, and Egypt also reveals important similarities and differences. The most striking commonality among them is program abandonment, notwithstanding the significant differences in the technical approaches that were pursued. Although Iraq, the Soviet Union, and the United States—unlike Britain and Egypt—were able to produce prototype radiological weapons and test them with some degree of success, all these programs failed to generate a new weapon that could be adopted for deployment by their respective militaries.

The Iraqi RW program was aimed at affording Baghdad options for area denial during its war with Iran. Regarding the military objectives that states anticipated could usefully be served by RWs in the context of their regional security postures, the Egyptian and Iraqi efforts—both case studies from the Middle East—reveal important nuances, with Cairo viewing RWs primarily as weapons to match and deter Israel and Baghdad coveting a radiological device for active battlefield use. The Iraqi program represents the only RW effort besides that of the United States that did not seek to emulate or match an adversary's nonconventional capability; rather, it was intended for concrete military use in an ongoing war.

The role of Hussein Kamel in championing Iraq's pursuit of RWs echoes the role of similar scientific entrepreneurs who proved essential as initial catalysts for exploring the viability of radiological warfare in the United States. In Egypt, an individual scientific entrepreneur was likely instrumental not only to kickstarting but also to sustaining the RW effort through its entire (albeit short) life cycle. In the Soviet Union, by contrast, early proposals by scientists to explore RWs had failed to resonate. Similar to British defense officials, Iraq's weaponeers viewed RWs as potentially complementing other nonconventional armaments including chemical and biological weapons. And like the U.S. and Soviet programs, Iraq's RW effort enlisted the expertise and support of chemical weaponeers, including in the development of ideas for weaponization and suitable munitions. Unlike the U.S. RW program, however, there is no evidence that the Iraqi RW program competed directly with the CW enterprise for resources and support.

Iraq's RW effort did not fall victim to a "substitution effect"—an abandonment of RWs in favor of nuclear arms—in the same manner as the U.S. program, since there was a greater availability of resources earmarked for military innovation in Saddam's Iraq. That said, the Iraqi RW program's somewhat awkward position at the nexus of the country's NW and CW programs might have reduced a sense of responsibility and accountability for the project. Finally, unlike in the Iraqi case, declining support in the United States and Soviet Union for RWs was not the result of poor performance in testing—initial tests in both countries initially yielded positive results—but rather of competition for financial resources and attention within the military-industrial establishment due to the perceived superior military effectiveness of alternative nonconventional weapons.

CONCLUSION
Patterns across Cases and Prospects for the Future

The preceding chapters have analyzed all known prior cases of state-level pursuit of radiological weapons. This final chapter looks for patterns across the cases and more general explanations for the rise, evolution, and demise of weapons innovation involving RWs. It also identifies new circumstances, such as the war in Ukraine, that might encourage other states to pursue RWs and assesses how the spread of such weapons would affect nuclear deterrence and the stability of the nuclear nonproliferation regime. The chapter concludes with a discussion of practical steps that could be taken by members of the international community to reduce the likelihood of a resurgence of interest in and pursuit of RWs by state actors.

Deconstructing the RW Life Cycle

One of the more curious aspects of the life cycle of RW innovation is the discrepancy between the relatively large number of states that we know pursued or at least flirted with RWs, five; the smaller but not inconsequential number of states that tested RWs, three; and the absence of any states that completed the weapons innovation process by deploying RWs in their military's arsenal.[1] Significantly, four of the five states that pursued RWs simultaneously conducted research on nuclear weapons, and all five had active chemical weapons programs during the time that they either initiated research and development of RWs or, in the case of Egypt, sought to secure RW precursor material from abroad.

No single theory, school of thought, or set of factors adequately explains these findings. Data limitations further impede our ability to draw definitive conclusions about the role of some likely drivers of and impediments to RW development and deployment. Nevertheless, our comparative analysis uncovers significant new insights about the previously obscure history of state-level RW programs.

Drivers

Scientific Discovery and the Technological Imperative

The fertile imagination of science fiction writer and editor John Campbell anticipated radiological weapons. Robert Heinlein, gifted contributor to his magazine and science enthusiast, expanded on the concept and provided a not implausible context for their development. However, the actual policy initiation or agenda-setting phase of the RW innovation process in the United States, while proximate in time to its science fiction counterpart, was the product of more informed scientific theorizing, albeit still based on incomplete information. In terms of Matthew Evangelista's conception of the U.S. weapons innovation process, the birth of RWs may be viewed as a form of technocratic (or technological) imperative, a new technical possibility with military applications, which was advocated by scientists.[2]

It is more difficult to make the case for the role of scientific discovery and the operation of a technological imperative with respect to the initiation of other state-level RW programs. In the Soviet Union, a time lag of at least several years appears to have separated the initial recognition by two physical mathematicians of the possible military applications of radioactive material and high-level Soviet interest in the development of RWs. A major intervening variable prompting Soviet interest was intelligence indicating that the United States was taking measures to defend against the use of radioactive poisons. Ironically, it was at about the same time in 1943 that the British government may have become more skeptical about the seriousness of the RW threat and U.S. efforts to counter it.[3] It is possible that a technological imperative involving RWs also was at work in Iraq, perhaps leading scientists in the mid-1980s to recommend the innovation to Hussein Kamel, who launched the Iraqi RW R & D program. Data are inconclusive, however, and it is as likely that military losses in the war against Iran were paramount in prompting the Iraqi regime to explore a variety of nonconventional weapons for battlefield use, of which RWs were one. It also is difficult to make the case that scientific discovery per se played a major role in prompting Egypt to explore radiological weapons. A fertile environment, however, was present that encouraged scientific entrepreneurs (including a large cadre of German scientists) to promote novel weapons, including nonconventional ones such as RWs.

Although the science underlying the RW programs in the five countries was often similar, the technologies employed to produce the radioactive material for weapons purposes were by no means uniform. That variation was a function of technical knowledge and infrastructure, military mission, anticipated production costs, and critical to the sustainability of the program, perceived opportunity costs related to competing weapons systems.

Basically, two alternative means were available for obtaining the necessary radioactive material for the novel weapon system. (A third alternative, pursued by Egypt, was to purchase the material abroad.) The first approach, adopted by the United States and Iraq, entailed irradiating an inert metal inside a nuclear reactor to produce radioactive isotopes for use in the weapon. The virtue of this approach for countries that already possessed reactors was that it did not require a major new investment in specialized facilities. In the United States, for example, the Hanford reactor that made plutonium for the Nagasaki bomb could, in principle, also be used to produce the radioactive isotope tantalum-182 during its normal operation. The problem with this approach was that the same Hanford reactor was needed to produce both plutonium-239, the fissile material for most of the early nuclear bombs, and polonium-210, a key component of the neutron initiators for the bombs. Even while running at full capacity, the reactor did not seem capable of sustaining production of both the necessary amounts of fissile material and radioactive isotopes. As such, the early cost-saving measure adopted by the U.S. ultimately deprived the RW program of a dedicated radioactive source production facility.

An alternative means to obtain radioactive material for RWs was to extract it from the spent fuel produced by the operation of a reactor. The trick, however, was to obtain an isotope with a useful half-life (neither too short nor too long) in a cost-effective fashion. U.S. scientists identified one such isotope (zirconium-niobium[4]) but determined that its extraction from the plutonium production reactor at Hanford was both difficult and expensive and decided not to pursue that path. The Soviet Union apparently attached less importance to the cost factor and opted to derive its radioactive material from spent fuel from which plutonium also was extracted. The preferred radioactive isotopes for its RWs were zirconium-95 and niobium-95. The UK approach also departed from that of the United States, and the radioactive material for its RW program was expected to be extracted from the spent fuel generated by nuclear reactors. As best we can tell, Iraqi scientists were unaware of U.S., Soviet, or British experimentation with different modes of production of radioactive materials or their preferred radioisotopes. In any case, perhaps because the production mode was relatively easy technologically, Iraq chose to irradiate zirconium oxide at its IRT-5000 research reactor to produce zirconim-95.

The third route to acquisition of radioactive isotopes for RWs was the one explored by Egypt. Lacking the technical means to produce such isotopes indigenously, it, not unreasonably, looked abroad, specifically to the country (Germany) that had provided other valuable military assistance and scientific expertise. According to the limited data to which we have access, the Egyptian RW program was unique in focusing on weaponization of the longer-lived isotopes of cobalt-60 and strontium-90, perhaps because of the different military mission envisaged, possibly due to a lack of scientific know-how and limited domestic production capability and conceivably due to the greater availability of those isotopes in foreign markets.

International Security Considerations

The process by which RWs first gained attention and then acquired traction in the five states under review varied considerably. Although one might have expected some learning to have transpired based on the experiences of those who first experimented with a new weapons technology, in the case of RWs there was very little diffusion effect or, with the possible exception of the Soviet experience, anything resembling the kind of action-reaction process often associated with arms racing. The absence of this dynamic was in large part due to the secrecy surrounding the RW programs, even among allies. It also was the result of the very different mix of international security threats, decision-making structures, economic resources, technological know-how, military objectives, and individual and organizational advocates in the five states. Thus, while the perception of external threats was a common driver, at least initially, in each case, the impact of the international security environment on the seriousness with which research and development of RWs was pursued was moderated in some instances by faulty intelligence, interservice rivalries, technical assumptions, economic constraints, the availability or pursuit of other nonconventional weapons, and the presence or absence of effective technological entrepreneurs.

In the U.S. case, for example, the initial decision to examine the potential of RWs was influenced by a concern that Nazi Germany might pursue such a weapon. Fairly soon, however, the U.S. became convinced that the threat—to the extent that it existed—did not extend directly to the continental United States. Because of poor intelligence and perhaps indifference, the U.S. also failed to recognize Soviet R & D related to radiological weapons.[5] As a result, the potential danger posed by Soviet activities in that domain never played a role in justifying U.S. investments to sustain its RW program.

The situation was different in the Soviet Union. Soviet officials received early information from both clandestine (Alan Nunn May) and open (the Smyth Report) sources about U.S. interests in and activities involving RWs. On balance, this knowledge probably encouraged their pursuit of this nonconventional weapon. Ironically, while Soviet spies may have informed their handlers about U.S. and British assessments of RWs, the same spies—who were deeply embedded in the British nuclear weapons program—appear to have been less enthusiastic about RW's potential than were their Soviet scientific and military counterparts.

As noted earlier, there is no evidence to suggest that the initiation of the Iraqi RW program was informed by the earlier U.S., Soviet, or British programs. The Iraqi effort, however, shared with the U.S. and British initiatives a general interest in the weapon for area-denial purposes and was driven by the specific objective of disrupting Iranian human-wave attacks. As with Iraq, there are no indications that Egyptian interest in radiological weapons was prompted by knowledge of prior work in the field. Unlike the other states that sought RWs, Egypt's interest in nonconventional weapons generally and RWs specifically was driven by a desire to counter a regional adversary's military applications of nuclear energy by means of a potential weapon of terror. In that respect, the Egyptian program differed from the four other cases, which were more focused on developing a nonconventional weapon for area-denial purposes.

Domestic Determinants

While technological and security-oriented explanations for military innovations tend to be straightforward, they may obscure equally important but less visible domestic sources of weapons acquisition. These internal drivers of policy include such categories as individual and institutional advocates, bureaucratic rivalries, and slack resources. In the U.S., Soviet, and Iraqi cases, for example, one can point to a relatively small number of "issue entrepreneurs" whose strong advocacy for RWs was responsible for building support within the military-technical community and securing initial funds for research and development. In the U.S., these advocates tended to be scientists, while in the Soviet Union and Iraq, they were government officials closely associated with the military and security services. The influence of an individual advocate was most pronounced in the Iraqi case, where the patron of the RW program was both the head of the Military Industrialization Corporation and, more importantly, the son-in-law of President Saddam Hussein. While one also can point to prominent individuals in the British and Egyptian cases, it is more difficult to establish their role as advocates and significant policy influencers as opposed to implementers (e.g., Marley in the case of the UK and Joklik in the case of Egypt).

It is not always easy to separate the impact of individual and institutional advocates. In the U.S., one often finds leading scientific, military, and industrial figures acting in concert to build consensus for the initiation of new weapons systems and their testing and production. Although one can identify informal coalitions that promoted RWs in the United States, often involving individuals with experience in radiochemistry and radiological defense during World War II,[6] these weapons never acquired a high-level political champion in either the executive or legislative branch. Their biggest ally initially was the Army Chemical Corps, which saw the atomic bomb as a challenge to the organization's existence and RWs as a means to get its fair share of the budding atomic business. The availability of funds for work in the nuclear sector can be thought of as slack resources—the opposite of resource scarcity or resource constraints—and a condition often identified by organizational theorists as a driver of innovation.

Consistent with the stages in the process of Soviet weapons innovation suggested by Matthew Evangelista, Soviet pursuit of RWs moved from several years of low-level preparatory work to high-level mobilization under the oversight of the Soviet Council of Ministers and involving several military services. The British RW program, in contrast, never attracted the attention of senior political officials or enjoyed the support of any of the UK's military services. Although the Iraqi RW program initially had the institutional support of the Military Industrialization Corporation, that support was linked entirely to the person of its leader. In Egypt's case, chief scientist Joklik reported to senior military figures who oversaw the country's rudimentary RW program, but it is impossible to determine from the available evidence the degree to which his superiors or the institutions they represented were involved. The same caveat applies to the Egyptian presidency.

Normative Considerations

Conceivably, normative factors may have both encouraged and discouraged the pursuit of RWs. They appear, however, to have had little or no impact on RW decision-making in the Soviet, Egyptian, and Iraqi cases. The comments by some RW advocates in the United States suggest that RWs were occasionally depicted as "more humane" than other weapons of war because they ostensibly gave their human targets a choice of whether to flee and live or stay and die.[7] This view was reportedly also voiced by members of the UK's atomic weapons program during World War II, although the argument lost its appeal after the bombing of Hiroshima and Nagasaki as more information became available about the effects of radiation.[8] There is little evidence, moreover, that the argument ever had many adherents in the United States or elsewhere. Normative considerations may have played a very different role in persuading the brilliant nuclear physicist and Soviet spy Alan Nunn May to share nuclear secrets, including those involving RWs, however. His espionage work appears to have been driven primarily by the conviction that no country should have a monopoly on nuclear violence.

The Role of Prestige

Considerations of international status and prestige have been identified by numerous studies as incentives for the acquisition of nuclear weapons by certain states. At least in the past, they were seen as a symbol of scientific expertise and technological innovation. There is little evidence that radiological weapons have ever held the same attraction, and prestige appears to have played little or no role in the RW programs of the United States, the Soviet Union, the United Kingdom, or Iraq. The picture is less clear, however, in the case of Egypt, where it is quite possible that Nasser viewed RWs—like other nonconventional weapons and also especially missiles—as a means to bolster his credentials as the leader of the Arab world, a position that was in jeopardy after the breakup of the United Arab Republic. While prestige is insufficient to explain Egypt's RW ambitions, it is a plausible reinforcing factor in the country's pursuit of a mix of nonconventional weapons, including RWs.

Inhibitors

The demise of the RW programs in the five countries under review was, in most instances, not abrupt. Although the precise factors responsible for the abandonment of the programs vary from country to country, the devolution processes also display a number of commonalities.

Technical Impediments

A major factor contributing to the demise of RWs across all cases was the inability of the novel weapons system to deliver what its promoters—including those in the scientific-technical community—promised. In part, this outcome was due to the specific technological paths pursued (i.e., the mode selected to produce radioactive sources), the RW capabilities that were required for specific military missions (e.g., the desired half-life of radioisotopes), and unanticipated safety and environmental risks associated with the production, transportation, testing, and delivery of RWs. For example, as noted in the previous section, the initial choices of the desired RW isotope and the means of production dimmed, if not doomed, the prospects for a viable radioisotope production line in the U.S. and Iraq. The situation was not much better in the Soviet Union, where the materials used in the weapons tests posed extreme hazards to the personnel involved and produced generally disappointing performance results. Over time these technological impediments contributed to the erosion of any lingering enthusiasm within the scientific-technical communities for continuation of work on RWs.[9]

Changes in the International Security Environment

In principle, just as a threatening international security environment might contribute to the pursuit of novel weapons systems such as RWs, the perceived diminution of external threats could lead to reduced support for production and deployment of new weapons. Our comparative analysis does not find instances in which reduced threat perceptions played a role in the demise of RWs, although the lack of accurate U.S. intelligence about Soviet efforts in the RW sphere probably removed a possible rationale for continued pursuit of the U.S. program. More importantly, the perceived need to respond in kind to the rise of new external threats posed by nuclear-armed adversaries likely drew resources away from RWs, at least in the cases of the United States, the Soviet Union, and the United Kingdom.

Domestic Impediments

The fate of RW programs in all the countries under consideration were intrinsically linked to competing organizational interests and bureaucratic infighting. This domestic political competition was especially pronounced among the different military services and often involved competing interests of those associated with RWs, chemical weapons, and nuclear weapons. These interests were not static and alliances shifted over time, sometimes favoring research, development, and testing of RWs, but ultimately dooming their deployment. Crucial to this outcome in each state-level program, with the possible exception of Egypt, was what we previously referred to as the "substitution effect." This phenomenon, proposed in the nonconventional weapons arena by Michael Horowitz and Neil Narang, hypothesizes that nuclear, chemical, and biological weapons are typically pursued simultaneously until a state has acquired a nuclear capability, at which point the state is unlikely to continue its CW or BW programs.[10] Although Horowitz and Narang do not address RWs in their study, the logic of their analysis would appear to extend to radiological weapons, which lost most of their key military advocates and budget support as greater reliance was placed on nuclear weapons, especially hydrogen bombs. Radiological weapons also came up short in the U.S., Soviet, British, and Iraqi cost-benefit comparisons with chemical weapons, which often were seen as having similar military missions.[11]

The degree of high-level individual and institutional support for RWs varied across the five cases, with the lowest degree of government support found in the United Kingdom and the highest degree present in the Soviet Union and Iraq.[12] That support, however, was very closely linked to specific individuals, and when they passed from the scene, they were not replaced by other effective advocates. The extreme secrecy and compartmentalization of work associated with the RW programs in all countries impeded the ability of RW advocates to build larger coalitions of supporters with access to different funding sources.

A different bureaucratic impediment to the military's adoption of RWs in every country we have reviewed is the operation of what may be thought of as a "kinetic warfare" bias. The basic argument advanced by Frank Smith is that military bureaucracies—at least in the United States—have a preference for innovations that resemble bullets and bombs and a corresponding aversion to arms such as neutron weapons that rely on less visible physical properties. While Smith does not focus on RWs per se, he does make the case with respect to neutron bombs, a weapons system that shares with RWs a reliance on effects other than blast and heat to achieve lethality.[13]

Normative Considerations

Norms may well have influenced the degree of support RWs enjoyed within the U.S. and British governments. In this respect, their frequent association with chemical weapons may have diminished their appeal for some policymakers, who found both categories of weapons to be "beyond the pale." From what we can discern from the available evidence, however, norms appear to have played at best a secondary role in influencing the demise of RW programs across the five cases. Even in the British experience in which scientists, according to William King, displayed greater uniformity of condemnation of RWs than was the case in the United States,[14] the final decision to forego further development of the novel weapon system was determined primarily by technical and economic considerations and the much greater punch for the pound delivered by nuclear weapons.

Implications for Nuclear Deterrence

As evident from the preceding chapters, the story of radiological weapons is both incomplete and largely unknown to most scholars and security policy practitioners. It is not surprising, therefore, that very little attention has been given by the academic and policy-making communities to the impact—if any—of RWs on the concept and operation of nuclear deterrence. A partial, early exception to this general phenomenon is the brief discussion of "super-dirty" bombs by Bernard Brodie in the 1958 RAND report "The Anatomy of Deterrence."[15] In the report, Brodie—arguably the preeminent postwar nuclear strategist—sought to "think through some of the peculiar and historically novel requirements of a deterrence posture."[16] In a section titled the "Choice of Weapons for Maximum Deterrence," he observes that the U.S. military would have been happy to do without the radioactive byproduct of nuclear explosion weapons and that considerable effort was made to develop a "clean bomb" that would produce a relatively small amount of radioactive fallout.[17] He also notes, however, that in principle it was feasible to produce super-dirty weapons, although support for such an innovation "was bound to be retarded by the feeling that they had little or no military utility and hence could not be morally justified."[18]

Brodie's focus on the relationship between the degree of radioactivity produced by a weapon and the effectiveness of deterrence is noteworthy for a number of reasons, including the fact that the issue was underexplored and remains so. According to Brodie, the case for a super-dirty bomb is founded on the premise that deterrence requires making the prospect of retaliation "as horrendous as possible."[19] Brodie's comments also are significant because he was very familiar with the early U.S. RW program, having served as the lead consultant for a 1949 RAND conference on "the psychological effects of unconventional weapons" at which RWs were discussed at length.[20] In one particularly candid intervention at the conference, Brodie wondered aloud about the extent to which "the propaganda of some of our own armed services in support of their own specific needs invalidated the impact which the atomic raids on Hiroshima and Nagasaki would have had otherwise." His response to the question, which is relevant to the role of bureaucratic politics in the pursuit of different nonconventional weapons after the war, was that "possibly some statement by high-ranking officers interested in other weapons minimized the value of what we have and blunted its effect on others."[21]

While Brodie's discussion of radioactivity and deterrence may help to explain Russia's development of its new "super torpedo" Poseidon, it does little to clarify either the question of how the use of RWs might be deterred or what policymakers perceive to be the relationship between RWs and other nonconventional weapons. In fact, as best we can discern, these issues have not been seriously examined by either scholars or contemporary national security policymakers, most of whom are unaware of their own country's historical record regarding RWs, much less that of other countries.

These issues are not only of theoretical interest if one believes, as do the authors, that additional states may well seek to acquire radiological weapons in the future. It may be important, for example, in attempting to deter the use by a future possessor of RWs to establish where RWs fall in the conventional weapons, chemical weapons, biological weapons, and nuclear weapons continuum. Absent such an understanding by both the intended target of deterrence and the would-be deterrer, there are likely to be major miscalculations about the credibility of the deterrent threat, the appropriate response if deterrence fails, and the means available to carry out the threatened action. As best we can ascertain, the U.S. government has not in many years considered either the possibility of state actor employment of radiological weapons as a distinct category of nonconventional weapons or how to deter the use of such arms.[22] While ambiguity sometimes may be a desirable feature in deterrent threats, it is not obvious that current U.S. nuclear doctrine is intentionally vague regarding whether an adversary state's use of RWs against

U.S. forces would be considered grounds for nuclear weapons retaliation. Similarly, it is not clear what retaliatory options would be "on the table" were RWs to be used against a civilian target, such as a major population center. As discussed below, these questions have moved from a theoretical realm to a very practical one as the war in Ukraine has revived the long-dormant concern that states might resort to the use of RWs.

While it would appear desirable for governments to at least think through the wisdom of trying to deter state-level use of (and threats to use) RWs, there are reasons to believe that achieving an effective RW deterrence capability would be extremely difficult. This conclusion is due to significant intelligence challenges (reinforced by prevailing organizational perspectives), the less-than-stellar record of U.S. efforts to deter chemical weapons use, and the potential counterproductive consequences of adopting a public RW deterrence policy.

As we have noted in our comparative case studies, the United States government consistently failed to detect foreign radiological weapons programs in a timely fashion. These intelligence shortcomings reflect the inherent difficulty of discerning clandestine nonconventional weapons activities, especially when they involve dual-use materials and technologies employed in legitimate civilian and military sectors. The failure of U.S. (and British) intelligence to detect the scope and nature of the Soviet RW program or to anticipate (or attach importance to) the British, Egyptian, and Iraqi RW programs also reflects the low regard U.S. analysts had of RWs—to the extent they were even aware of the U.S. RW experience. This negative assessment can be explained logically by the demise of the U.S. program due to technical difficulties, limited military benefits, and the absence of strong institutional and leadership advocacy. In other words, as is often the case, intelligence analysts assumed that if RWs were unattractive to the U.S. military, they should not be more attractive to other state actors.[23]

The literature on deterring chemical weapons use also suggests that developing an effective policy for deterring RW attacks by state actors will be difficult. Two cases frequently cited in this regard are the deterrence "success" against Iraq in 1991 and the failure against Syria beginning in 2012.[24] In the first case, a threat was made by the Bush administration in January 1991 in the form of a letter to Saddam Hussein delivered by Secretary of State James

Baker to Iraqi foreign minister Tariq Aziz. The letter, which Aziz appears never to have shown to the Iraqi president, stated that "the United States will not tolerate the use of chemical or biological weapons or the destruction of Kuwait's oil fields." Baker also issued a more forceful verbal warning to Aziz that if Iraq used chemical or biological weapons, "the American people would demand vengeance. And we have the means to exact it."[25] Although these threats sometimes are cited as instances of successful deterrence, more recent research based on recordings of Saddam's meetings with his advisors recovered after his capture in 2003 indicates that U.S. threats were not responsible for Iraqi chemical weapons restraint. Instead, Saddam appears to have regarded chemical weapons as his own weapon of last resort and means of deterrence against U.S. (or Israeli) use of nonconventional weapons.[26]

The second widely studied case involves the ill-fated attempt by the Obama administration in 2012 to deter the use of CWs by Syrian president Bashar al-Assad. In August of that year, President Barack Obama warned Syria that use of chemical weapons would be a "red line for the U.S.," but to no avail, and by the end of the year, reports began to emerge of Syrian CW attacks, culminating in a deadly sarin-laced rocket attack on the Damascus suburb of Ghouta in August 2013.[27] Not only did the American attempt at deterrence fail miserably, but it likely has undermined future U.S. efforts to deter the use of CWs by means of vague threats.[28] The danger of drawing stark "red lines" without a clear plan of action if they are crossed again confronts U.S. policymakers who seek to deter Russian use of CW in Ukraine.[29]

Attempts at deterrence of chemical weapons in the cases of Iraq and Syria suggest that efforts to deter the use of RWs—nonconventional weapons whose characteristics and military missions resemble CWs in some important respects—point to the difficulties of designing effective deterrent strategies. In the two cases mentioned above, situational factors involving immediate military needs, available conventional options, the "fog of war," uncertainties regarding the credibility of threats, and the difficulty of accurately discerning the interplay of domestic and international political pressures on the decision-making calculus of the targets of deterrence threats greatly complicate a straightforward assessment of the likelihood that deterrence will be achieved. These difficulties are apt to be compounded if the target of deterrence is a nuclear weapons state.

Effective RW deterrence faces at least two additional problems. The first is what international relations scholar Scott Sagan has termed "the commitment trap." Writing with reference to U.S. efforts to deter chemical weapons attacks, Sagan argues that if deterrence were to fail, U.S. policymakers would be under pressure to follow through with the threats even if they were not in the best interests of the United States.[30] While one could escape the trap in the fashion pursued by President Obama, that evasion came with high reputational and credibility costs that future policymakers may not be prepared to incur.

A second challenge for RW deterrence is making credible threats without calling attention to what might otherwise not be viewed by many potential RW proliferators as an attractive nonconventional weapons option. In other words, at what point does a public policy of RW deterrence undermine efforts to disseminate information about the substantial military limitations of and technical obstacles involving RWs, such as those highlighted in this volume? This deterrence dilemma—a form of what Robert Jervis referred to as "self-inflicted wounds"—involves balancing the need to persuade one audience that the United States would be willing to follow through on a threat of punishment without giving other audiences the impression that RWs have substantial value.[31]

This dilemma is not merely a theoretical one. There is some evidence, for example, that in attempting to make the case for preparedness against biological attacks, U.S. officials drew the attention of al-Qaeda to these very weapons. A computer captured in Afghanistan that belonged to al-Qaeda leader Ayman al-Zawahiri contained a 1999 memorandum recommending the pursuit of biological weapons and noted that "we only became aware of them when the enemy drew our attention to them by repeatedly expressing concern that they can be produced simply."[32] A public campaign to deter the use of RWs runs a similar risk of raising the profile of these weapons. In fact, Russia's duplicitous propaganda efforts to justify its invasion of Ukraine as necessary to prevent "the terrorist regime" from acquiring radiological weapons may already have raised the salience of RWs as a nonconventional weapon of possible interest to state actors, especially those who have not acquired nuclear weapons.[33] Indeed, it would not be surprising if Ukraine, which, as far as we know, never displayed any interest in RWs during the post-Soviet period, were to examine carefully the fabrications promoted by Russia with an eye to exploring their feasibility given the degree to which they appeared to be of concern to the Kremlin.[34]

The War in Ukraine and the Future of Radiological Weapons

No nation has ever used radiological weapons in war, although Russian attacks on and occupation of several Ukrainian civilian nuclear facilities in 2022 raised the specter of the unintended dispersal of radioactive material in a fashion that might have resembled the battlefield effects of RWs.[35] These attacks first occurred almost immediately after the outset of the war when Russia seized the non-operational Chernobyl nuclear power plant, most likely due to its location, about twelve miles from the Belarussian-Ukrainian border along the northern invasion route to Kyiv.[36] Russia subsequently attacked and then occupied the Zaporizhzhia nuclear power station, which it has controlled since March 4, 2022. According to some analysts, Russia is using nuclear power plants "as a shield for their offensive operations" and regards them as "pre-positioned nuclear weapon[s]" for the purpose of threatening and intimidating adversaries both within Ukraine and in Europe.[37] Others see the Russian targeting of nuclear facilities as a means to freeze the inhabitants of Ukraine into submission by eliminating their electricity—action consistent with the barrage on other critical Ukrainian infrastructure.

Interestingly, in terms of the focus of our study, some Russian publications also have suggested that Russian military operations against nuclear power facilities were necessary in order to prevent Ukrainian development of radiological weapons. Russian media reported, for example, that the Chernobyl plant was a source of material for a covert Ukrainian "dirty bomb," work on which was masked by the elevated radiation background at the Chernobyl facility.[38] Similar arguments were advanced to justify the seizure of the Zaporizhzhia nuclear plant and the attack on the Kharkiv Institute of Physics and Technology, a nuclear research facility that housed a subcritical assembly.[39] News reports of this nature were fairly frequent in the first months of the war and tended to appear in clusters. They were usually attributed to little-known commentators and largely disappeared from the media scene by summer 2022. The accusations, however, resurfaced again in October 2022 and were made by the most senior Russian officials. On October 23, Russian defense minister Sergey Shoigu warned of a dirty bomb provocation by Ukraine in phone calls to his British, French, and Turkish counterparts;[40] on October 25, Foreign Minister Sergey Lavrov reiterated Shoigu's assertion and indicated that Russia would raise the issue at the UN Security Council;[41] and on October 26 President Vladimir Putin repeated the unsubstantiated warning.[42] The U.S. and its allies were quick to discredit the claims, and the foreign ministers of France, the United Kingdom, and the United States issued a joint statement to that effect on October 23 in which they made clear that they rejected "Russia's transparently false allegations that Ukraine is preparing to use a dirty bomb on its own territory" and warned that the "world would see through any attempt to use this allegation as a pretext for escalation."[43]

The most detailed formal accusations about alleged Ukrainian RW plans were presented in a letter from the Russian ambassador to the United Nations Vassily Nebenzia to UN Secretary General António Guterres and the president of the UN Security Council Ambassador Michel Havier Biang on October 24, 2022. It described the basic features of a dirty bomb and purported to identify the facilities and material Ukraine would employ for its manufacture. It also asserted, without evidence, that the Russian Ministry of Defense possessed information that the Institute for Nuclear Research of the National Academy of Sciences and the Vostochniy Mining and Processing Plant "have received direct orders from Zelenskiy's regime to develop such a 'dirty bomb,'" work on which is at a "concluding stage." Moreover, the letter alleged that the Russian Ministry of Defense had received "information that this provocation may be carried out with the support of the Western countries."[44]

As Matthew Bunn convincingly argues in his annotated critique of the Nebenzia letter, the Russian assertions are so technically flawed that it is hard to imagine that they were reviewed by competent experts. The letter, for example, dwells on the potential for Ukraine to draw upon its production of uranium ore at the Vostochniy Mining and Processing Plant although that material is neither very radioactive nor useful for purposes of a radiological dispersal.[45] Moreover, by naming specific "suspect" Ukrainian nuclear facilities, the letter enabled Kyiv to invite the IAEA to inspect them. Not surprisingly, the Agency's missions found nothing suspicious at the nuclear sites.[46]

The most difficult question to answer is why so many senior Russian officials, including President Putin, chose to propagate a bogus charge in a sloppy fashion that they should have known would be discredited. Bunn also is stymied by that question, at least at this time. It is one thing, for example, for relatively obscure figures to mouth propaganda about Ukrainian intentions to acquire and/or employ biological, nuclear, and radiological weapons. It is quite another matter for the Russian president to make such assertions and sanction their communication officially to senior foreign government and international officials.

One possible explanation for the false narrative, which appeared frequently during the early phase of the war in Ukraine, is that it may have been directed as much to a domestic as an international audience for the purpose of justifying and bolstering support for the regime's use of a much larger degree of military force than was anticipated by most analysts. It is conceivable that a return to this narrative by very senior Russian officials in fall 2022 also may have been driven in part by domestic considerations following the unpopular and poorly implemented mobilization of 300,000 Russian recruits. Another interpretation for the series of high-level prevarications is that it was conceived in preparation for a "false flag" operation in which the detonation of a Russian radiological device would be portrayed as one concocted by Ukraine. It is the kind of tactic that Western intelligence services increasingly attribute to Russia, and the United States and its allies have become adept at publicly trumpeting the plan as a means to forestall its occurrence. It is unclear, however, what miliary or political gains Russian policymakers believe they would derive from a detonation, which would probably only increase international demands for the withdrawal of Russian forces from the Zaporizhzhia nuclear plant and the creation of a demilitarized zone around the facility.

Perhaps most worrisome is the possibility that renewed high-level affirmation of the false narrative about Ukrainian RW ambitions was a ploy by which Russia sought to shift attention away from its own preparations for the use of nuclear weapons in the war in Ukraine. The timing of the Russian accusations in October 2022, following the sixtieth anniversary of the Cuban missile crisis, coincided with increasingly bellicose statements by Russian officials about the possibility of a confrontation between Russian and the United States. On the occasion of the signing of presidential decrees asserting Moscow's claim to Ukrainian territories of Luhansk, Donetsk, Kherson, and Zaporizhzhia, Putin recalled that the United States was the only country in the world to have used nuclear weapons and declared that the bombing of Hiroshima and Nagasaki had created a precedent.[47] In his remarks at the annual Valdai forum in late October, he returned to the theme and asserted that "Ukraine has moved from irresponsible statements to the practical preparation of a nuclear provocation" (i.e., plans for a dirty bomb). He further accused the United States and the United Kingdom "of making statements with suggestions of the possible use of nuclear weapons."

At this time, it is impossible to know how seriously the Russian leadership regarded the potential for nuclear escalation in fall 2022 or the circumstances under which it was prepared to authorize the use of nuclear weapons in one fashion or another in Ukraine. It is likely, however, that the high-level dirty-bomb accusations were part of a series of nuclear saber-rattling initiatives conceived by the Kremlin with the objective of inducing the West to take more seriously the risks it faced by continuing to arm and otherwise assist Ukraine.

Whatever the intentions of Russian policymakers, the war in Ukraine has led many commentators to suggest that the conflict has eroded the taboo or norm against nuclear weapons use and undermined the Treaty on the Non-Proliferation of Nuclear Weapons (or NPT) and the international nonproliferation regime. As a result, it is argued, some non-nuclear weapon states may reconsider the possible deterrent benefits often ascribed to the possession of nuclear arms.[48] Jeffrey Knopf, however, makes a powerful counterargument against accepting that logic and points to the tendency to overstate the benefits of a nuclear arsenal while ignoring the costs and risks associated with its acquisition.[49] A substantial body of scholarly research also demonstrates that prior forecasts of rampant nuclear proliferation due to major shocks to the international system have not materialized. In fact, the number of nuclear weapons possessors remains limited, and the pace of proliferation has been slow. As such, it remains uncertain if recent international developments will significantly alter this trendline. Nevertheless, one cannot dismiss out of hand the possibility that the war in Ukraine may affect proliferation dynamics generally and/or for specific states. Similarly, it is conceivable that policymakers in some states may reassess the perceived deterrent value of nonconventional weapons even if they conclude that the economic, technical, normative, and political costs of pursuing nuclear weapons are prohibitive. For these states, RWs may appear, at least before careful examination, to offer a more viable option, especially if their proponents are unaware of the difficulties that prior RW aspirants encountered in their quest for these weapons.

It is unclear who, if any, these states might be. It also is not obvious what the mix of new and prior incentives and inhibitors could be for those states who might be inclined to revisit a nuclear weapons option and/or one involving radiological weapons. There is circumstantial evidence, for example, that North Korea considered RWs before obtaining a more robust nuclear weapons capability.[50] That "substitution effect" would be consistent with the behavior of prior radiological and nuclear weapons aspirants, at least with respect to the perceived utility of RWs as a deterrent. Nevertheless, Pyongyang might still consider RWs as having some meaningful offensive or area-denial benefits. For example, given North Korea's historical focus on commando operations and proximity to Seoul, it might view RWs as useful for area-denial purposes such as impeding U.S. and South Korean military operations or for instigating social and economic chaos in the South Korean capital. If so, this perception may be reinforced by the absence of contemporary U.S., Russian, or other state policies designed to deter the use of RWs or develop norms against their use.

It also is intriguing to consider if other countries that previously actively pursued nuclear activities with a military focus before joining the NPT as non-nuclear weapon states might now turn their attention to a poor man's weapon that is not currently prohibited by any treaty—namely, radiological weapons—or in the case of Egypt and Iraq perhaps revisit their abandoned RW programs. While one might presume that these countries—especially those who experienced firsthand RW disincentives—would be reluctant to seriously explore an RW option, much might depend on the behavior of other regional hegemons or adversaries, including states such as Iran, Saudi Arabia, and China. Given the fact that policymakers in Taiwan and South Korea previously pursed covert research activities related to nuclear weapons, it would be imprudent to exclude the possibility of their future interest in RWs as well, assuming that they did not already explore and abandon that option in the past.

As mentioned above, the Russian disinformation campaign alleging Ukrainian pursuit of RWs (as well as biological and nuclear weapons) also may be exploited by some critics of Kyiv's past nuclear renunciation decision to advance the case that some form of nonconventional weapon—possibly including RWs—is necessary to deter future Russian aggression. This possibility will increase if the perception grows among defense policymakers and analysts that possession of a nuclear arsenal, possibly including RWs, provides significant security benefits that outweigh traditional proliferation inhibitors. The purpose of this conjecture is not to endorse this argument, which we regard as suspect. Rather, it is to caution against presuming that past behavior with respect to RWs will prove a reliable guide to future decisions, especially for those states for whom nuclear weapons remain an unlikely option.

Finally, it is possible that if the nuclear taboo is further eroded, some state actors, including Ukraine, may come to regard RWs less as military weapons in the traditional sense and more as terrorist-style instruments to instill fear in the minds of noncombatants and disrupt the economic and social fabric of society. In that regard, the differences in the missions of radiological dispersal devices for state and non-state actors may be reduced, although states will retain a huge advantage in their technical capacity to manufacture and disperse potent devices.

Preventive Measures/Mitigating Strategies

Deterrence does not seem to be a very promising avenue for preventing future RW development or use, although the United States needs to direct more attention to the study of this issue. States that choose to pursue RWs through the testing phase are apt to be led by or have influential institutional advocates who believe radiological weapons offer an advantage on the battlefield. If the efficacy of deterrence is likely to be situational, it would appear to be difficult to tailor deterrent threats to prevail in situations in which an adversary sees a compelling tactical advantage to the use of RWs. The U.S.'s experience in failing to deter chemical weapons use may be instructive in this regard.

The U.S.'s ability to deter RW use also assumes a degree of knowledge about an adversary's possession of and plans for employing RWs that would be challenging at best to obtain and is not borne out by the historical record. Indeed, there is little reason to assume that the United States or other states would be able to detect RW programs and policies for RWs prior to their testing and deployment unless they were looking carefully for such developments. If this analysis is correct, it suggests that efforts at deterrence will have a difficult time overcoming situational factors likely to dominate an adversary's calculations. They also could have the unintended effect of increasing the perceived attractiveness of RWs for targeted states. As indicated above, this is a possible consequence of Russia's bogus claims about Ukraine's RW activities.[51]

Given the challenges in deterring RWs' use, what are other potential means to prevent and/or mitigate their proliferation and use? The list of practical measures is not long but it includes a variety of legal, normative, and educational approaches. None of them is likely to be transformative, but if pursued collectively, they could improve the prospects for retaining the current record in which no nation has ever used RWs in war or moved beyond the testing and protype phase and deployed them as operational weapons.

Legal Restraints

Among the many disturbing features of the contemporary international scene is the diminished support for international law, multilateral institutions, and much of the legally binding arms control infrastructure that was erected in the decades following the Cuban missile crisis. In the context of this study about the rise and demise of radiological weapons, therefore, it is useful to recall a prior but largely forgotten joint effort by the United States and the Soviet Union in the 1970s to prohibit radiological warfare. In a significant display of superpower cooperation, the two Cold War rivals negotiated a joint initiative on RWs, which they submitted to the Committee on Disarmament (CD) in Geneva in July 1979.

Under the terms of the draft treaty, states parties would undertake "not to develop, produce, stockpile, otherwise acquire or possess, or use radiological weapons."[52] Notwithstanding agreement between Moscow and Washington, however, the initiative foundered over scope and definitional issues and because of the low priority most delegations attached to the subject. Particularly contentious was the question of whether to extend the RW prohibition to attacks on nuclear facilities, a subject that was no longer academic after Israel destroyed the Iraqi Osirak reactor in June 1981. Although the CD maintained an ad hoc committee on RWs for more than a decade, the draft prohibition languished and was removed from the body's agenda of work in 1992.

The CD has been deadlocked since 1996, and there are no signs that it will soon resume business as a negotiating forum. Although prospects for U.S.-Russian nuclear arms control negotiations improved briefly after the election of President Joseph Biden—and a U.S.-Russia strategic dialogue appeared to make headway following the meeting of Presidents Putin and Biden in Geneva in June 2021—the outlook for bilateral arms control deliberations of any sort in the near term is virtually nonexistent in the wake of the Russian invasion of Ukraine. Prospects for multilateral arms control and disarmament negotiations are only marginally better, and there is little reason to believe that an RW ban will be the subject of deliberations in any multilateral fora. Nevertheless, one should not exclude altogether the possibility that should a radiological weapon be used in Ukraine or elsewhere, states might display interest in negotiating a treaty banning RWs along the lines of the Treaty on the Prohibition of Nuclear Weapons.

Prior to the invasion of Ukraine in February 2022, the most promising forum for consideration of restraints on RWs was the P-5 Process, a more than decade-long series of nuclear disarmament consultations among the five NPT-recognized nuclear weapon states: China, France, Russia, the United Kingdom, and the United States. At least one P-5 member had expressed interest in an RW ban during the 2020 NPT review process cycle to signal support by the nuclear weapon states for their disarmament commitments in advance of the Tenth NPT Review Conference, originally scheduled for 2020. However, it is unclear if the idea currently enjoys any support. If the P-5 members were to renounce RWs sometime in the future, that action would almost certainly not be in the form of a treaty. Still, even an informal five-party declaration could help to raise the political costs of proliferation in this specific nuclear realm.

Normative Restraints

It is difficult to gauge the strength of the norm against radiological weapons and their use. As noted previously, we found that normative factors played a relatively minor role in influencing decisions to pursue or abandon RW programs in the five cases we analyzed. There also is little evidence to suggest that any form of taboo or aversion to RWs based on shared standards of acceptable behavior has increased in recent years.[53] If anything, the opposite trend would appear to be the case given the increased frequency and almost fatalistic manner in which nuclear weapons threats have emanated from the Kremlin. Regardless of their intent, they have had the effect of eroding the barrier separating conventional and nonconventional weapons, a development that has been reinforced by the disinformation campaign involving alleged Ukrainian preparations to employ biological, chemical, and radiological weapons.[54] The more often the pursuit of and potential use of these nonconventional weapons are discussed, the less exceptional these events appear and the more difficult it becomes to stigmatize the possession and use of these weapons.

As recently as January 2022, international sentiment appeared to be turning in the direction of greater nuclear restraint, at least at the declaratory level. In advance of the anticipated convening of the NPT Review Conference in New York that month, the P-5 collectively endorsed the Reagan-Gorbachev principle that a nuclear war could not be won and must never be fought. At that time, there was some optimism that at the long-delayed Review Conference, the nuclear weapon states might support more concrete steps involving nuclear risk reduction consistent with the declaration. However, the conference was again postponed due to the pandemic, and the war in Ukraine ensued, accompanied by incautious nuclear saber-rattling and attacks on nuclear facilities without apparent regard for the potential release of radioactive material.

It is conceivable that these normative transgressions will spur greater international consciousness about the dangers of nuclear war and the risks posed by radioactive contamination, be it from the inadvertent release of radioactive material at nuclear power plants and spent fuel storage sites or by design involving RWs. The International Atomic Energy Agency has played an active role in trying to mitigate the dangers at Ukraine's nuclear facilities, and it is possible that perceived common interests on the part of all states possessing civilian nuclear power plants may yield meaningful new normative and legal restraints to protect their safe operation. Such a convergence of perceived shared interests, however, is more difficult to envisage in the short term regarding RWs unless a number of key states and civil society identify the issue as a priority and promote an initiative to stigmatize RW possession and use.

The Role of Popular Culture and Education

Both popular culture and more formal educational activities could, in principle, assist in raising the salience of the risks posed by radiological weapons and promoting the adoption of measures to inhibit their spread and use, although their impact likely would vary significantly across societies.[55] Popular science fiction, including the powerful work of Robert Heinlein and Ray Bradbury, played this role in the United States, as did Al Capp's widely read comic strip *Li'l Abner*. Largely forgotten today but noteworthy is the comic strip segment that ran from December 11, 1947, to January 24, 1948. In it, Capp depicts the unanticipated effects of the aerial dumping of accumulated atomic rubbish on the population of the fictional community of Dogpatch.[56] Although anti-nuclear weapons themes in U.S. popular culture waned in the early 1950s as the U.S.-Soviet arms race accelerated, they experienced a major renaissance in the late 1950s with such popular post-apocalyptic-themed novels and films as *On the Beach*, *Alas Babylon*, and *A Canticle for Leibowitz*.[57] Also noteworthy in this genre is *The War Game*, a British pseudo-documentary film produced in 1965 that depicts a nuclear war and its aftermath. Although banned from British television for twenty years on the grounds that it was "too horrifying," it has since proved to be "a highly effective recruiting tool for international peace groups."[58]

By far the most widely viewed and influential fictional account of the radiation effects of nuclear war is the 1983 U.S. television film *The Day After*.[59] More than 100 million people watched the ABC TV drama in its initial broadcast, and one of the authors recalls participating in a pre-release experts discussion group in Los Angeles convened by the film's director to strategize how to maximize the "public service" impact of the movie. President Ronald Reagan, who screened the film before its airing on TV, was also very deeply affected by the film and was concerned about its potential impact. He noted in his diary that the fictional account left him "greatly depressed" and convinced that "we had to do all we can to have a deterrent & to see there is never a nuclear war."[60]

Although *The Day After* appears to have deeply affected President Reagan, its impact on the general viewing public is less evident.[61] An analysis of public opinion polls found that the film had a "statistically nonsignificant effect on perceptions of the likelihood of nuclear war" and "no effect on the salience of defense policy or on support for nuclear arms limitations."[62]

As we know from both the U.S. and Soviet experience, popular culture also can be used as a tool by the state to portray RWs as abhorrent weapons when in the hands of an adversary or as merciful innovations that enable one to kill without bloodshed and while preserving critical infrastructure. The former aspect was highlighted in a number of mainstream U.S. publications such as *Colliers*, *Coronet*, and *Time* and in the Soviet film *Serebristaya pil'* (Silver dust), while the latter was reflected in both popular magazines and more specialized publications, including the *Bulletin of the Atomic Scientists*, and *Officer's Call*.[63] Popular culture thus both reflects and influences the attitudes of a country's policymakers and citizens at large.

Like popular culture, more formal disarmament and nonproliferation education has the potential to counter apathy and ignorance about nuclear issues. More specifically, it can be helpful in raising awareness about the dangers posed by radiological weapons, as well as the need to reinforce legal and normative means to inhibit their spread and use. Regrettably, the public's overall knowledge base with respect to nuclear matters is very low and is practically nonexistent regarding RWs. Indeed, as this volume has detailed, the paucity in expert knowledge about past state RW programs differs little from the knowledge deficit of the public at large. While it is unrealistic to expect this situation to change significantly in the short term, much more can and should be done to expand opportunities for the study of nuclear proliferation and disarmament at the high school, undergraduate, and graduate levels. At a minimum, to the extent that the topic of "dirty bombs" is considered in courses dealing with nuclear dangers, the discussion should be expanded from the typical exclusive focus on non-state actors (i.e., terrorists) to the broader historical record involving state-level pursuit of radiological weapons and the potential for future RW proliferation. Hopefully, our comparative analysis of the rise and demise of five past RW programs will contribute to this expanded nonproliferation curriculum.

An analysis of U.S, Soviet, British, Egyptian, and Iraqi pursuit of radiological weapons offers insights into a previously neglected but important chapter of nonconventional weapons development, testing, and eventual termination. It also highlights the remarkable parallels between prescient science fiction treatments of atomic warfare and preternatural, "real world" military developments, beginning with the literary specter of "death dust" in the early 1940s and culminating in unsubtle Russian threats to launch massive radioactive-spewing torpedoes against the British Isles in spring 2022.[64]

In this regard, it is timely to recall the editorial comment by John Campbell at the end of the story "Solution Unsatisfactory," published in May 1941. It observes that MacDonald's (aka Heinlein's) science fiction story "presents a logical possibility of the near future" in which "atomic power plants, in burning atomic fuel[,] will automatically and inevitably produce radioactive ashes." "The story," Campbell argues, "presents the problem mankind must solve some day" and is generalizable "to cover any irresistible weapon"—namely, "*how can it be controlled.*"[65] A compelling answer to that question continues to elude science fiction authors, policymakers, and academic experts, while the urgency of finding a satisfactory solution grows.

Notes

Preface

1. William C. Potter and Jeffrey Lewis, "Cheap and Dirty Bombs," *Foreign Policy*, February 17, 2014, https://foreignpolicy.com/2014/02/17/cheap-and-dirty-bombs/.

2. Samuel Meyer, Jeffrey Lewis, Sarah Bidgood, and William Potter, "Final Performance Report for 'Addressing the Threat of State-Level Radiological Weapons Programs,'" Grant No. FA7000-17-0022 (March 5, 2019).

3. Samuel Meyer, Sarah Bidgood, and William C. Potter, "Death Dust: The Little-Known Story of U.S. and Soviet Pursuit of Radiological Weapons," *International Security*, 45, No. 2 (Fall 2020): 51–94, copyright 2020 by the President and Fellows of Harvard College and the Massachusetts Institute of Technology. Some portions of the present book first appeared in that article and are reprinted with permission.

Introduction

1. See Anson MacDonald, "Solution Unsatisfactory," *Astounding Science Fiction*, 27, No. 3 (May 1941): 56–86. The story by Robert A. Heinlein was published under the pseudonym "Anson MacDonald."

2. For a discussion of the Russian weapon, see Jill Hruby, *Russia's New Nuclear Weapons Delivery Systems: An Open Source Technical Review* (Washington, DC: Nuclear Threat Initiative, 2019), 30–32, https://media.nti.org/documents/NTI-Hruby_FINAL.PDF. See also Steve Weintz, "Why Russia's Status-6 Torpedo Is Really

a 100-Megaton Cruise Missile," *National Interest*, July 7, 2018; and Hanna Notte, Sarah Bidgood, Nikolai Sokov, Michael Duitsman, and William Potter, "Russia's Novel Weapons Systems: Military Innovation in the Post-Soviet Period," *The Nonproliferation Review*, 28, No. 1–3 (2021): 61–93, https://doi.org/10.1080/10736700.2021.194627.

3. The accusation about Sakharov, for which little evidence is presented, is made by Evgeny Krutitkov, "Sverhsekretnyj proekt 'Status-6' napominayut ideyu akademika Sakharova" [Top-secret project "Status-6" recalls an idea of Academician Sakharov], *Vzglyad*, November 12, 2015, https://vz.ru/society/2015/11/12/777703.html; and is repeated by many Russian commentators. Alex Wellerstein also refers to the connection in "An Untold Story of the World's Biggest Nuclear Bomb," *Bulletin of the Atomic Scientists*, October 29, 2021, https://thebulletin.org/2021/11/the-untold-story-of-the-worlds-biggest-nuclear-bomb/.

4. Indeed, in some cases, civilians were envisaged as the primary target. We are grateful to William King for highlighting this point.

5. See Owen Sirrs, *Nasser and the Missile Age in the Middle East* (London: Routledge, 2006), 112.

6. For a discussion of the possibility that North Korea considered RW before obtaining a more robust nuclear weapons capability, see Potter and Lewis, "Cheap and Dirty Bombs."

7. See Matthew Goldenberg and William C. Potter, "Russian Misinformation about Ukrainian Radiological Weapons Capabilities and Intentions," CNS Research Note, March 10, 2022, https://nonproliferation.org/russian-misinformation-about-ukrainian-radiological-weapons-capabilities-and-intentions/.

8. For an extended analysis of the terrorist risks posed by radiological dispersal devices, see Charles D. Ferguson and William C. Potter, *The Four Faces of Nuclear Terrorism* (New York: Routledge, 2005), 259–317.

9. Meyer, Bidgood, and Potter, "Death Dust: The Little-Known Story of U.S. and Soviet Pursuit of Radiological Weapons."

10. Notte et al., "Russia's Novel Weapons Systems."

11. Matthew Evangelista, *Innovation and the Arms Race: How the United States and the Soviet Union Develop New Military Technology* (Ithaca, NY: Cornell University Press, 1988), 52.

12. Lesley Kucharski, Sarah Bidgood, and Paul Warnke, "Negotiating the Draft Radiological Weapons Convention," in *Once and Future Partners: The United States, Russia and Nuclear Non-Proliferation*, ed. William C. Potter and Sarah Bidgood (London: IISS, 2018), 187–216.

13. A radiation emission device would not require a conventional explosive to disperse radiation and might consist simply of a radioactive source placed near a target, such as a heavily traversed area.

14. See James Arnold, "The Hydrogen-Cobalt Bomb," *Bulletin of the Atomic Scientists*, 6, No. 10 (1950), republished online on September 15, 2015, https://www.tandfonline.com/doi/abs/10.1080/00963402.1950.11461290F. The article is based on a February 1950 Chicago Round Table presentation by Dr. Leo Szilard.

15. The idea for a neutron bomb usually is attributed to Samuel Cohen, who developed the concept in 1958. See Thomas H. Maugh II, "Samuel T. Cohen Dies at 89; Inventor of the Neutron Bomb," *Los Angeles Times*, December 2, 2010, https://latimes.com/local/obituaries/la-me-sam-cohen-20101202-story.html.

16. See, for example, G. M. Moore, "Radiological Weapons: How Great Is the Danger?" UCRL-ID-1544879 (Livermore, CA: Lawrence Livermore National Laboratory, June 1, 2003); Graham Allison, *Nuclear Terrorism: The Ultimate Preventable Catastrophe* (New York: Henry Holt, 2004); and Ferguson and Potter, *The Four Faces of Nuclear Terrorism*. For more recent analyses, see Ioanna Iliopulos and Christopher Boyd, "Preventing a Dirty Bomb: Case Studies and Lessons Learned" (Washington, DC: Nuclear Threat Initiative, 2019); and BreAnne K. Fleer, "Radiological-Weapons Threats: Case Studies from the Extreme Right," *The Nonproliferation Review*, 27, No. 1–2 (June 2020): 1–18.

17. Radioactive sources around the world are estimated to number in the millions. There is little information however, about the number of "orphaned sources"—those no longer subject to institutional or national control because they have been lost, abandoned, or stolen. Fortunately, although many orphaned sources pose a significant health and safety hazard for individuals who may be exposed to them inadvertently, relatively few lend themselves to use as terrorist weapons. In a 2003 study, the Center for Nonproliferation Studies identified the following seven reactor-produced radioisotopes as posing the greatest security risks: californium-252, cobalt-60, cesium-137, iridium-192, strontium-90, americium-241, and plutonium-238. While these same radioisotopes have been available to some state-level RW programs in the past and remain a potential source of material for a contemporary state-level RW program, as the case studies in this book indicate, their characteristics did not lend themselves to the military missions envisaged by past RW aspirants. See "Inadequate Control of World's Radioactive Sources," International Atomic Energy Agency press release, June 24, 2002, https://www.iaea.org/newscenter/pressreleases/inadequate-control-worlds-radioactive-sources; and Charles D. Ferguson, Tahseen Kazi, and Judith Perera, "Commercial Radioactive Sources: Surveying the Security Risks," Occasional Paper No. 11 (Monterey, CA: Center for Nonproliferation Studies, January 2003), especially 16–18.

18. These characteristics, discussed in more detail in subsequent chapters, include high energy gamma emission and a half-life that is at least several weeks but no longer than approximately one year.

19. William King, "A Weapon Too Far: The British Radiological Warfare Expe-

rience, 1940–1955," *War in History*, 29, No. 1 (January 11, 2021): 1–23, https://doi.org/10.1177/0968344520922565.

20. This literature review draws heavily on the article by three of the authors, Meyer, Bidgood, and Potter, "Death Dust: The Little-Known Story of U.S. and Soviet Pursuit of Radiological Weapons."

21. This list is not exhaustive. One scholar reviewing the literature has proposed that schools of military innovation research should be thought of in terms of "civil-military," "interservice," "intra-service," and "cultural" models. See Adam Grissom, "The Future of Military Innovation Studies," *Journal of Strategic Studies* 29, No. 5 (2006): 905–34. Several of these categories could be subsumed under the heading of "bureaucratic political." See also Owen Reid Cote, Jr., "The Politics of Innovative Military Doctrine: The U.S. Navy and Fleet Ballistic Missiles" (PhD diss., Massachusetts Institute of Technology, 1996). A relatively recent contribution to the literature on the factors influencing the sources and retention of different types of weapons of mass destruction (WMD) innovation is "weapons substitution theory." It does not fit neatly into traditional categories of explanations for the pursuit of new weapons but has a basis in economic theory dealing with the cross elasticity of demand. Most relevant to the authors' work on RW is the article by Michael C. Horowitz and Neil Narang, "Poor Man's Atomic Bomb? Exploring the Relationship between 'Weapons of Mass Destruction,'" *Journal of Conflict Resolution*, 58, No. 3 (April 2014): 509–535.

22. Stephen Peter Rosen, *Winning the Next War: Innovation and the Modern Military* (Ithaca, NY: Cornell University Press, 1991), 45.

23. Ibid., 45.

24. See, for example, Morton H. Halperin, "The Gaither Committee and the Policy Process," *World Politics*, 13, No. 3 (April 1961): 360–384, doi.org/10.2307/2009480; Morton Halperin, Priscilla Clapp, and Arnold Kanter, *Bureaucratic Politics and Foreign Policy* (Washington, DC: Brookings Institution Press, 1974); Graham T. Allison, "Conceptual Models and the Cuban Missile Crisis," *American Political Science Review*, 63, No. 3 (September 1969): 689–718, doi.org/10.1017/S000030554002583X; and Graham T. Allison, *Essence of Decision: Explaining the Cuban Missile Crisis* (Boston: Little, Brown, 1971).

25. Case studies with a bureaucratic politics focus include Michael H. Armacost, *The Politics of Weapons Innovation: The Thor-Jupiter Controversy* (New York: Columbia University Press, 1969); Edmund Beard, *Developing the ICBM: A Study in Bureaucratic Politics* (New York: Columbia University Press, 1976); and Robert J. Art and Stephen E. Ockenden, "The Domestic Politics of Cruise Missile Development, 1970–1980," in *Cruise Missiles: Technology, Strategy, Politics*, ed. Richard Betts (Washington, DC: The Brookings Institution, 1981), 359–413. A more recent extension of this literature, but with a focus on organizational frames of reference and

stereotypes, is Frank L. Smith, *American Biodefense: How Dangerous Ideas about Biological Weapons Shape National Security* (Ithaca, NY: Cornell University Press, 2014). It suggests that the military's preference for "kinetic weapons" is an obstacle to the adoption of systems that do not resemble traditional bullets or bombs—an insight relevant to the fate of RW.

26. See Mary Kaldor, "The Weapons Succession Process," *World Politics*, 38, No. 4 (July 1986): 580, doi.org/10.2307/2010167.

27. Solly Zuckerman, *Nuclear Illusion and Reality* (New York: Viking, 1982), 143, quoted in Matthew Evangelista, *Innovation and the Arms Race*, 13. Another major exponent of technology as a driver of military innovation—and arms races—is Herbert F. York. See York, *Race to Oblivion: A Participant's View of the Arms Race* (New York: Simon & Schuster, 1970).

28. For a discussion of the role of change agents in the innovation and diffusion process, see Everett M. Rogers and F. Floyd Shoemaker, *Communication of Innovations: A Cross-Cultural Approach*, rev. ed. (New York: Free Press, 1971), 233–248.

29. A rarely cited but important study of this phenomenon in the Soviet context is Andrew Aldrin, "Innovation, the Scientists and the State: Programmatic Innovation and the Creation of the Soviet Space Program" (PhD diss., University of California, Los Angeles, 1996).

30. Studies emphasizing the role of economic drivers in the weapons acquisition process include Jacques S. Gansler, *The Defense Industry* (Cambridge: MIT Press, 1980); J. Ronald Fox, *Arming America: How the U.S. Buys Weapons* (Cambridge, MA: Harvard University Press, 1974); and "How Defense Industries Keep the Business Coming," *Bulletin of the Atomic Scientists* (May 1976): 44–46. For a review of other economic explanations, see Michael E. Brown, *Flying Blind: The Politics of the U.S. Strategic Bomber Program* (Ithaca, NY: Cornell University Press, 1992).

31. The most fully developed explanation for military innovations emphasizing economic resources and organizational capacity is Michael C. Horowitz's "adoption-capacity theory." See Horowitz, *The Diffusion of Military Power: Causes and Consequences for International Politics* (Princeton, NJ: Princeton University Press, 2010). Jon Schmid also develops a related explanatory framework, which he calls "threat-capacity theory." See Schmid, "The Determinants of Military Technology Innovation and Diffusion" (PhD diss., Georgia Institute of Technology, 2018), 31–36.

32. Horowitz, *The Diffusion of Military Power*, 8–12.

33. See, for example, Brad Roberts, *Weapons Proliferation and World Order after the Cold War* (The Hague: Kluwer Law International, 1996); and Martin Wright, *Power Politics* (London: Royal Institute of International Affairs, 1978).

34. Roberts, *Weapons Proliferation and World Order after the Cold War*, 120.

35. Ibid.

36. See William C. Potter, *Nuclear Power and Nonproliferation: An Interdisciplin-*

ary Perspective (Cambridge, MA: Oelgeschlager, Gunn, & Hain, 1982), 139–140; and Scott Sagan, "Why Do States Build Nuclear Weapons? Three Models in Search of a Bomb," *International Security*, 21, No. 3 (Winter 1996/97), 73–80.

37. See, for example, Ciro Zoppo, "France as a Nuclear Power," in *The Dispersion of Nuclear Weapons*, ed. R. N. Rosecrance (New York: Columbia University Press, 1964), 113–156.

38. W. Seth Carus, *Ballistic Missiles in Modern Conflict* (New York: Praeger, with the Center for Strategic and International Studies, 1991); and Sirrs, *Nasser and the Missile Age in the Middle East*.

39. As noted above, the only extended analysis on the British experience is the 2021 journal article by William King (see note 19).

40. C. L. Sulzberger, "The Little Old Man in the Desert Using Nuclear Energy," Foreign Affairs, *New York Times*, November 16, 1963, 21.

41. C. L. Sulzberger, "The Problem of a Garbage Bomb: Neither Missiles Nor Funds," Foreign Affairs, *New York Times*, November 20, 1963, 42.

Chapter 1

1. H. G. Wells, *The World Set Free* (London: MacMillan, 1914). He also believed that atomic weapons might have the redeeming quality of compelling states to come together in a form of world government.

2. H. Bruce Franklin notes that there were several earlier works of fiction to imagine radioactivity as a weapon of war, including Roy Norton, *The Vanishing Fleets* (serialized in the *Associated Sunday Magazines* in 1907); and Hollis Godfrey, *The Man Who Ended War* (Boston: Little, Brown, 1908). These writings, however, bore little resemblance to radiological weapons as we have come to know them. See Franklin, "Fatal Fiction: A Weapon to End All Wars," *Bulletin of the Atomic Scientists*, November 1989, 20.

3. Campbell later alienated many of the authors whose careers he had launched by his embrace of pseudoscience and segregation. For details on Campbell's influence on science fiction, see Rob Latham, "How Science Fiction Grew Up," *Nature*, October 10, 2018.

4. Perry A. Chapdelaine, Sr., "John Wood Campbell, Jr.," in *The John W. Campbell Letters*, vol. 1, ed. Perry A. Chapdelaine, Sr., Tony Chapdelaine, and George Hay (Franklin, TN: AC Projects, 1985), 25.

5. Heinlein to Campbell, May 1, 1939, Box 27-4, Robert A. and Virginia G. Heinlein papers, MS 95, Special Collections and Archives, University Library, University of California, Santa Cruz.

6. Campbell to Heinlein, January 15, 1940, 2, Box 27-5, Robert A. and Virginia G. Heinlein papers, MS 95, Special Collections and Archives, University Library, University of California, Santa Cruz.

7. Ibid.

8. Heinlein to Campbell, January 20, 1940, 2 Box 27-5, Robert A. and Virginia G. Heinlein papers, MS 95, Special Collections and Archives, University Library, University of California, Santa Cruz.

9. Campbell to Heinlein, January 23, 1940, Box 27-5, Robert A. and Virginia G. Heinlein papers, MS 95, Special Collections and Archives, University Library, University of California, Santa Cruz.

10. Heinlein to Campbell, January 31, 1940, Box 27-5, Robert A. and Virginia G. Heinlein papers, MS 95, Special Collections and Archives, University Library, University of California, Santa Cruz; Campbell to Heinlein, October 29, 1940, Box 27-5, Robert A. and Virginia G. Heinlein papers, MS 95, Special Collections and Archives, University Library, University of California, Santa Cruz.

11. Robert Heinlein, "Science Fiction: Its Nature, Faults and Virtues," in *Turning Points: Essays on the Art of Science Fiction*, ed. Damon Francis Knight (New York: Harper & Row, 1977), 10–11, https://archive.org/details/turningpointsessooknig/page/n19/mode/2up?q=%22solution+unsatisfactory%22.

12. It was at this meeting that the Radiation Laboratory recruited most of its core staff. See "MIT Radiation Laboratory," MIT Lincoln Laboratory, n.d., https://www.ll.mit.edu/about/history/mit-radiation-laboratory. Text adapted from T. A. Saad, "The Story of the M.I.T. Radiation Laboratory," *IEEE Aerospace and Electronic Systems Magazine*, 5, No. 10 (October 1990): 46–51.

13. Campbell to Heinlein, October 29, 1940.

14. See, for instance, Jack Hatcher, "Transmutation, 1939," *Astounding Science Fiction* 24, No. 5 (1940): 69–78, https://archive.org/details/Astounding_v24n05_1940-01_dtsgo318/; and Jack Hatcher, "Fuel for the Future," *Astounding Science Fiction* 25, No. 1 (1940): 68–83, https://archive.org/details/Astounding_v25n01_1940-03_AK/.

15. John Waugh, "Don Merlin Lee Yost: 1893–1977" (Washington, DC: National Academy of Sciences, 1993), 47.

16. Harold Johnston, *A Bridge Not Attacked: Chemical Warfare Civilian Research during World War II* (River Edge, NJ: World Scientific Publishing Company, 2003), 60.

17. Campbell to Heinlein, c. December 15, 1940, Box 27-5, Robert A. and Virginia G. Heinlein papers, MS 95, Special Collections and Archives, University Library, University of California, Santa Cruz.

18. Ibid.

19. Heinlein to Campbell, December 17, 1940, Box 27-5, Robert A. and Virginia G. Heinlein papers, MS 95, Special Collections and Archives, University Library, University of California, Santa Cruz.

20. MacDonald, "Solution Unsatisfactory," 63–64.

21. Ibid., 65.

22. Ibid. One approach to the problem posed by death dust that is considered but rejected by U.S. policymakers after its initial use resembles the Baruch Plan. See ibid., 75.

23. Gregory Benford, "A Scientist's Notebook: The Science Fiction Century: A Brief Overview," *Fantasy & Science Fiction*, 97, No. 3 (1999): 133, https://archive.org/details/Fantasy_Science_Fiction_v097n03_1999-09_DaisyChainsaw/.

24. John W. Campbell, "Is Death Dust America's Secret Weapon?," *PIC*, July 22, 1941, 6–8. A copy of Campbell's article appears among Leo Szilard's files, suggesting that the famed Hungarian physicist had read it. See Leo Szilard Papers, Box 53, Folder 8, Call #MSS 0032, UC San Diego Library.

25. Campbell, "Is Death Dust America's Secret Weapon?," 7. Although the U.S. government attempted to block publication about atomic research in the popular press as early as the fall of 1940, it initially ignored science fiction. According to Franklin, "Fatal Fiction," 24, this neglect was due to its view of that genre "as a subliterary ghetto inhabited by kids and kooks."

26. Campbell, "Is Death Dust America's Secret Weapon?," 6–7.

27. Arthur H. Compton, "Report of National Academy of Sciences Committee on Atomic Fission," to Frank Jewett, President, National Academy of Sciences, May 17, 1941, 2, https://nsarchive.gwu.edu/sites/default/files/documents/3913457/Report-of-the-Uranium-Committee-Arthur-H-Compton.pdf. The other two possible applications were "a power source on submarines and other ships" and "violently explosive bombs."

28. Ibid. The report indicated that it would take at least three years after a chain reaction to produce a nuclear power source, whereas a bomb based on U-235 or plutonium would unlikely be available before 1945.

29. E. P. Wigner and H. D. Smyth, "Radioactive Poisons," December 10, 1941, Department of Energy, OSTI OpenNet, https://www.osti.gov/opennet/servlets/purl/16385496.pdf.

30. Richard Rhodes, *The Making of the Atomic Bomb* (New York: Simon & Schuster, 1986), 510. Barton J. Bernstein cites a communication from Arthur Compton to James Conant in July 1942 expressing the view that there was a real danger that Germany might attack the United States with bombs designed to disperse radioactive material. See Bernstein, "Radiological Warfare: The Path Not Taken," *Bulletin of the Atomic Scientists*, 41, No. 7 (August 1985): 45, doi.org/10.1080/00963402.1985.11455998.

31. Subcommittee of S-1 Committee, "Use of Radioactive Material as a Military Weapon," n.d., ACH1.000003.006.e, Department of Energy, OSTI OpenNet, 1, https://www.osti.gov/opennet/servlets/purl/16384400.pdf. The memo has no date, but it appears to have been prepared during the summer of 1943. See "Foreign Intelligence Supplement No. 2," July 31, 1952, *Manhattan District History*, book 1: Gen-

eral, vol. 14: *Intelligence and Security*, DOE OSTI OpenNet, 3, https://www.osti.gov/includes/opennet/includes/MED_scans/Book%20I%20-%20General%20-%20Volume%2014%20-%20Intelligence%20-%20Foreign%20Intell.pdf.

32. Subcommittee of S-1 Committee, "Use of Radioactive Material as a Military Weapon," 2.

33. Ibid., 3.

34. Ibid., 2.

35. See J. Robert Oppenheimer to Enrico Fermi, March 11, 1943, *Restricted Data: Nuclear Secrecy Blog*, http://blog.nuclearsecrecy.com/wp-content/uploads/2013/09/1943-Oppenheimer-to-Fermi.pdf. See also Rhodes, *The Making of the Atomic Bomb*, 511.

36. Oppenheimer to Fermi, March 11, 1943. See also Alex Wellerstein, "Fears of a German Dirty Bomb," *Restricted Data: Nuclear Secrecy Blog*, September 6, 2013, http://blog.nuclearsecrecy.com/2013/09/06/fears-of-a-german-dirty-bomb/.

37. See Sean L. Malloy, "'A Very Pleasant Way to Die': Radiation Effects and the Decision to Use the Atomic Bomb against Japan," *Diplomatic History*, 36, No. 3 (June 2012): 527, doi.org/ 10.1111/j.1467-7709.2012.01042.x. He suggests that Groves, as well as Conant, Compton, and Urey, were reluctant to support radiological warfare because of its resemblance to chemical warfare.

38. See "Foreign Intelligence Supplement No. 2," July 31, 1952, *Manhattan District History*, 7–10. See also Wellerstein, "Fears of a German Dirty Bomb."

39. Joseph G. Hamilton to Col. E. B. Kelly, August 28,1946, Research Program for Contract W-7405-eng-48-A, DOE OSTI OpenNet, https://www.osti.gov/opennet/servlets/purl/16004198.pdf.

40. Oppenheimer to Fermi, March 11, 1943.

41. Barton Bernstein notes that there are no references to such a discussion in the papers of either Hamilton or Oppenheimer. See Bernstein, "Radiological Warfare," 46.

42. Ibid.

43. Leo Szilard, *The Collected Works of Leo Szilard* (Cambridge, MA: MIT Press, 1972).

44. Glenn T. Seaborg, "Wednesday, December 8, 1943," in *Journal of Glenn T. Seaborg: Chief, Section C-1, Metallurgical Laboratory, Manhattan Engineer District, 1942–46*, vol. 1 (Berkeley, CA.: Lawrence Berkeley National Laboratory, 1992), https://escholarship.org/content/qt8t99r79q/qt8t99r79q.pdf.

45. Evangelista, *Innovation and the Arms Race*, 52–59.

46. Bernstein, "Radiological Warfare," 48.

47. K. D. Nichols, memo to Area Engineer, Subject: Administration of Radioactive Substances to Human Subjects, December 23, 1946, Department of Energy, OpenNet, https://www.osti.gov/opennet/detail?osti-id=16369252.

48. Ibid. See handwritten note presumably from Nichols.

49. Memorandum from Joseph G. Hamilton, M.D., to Colonel K. D. Nichols, "Radioactive Warfare," December 31, 1946, Radiation Laboratory, Berkeley, CA, DOE OSTI OpenNet, https://www.osti.gov/opennet/servlets/purl/16367341.pdf.

50. W. S. Hutchinson to J. McCormack, "Proposal for an Initial Evaluation," April 16, 1947, OSTI OpenNet. https://www.osti.gov/opennet/detail?osti-id=16359297.

51. Carroll Wilson to Joseph Hamilton, January 22, 1948, OSTI OpenNet, https://www.osti.gov/opennet/detail?osti-id=16110844.

52. D. F. Carpenter, "Minutes of the 1st Meeting of an Ad Hoc Panel on RW," May 23, 1948, DOE Information Center, Oak Ridge, TN, DOE OSTI OpenNet, 5, https://www.osti.gov/opennet/detail?osti-id=16142313.

53. Karl Z. Morgan, "Uniformly Distributed Source, ARUU Program," August 25, 1948, Oak Ridge National Laboratory, Health Physics Division, DOE OSTI OpenNet, https://www.osti.gov/opennet/servlets/purl/16125584.pdf.

54. One of the less polemical, if also flawed, accounts is Alden P. Armagnac, "What You Should Know about 'RW,'" *Popular Science*, February 1951, 144–148.

55. Lt. Col. David B. Parker, "War without Death," *Coronet*, July 1950, 93–98.

56. Robert De Roos, "What Are We Doing about Our Deadly Atomic Garbage?," *Colliers*, August 20, 1954, 28–34.

57. J. Alvin Kugelmass, "Our Silent Mystery Weapon: Death Sand," *Real Magazine* ("the exciting magazine FOR MEN"), January 1952. It is catalogued by the Command Historical Office, CBDCOM, Edgewood Arsenal, Maryland, Row 3, File cabinet 55, Drawer 1. Interestingly, this note has been typed on the government copy: "This article is absolutely unreliable. Contains no official Cml C [Chemical Corps] info whatever. The author, Kugelmass, has also been found to be utterly sensationalist, failing entirely——."

58. According to one caption (December 26, 1947), "This darkness was caused by atomic rubbish, dumped over your valley. . . . This may take a thousand years [to clear up.] . . . We boys at Oak Ridge are mighty sorry about this—but—chin up—keep smiling!!" At its peak, *Li'l Abner* was estimated to have a daily readership of over 60 million. The relevant episodes are available at https://www.gocomics.com/lil-abner/1947/12/11,. December 11, 1947–January 19, 1948.

59. Colonel John Hinds, National Military Establishment, to Atomic Energy Commission, May 24, 1948, OSTI OpenNet, https://www.osti.gov/opennet/detail?osti-id=16007062.

60. Joint NME-AEC Panel on Radiological Warfare, "Radiological Warfare Staff Study, June–August 1948," August 29, 1948, DOE OSTI OpenNet, https://www.osti.gov/opennet/servlets/purl/16359248.pdf.

61. Memorandum from John C. MacArthur to General Alden H. Waitt, "Post-hostilities Organiza tion," August 13, 1945, Record Group [RG] 373, Department

of Defense, Department of the Army, U.S. Army Chemical Corps Research and Development Command, National Archives at College Park, MD.

62. See the commentary by William Porter, a subordinate officer to the chief of the Chemical Weapons Service. Porter to Commanding General, Army Service Forces, "Post-War Research and Development Activities of the Chemical Warfare Service," August 22, 1945, RG 373, National Archives at College Park, MD.

63. For example, in fiscal year 1950, $4.3 million was earmarked for Radiological Research and Development, representing almost one quarter of the ACC R & D budget. See Director of Logistics, GSUSA, Attn: Deputy Dir. for R&D, "Breakdown of Chemical Corps Research & Development Funds, FY1950 in Basic Fields," August 16, 1948, RG 373, National Archives at College Park, MD.

64. William Creasy, memo to Chief, Armed Forces Special Weapons Project, Subject: Facilities for Field Testing of RW Munitions, February 14, 1949, OSTI OpenNet, https://www.osti.gov/opennet/detail?osti-id=16004858.

65. C. B. Marquand, "Report of Visit with Dr. Joseph G. Hamilton Concerning the RW Test Safety Panel," May 25, 1949, OSTI OpenNet, https://www.osti.gov/opennet/detail?osti-id=16006436.

66. William Creasy, memo to Director of Logistics, General Staff, U.S. Army, Subject: Public Release on RW Tests at Dugway Proving Ground, October 3, 1949, OSTI OpenNet, https://www.osti.gov/opennet/detail?osti-id=16385512.

67. Atomic Energy Commission—Military Liaison Committee, Minutes of 38th Conference, October 26, 1949, OSTI OpenNet, https://www.osti.gov/opennet/detail?osti-id=16359134.

68. Harry Wexler to Joseph Hamilton, December 8, 1949, OSTI OpenNet, https://www.osti.gov/opennet/detail?osti-id=16388840.

69. Joseph Hamilton to C. B. Marquand, June 1, 1950, OSTI OpenNet, https://www.osti.gov/opennet/detail?osti-id=16388850.

70. Ernest Lawrence to James McCormack, September 20, 1950, OSTI OpenNet, https://www.osti.gov/opennet/detail?osti-id=16110892.

71. Command Historical Office, CBDCOM, "Disposition Form, Radiological Warfare," June 30, 1954, DOE OSTI OpenNet, https://www.osti.gov/opennet/servlets/purl/16007717.pdf.

72. Office, Chief Chemical Officer, "Estimate of the CBR Situation," October 1, 1956, DOE OSTI OpenNet, https://www.osti.gov/opennet/servlets/purl/16007341.pdf. Bernstein asserts that the U.S. "radiological warfare program seems to have died officially in 1954, under the Eisenhower Administration's budget cutbacks." Bernstein, "Radiological Warfare," 48.

73. See the excellent catalogue and commentary of works on atomic fiction by Paul Brians, *Nuclear Holocausts: Atomic War in Fiction, 1895–1984* (Kent, OH: Kent State University Press, 1987).

74. Parker, "War without Death." Italics in the original.

75. Memorandum from Joseph G. Hamilton, M.D., to Colonel K. D. Nichols, "Radioactive Warfare," December 31, 1946, 3.

76. Joint NME-AEC Panel on Radiological Warfare, "Radiological Warfare Staff Study, June–August 1948," 22–23.

77. Columbium is now known as niobium.

78. See, for example, Stephen I. Schwartz, *Atomic Audit: The Costs and Consequences of U.S. Nuclear Weapons since 1940* (Washington, DC: Brookings Institution Press, 1998), 361.

79. Joint NME-AEC Panel on Radiological Warfare, "Radiological Warfare Staff Study, June–August 1948," 49.

80. Carpenter, "Minutes of the 1st Meeting of an Ad Hoc Panel on RW," May 23, 1948, 5. One can imagine the dollar signs in Lawrence's eyes.

81. A. H. Holland, "Production of Materials for Radiological Warfare," January 25, 1949, 2, Box 49-1-239, Central Files, Nuclear Testing Archive, Las Vegas, NV. Approved for public release April 1, 2016.

82. From 1949 to 1952, the Chemical Corps conducted sixty-five field tests at Dugway, releasing 13,000 curies of tantalum-182 into the atmosphere. Advisory Committee on Human Radiation Experiments [ACHRE], part 2, "Intentional Releases: Lifting the Veil of Secrecy: What We Now Know," in *Final Report of the Advisory Committee on Human Radiation Experiments*, DOE Openness: Human Radiation Experiments, https://ehss.energy.gov/ohre/roadmap/achre/chapii_2.html.

83. A very different picture of the scope and duration is depicted in Lisa Martino-Taylor, *Behind the Fog: How the U.S. Cold War Radiological Weapons Program Exposed Innocent Americans* (New York: Routledge, 2018).

84. See "Static Test of Full-Diameter Sectional Munitions, E83," Defense Technical Information Center, May 7, 1953, https://apps.dtic.mil/sti/tr/pdf/AD0596085.pdf.

85. General McCormack was insistent that RW activities fall under the purview of the AEC. See Atomic Energy Commission, "Decision on AEC 28/1, Application of Certain Materials for Military Use: Report by the Director of Military Application in Collaboration with the Director of Biology and Medicine," March 18, 1948, DOE OSTI OpenNet, https://www.osti.gov/opennet/servlets/purl/16359831.pdf.

86. "Texts of Accounts by Lucas and Considine on Interviews with MacArthur in 1954," *New York Times*, April 9, 1964, https://www.nytimes.com/1964/04/09/archives/texts-of-accounts-by-lucas-and-considine-on-interviews-with.html.

87. Colonel M. E. Barker, "Chemical Weapons of the Future," *Military Review*, 27, No. 3 (June 1947). Adri Albert de la Bruheze also cites this source but refers to the author as "Baker." De la Bruheze, "Radiological Weapons and Radioactive

Waste in the United States: Insiders' and Outsiders' Views, 1941–55," *British Journal for the History of Science*, 25, No. 2 (June 1992): 212–213, doi.org/10.1017/S000708740 0028776.

88. Bernstein attributes this view to a group of physicists at Berkeley, including Luis Alvarez. Bernstein, "Radiological Warfare," 48. Edward Teller, Bernstein notes, continued to advocate the use of a cobalt-based RW as late as 1968, also ostensibly on grounds that it would be more humane. Ibid., 48–49.

89. "Radiological Warfare," *Officers' Call*, 2, No. 6 (1949): 1–12. The precise month of the publication is difficult to discern as it does not appear on the journal. No author is credited.

90. See statement by Lawrence in 1948, as relayed by Oak Ridge engineer William Becker and cited in John Shilling, Jr., "Meeting Notes on Radiological Warfare Conferences, June 28 and 29, 1948," Oak Ridge Operations Office, Records Holding Task Group, Classified Documents, RHTG #26,040, Box 51, DOE OSTI OpenNet, www.osti.gov/opennet/servlets/purl/906491.pdf.

91. For a discussion of the bureaucratic and organizational politics associated with the development of these systems, see Beard, *Developing the ICBM*; and Brown, *Flying Blind*. See also Jacob Neufeld, *The Development of Ballistic Missiles in the United States Air Force, 1945–1960* (Washington, DC: GPO, 1990), https://apps.dtic .mil/sti/citations/ADA439957.

92. See discussion of RW agent acquisition in Shilling, "Meeting Notes on Radiological Warfare Conferences, June 28 and 29, 1948," 2.

93. "Report of the Secretary of Defense's Ad Hoc Committee on Chemical, Biological and Radiological Warfare," June 30, 1950, DOE OSTI OpenNet, https: //www.osti.gov/opennet/servlets/purl/16008529.pdf. The outbreak of the Korean War on June 25, 1950, lent additional weight to the committee's recommendations. See Jonathan Tucker, *War of Nerves: Chemical Warfare from World War I to Al-Qaeda* (New York: Pantheon Books, 2006), 126

94. "Report of the Secretary of Defense's Ad Hoc Committee on Chemical, Biological and Radiological Warfare," June 30, 1950, 18–20.

95. Smith, *American Biodefense*, 3–4. Smith discusses the applicability of his kinetic frame thesis to neutron bombs, a non-RW example of weaponized radiation. See especially pages 33–34.

96. Memorandum from Joseph G. Hamilton, M.D., to Colonel K. D. Nichols, "Radioactive Warfare," December 31, 1946, 7.

97. W. Seth Carus, *Defining "Weapons of Mass Destruction,"* Center for the Study of Weapons of Mass Destruction, Occasional Paper, No. 8 (Washington, DC: National Defense University Press, 2012), https://wmdcenter.ndu.edu/Publications/ Occasional-Papers/.

98. The German word *Blausauere* is hydrogen cyanide, the B in Zyklon-B gas. Hans Thirring, *Atomkrieg und Weltpolitik* [Atomic war and world politics] (Vienna: Danubia-Verlag, 1948). Thirring also made reference to the dangers of radioactive dust in his lectures and in an influential article "Ueber das moegliche Ausmass einer radioacktiven Verseuchung durch die Spaltprodukte des U-235" [On the possible extent of radioactive contamination through fission products of U-235] *Acta Physica Austriaca*, 2 (1948): 379–400.

99. Brigadier General James McCormack, Memo to Carroll Wilson, Subject: Radiological Warfare, April 16, 1947, National Archives and Records Division, Atomic Energy Commission, DOE OSTI OpenNet, https://www.osti.gov/opennet/servlets/purl/16359294.pdf.

100. Louis N. Ridenour, "How Effective Are Radioactive Poisons in Warfare?," *Bulletin of the Atomic Scientists*, 6, No. 7 (July 1950): 199–202, 224, doi.org/10.1080/00963402.1950.11461264.

101. Ibid., 200.

102. E. B. White, "Comment," *The New Yorker* August 26, 1950, 17.

103. Ibid.

104. Ibid.

105. "Report of the Secretary of Defense's Ad Hoc Committee on Chemical, Biological and Radiological Warfare," June 30, 1950.

106. "Intelligence Memorandum No. 225," included as an annex to Central Intelligence Agency, "Soviet Potentialities to Conduct Radiological Warfare," February 23, 1950, DOE OSTI OpenNet, https://www.osti.gov/opennet/servlets/purl/16384715.pdf.

107. Ibid., 2.

108. Ibid., 3.

109. Ibid., 6. "They" is crossed out by hand and "RW materials" is inserted in the original. A handwritten note at the bottom of the page indicates that the inserts were made after the presentation to the committee on February 24, 1950.

110. See Army Emergency War Planning, *Chemical Warfare—Biological Warfare—Radiological Warfare*, vol. 2, Annex PP, August 4, 1952, RG 373, National Archives at College Park, MD.

Chapter 2

1. Boris Chertok, *Rockets and People*, vol. 1 (Washington, DC: NASA History Division, 2006), 36.

2. Anindita Banerjee, *We Modern People: Soviet Science Fiction and the Making of Russian Modernity* (Middletown, CT: Wesleyan University Press, 2012), 2.

3. V. P. Vizgin, "Fenomen 'Kul't atoma' v SSSR (1950–1960-e gg)" [The phenom-

enon of the "cult of the atom" in the Soviet Union (1950–1960)], in *Istoria Atomnogo Proekta* [The history of the atomic project] (St. Petersburg: Russian Christian Humanitarian Institute, 2002), 462, 478, http://elib.biblioatom.ru/text/istoriya-sovets kogo-atomnogo-proekta_v2_2002.

4. Boris Chertok, *Rockets and People*, vol. 2: *Creating a Rocket Industry* (Washington, DC: NASA History Division, 2006), 245.

5. Although there are only a few published accounts by actual participants in the Soviet RW program, a significant number of interviews with participants were conducted by Victor Tereshkin for the Bellona Foundation. These interviews, in Russian, are summarized in Tereshkin, "'Gryaznaya bomba' Leningrada" ["Dirty bomb" of Leningrad], *Bellona*, December 27, 2006, https://bellona.ru/2006/12/27/gryaznaya-bomba-leningrada/; the only academic literature in Russia or English on this program to date is that which the authors of this volume previously produced. See Meyer, Bidgood, and Potter, "Death Dust: The Little-Known Story of U.S. and Soviet Pursuit of Radiological Weapons."

6. Aldrin, "Innovation, the Scientists and the State"; Peter Almquist, *Red Forge: Soviet Military Industry Since 1965* (New York: Columbia University Press, 1990); Harley D. Balzer, *Soviet Science on the Edge of Reform* (Boulder, CO: Westview Press, 1989); John G. Hines, Ellis M. Mishulovich, and John F. Shull, *Soviet Intentions 1965–1985*, vol. 1: *An Analytical Comparison of U.S.-Soviet Assessments during the Cold War*, Department of Defense contract #MDA903–92-C-0147 (McLean, VA: BDM Federal, 1995).

7. Evangelista, *Innovation and the Arms Race*.

8. Tereshkin, "'Dirty Bomb' of Leningrad."

9. See "Zayavka na izobretenie V. A. Maslova i V. C. Shpinelya 'Ob ispol'zovanii urana v kachestve vzryvchatogo i otravliayushchego veshchestva'" [Claim for an Invention from V. Maslov and V. Shpinel, "About Using of Uranium as an Explosive and Toxic Agent"], October 17, 1940, in *Atomic Project of USSR: Documents and Materials*, vol. 1, *1938–1945*, book 1, 193–196.

10. Ibid.

11. Ibid.

12. See "Conclusion of National Institute of Chemical Studies of Soviet National Committee of Defence on Invention of UIPhT Fellows Which Was Sent to Agency of Military Chemical Defense," February 1941, doc. no. 89, *Atomic Project of USSR: Documents and Materials*, vol. 1, part 1, 220, Wilson Center History and Public Policy Program Digital Archive, https://digitalarchive.wilson center.org/document/121634. Obtained and translated for NPIHP by Oleksandr Cheban.

13. "Conclusion of Radium Institute of Academy of Sciences on Invention of

UIPhT Fellows Sent to Agency of Military Chemical Defense," April 17, 1941, doc. no. 96, *Atomic Project of USSR: Documents and Materials*, vol. 1, part 1, 228–229, Wilson Center History and Public Policy Program Digital Archive, https://digital archive.wilsoncenter.org/document/121635. Obtained and translated for NPIHP by Oleksandr Cheban.

14. Evangelista, *Innovation and the Arms Race*, 69.

15. "Iz spravki 'Ispol'zovanie reaktsii rasshchepleniya urana dlya voennykh tselej,' podgotovlennoj po agenturnym dannym" [From the reference "The use of the uranium fission reaction for military purposes," prepared using data from agents], January 13, 1943, in *Atomic Project of the USSR*, vol. 1, *1938–1945*, book 1, 291, http://elib.biblioatom.ru/text/atomny-proekt-sssr_t1_kn1_1998/go,291/.

16. Ibid.

17. "Spravka V. A. Makhneva o rassylke knigi G. D. Smita 'Atomnaya energiya dlya voennykh tselej'" [V. A. Makhneva's reference to the distribution of G. D. Smyth's report *Atomic Energy for Military Purposes*], January 23, 1946, doc. no. 164, in *Atomic Project of the USSR*, vol. 2, *1945–1954*, book 2 (Moscow: Science, FizMatLit, 2000), 404, http://elib.biblioatom.ru/text/atomny-proekt-sssr_t2_kn2_2000/go,404.

18. "Prilozhenie No. 1 Tematicheskij perechen' nauchno-issledovatel'skikh rabot po yadernoj fizike, podlezhashchikh vypolneniyu sekretnym poryadkom" [Appendix no. 1: Thematic list of scientific research work on nuclear physics to be carried out by secret order], in *Atomic Project of the USSR*, vol. 2, *Atomic Bomb, 1945–1954*, book 3 (Moscow: FizMatLit, 2002), 91, http://elib.biblioatom.ru/text/atomny-proekt-sssr_t2_kn3_2002/go,91/.

19. Thomas B. Cochran and Robert Standish Norris, "Russian/Soviet Nuclear Warhead Production" (Washington, D.C.: National Resource Defense Council, 1993), 33, https://fas.org/nuke/cochran/nuc_090893o1a_114.pdf.

20. "Otchet o rabote 9-go Upravleniya MVD SSSR po sostoyaniyu na 1 sentyabrya 1947 g." [Report on the work of the 9th directorate of the Ministry of Internal Affairs of the USSR as of September 1, 1947], doc. no. 345, in *Atomic Project of the USSR*, vol. 2, *Atomic Bomb, 1945–1954*, book 3, 698, http://elib.biblioatom.ru/text/atomny-proekt-sssr_t2_kn3_2002/go,698/.

This preliminary research effort aligns with a second stage of Soviet weapons innovation that Evangelista terms "preparatory measures," which are "often instituted in response to events abroad." See Evangelista, *Innovation and the Arms Race*, 71.

21. Prilozhenie 7. "Pis'mo B. L. Vannikova I. V. Stalinu po voprosam zashchity ot atomnogo oruzhiya ot 17 dekabrya 1947 g." [Appendix 7: Letter to V.B. Stalin from B.L. Vannikov on the issue of protection against atomic weapons dated December 17, 1947], in A. K. Chernyshyov, *Tvorets istorii XX veka Nikolaj Nikolaivich Semyonov v atomnom proekte SSSR* [History maker of the 20th century Nikolai Ni-

kolaevich Semyonov in the atomic project of the USSR] (Moscow: Torus, 2016), 133, http://elib.biblioatom.ru/text/chernyshev_tvorets-istorii-semenov_2016/go,135/.

22. Klaus Fuchs, "Letter to William Marley, HP/R352," *Military Liaison with Porton—Fission Product Warfare—General (1949–1951)*, June 1, 1949, box AB 6/544, National Archives, London, United Kingdom. The archive was accessed before its withdrawal from public view by the UK Nuclear Decommissioning Authority in December 2018.

23. M. W. Perrin, "Record of Interview with Dr. K. Fuchs on 30th January, 1950," Michael W. Perrin Interviews with Dr. Klaus Fuchs Following His Arrest for Espionage, January to March 1950, box AB 1/695, National Archives, London, United Kingdom.

24. Perrin, "Record of Interview with Dr. K. Fuchs on 30th January, 1950."

25. Andrew Brown, "The Viennese Connection: Engelbert Broda, Alan Nunn May and Atomic Espionage," *Intelligence and National Security* 24, No 2 (2009): 189.

26. For the most comprehensive study of these scientists, see Pavel Oleynikov, "German Scientists in the Soviet Atomic Project," *The Nonproliferation Review* 7, No. 2 (2000): 1–30.

27. "Pis'mo A. P. Zavenyagina L. P. Beriya s predstavleniem spravki o sostoyanii rabot po ispol'zovaniyu atomnoj energii v Germanii i spiska nemetskikh spetsialistov, rabotayushchikh v Sovetskom Soyuze" [Letter from A. P. Zavenyagin to L. P. Beria with the submission of an inquiry on the status of work on the use of atomic energy in Germany and a list of German specialists working in the Soviet Union], doc. no. 158, in *Atomic Project of the USSR*, vol. 2, *Atomic Bomb, 1945–1954*, book 2, 374, http://elib.biblioatom.ru/text/atomny-proekt-sssr_t2_kn2_2000/go,374/.

28. Oleynikov, "German Scientists in the Soviet Atomic Project," 4.

29. Letter from A. P. Zavenyagin to L. P. Beria.

30. "Prolozhenie No. 2. Spisok nemetskikh spetsialistov, rabotayushchikh v Sovetskom Soyuze" [Appendix 2. List of German specialists working in the Soviet Union], in *Atomic Project of the USSR*, vol. 2, *Atomic Bomb, 1945–1954*, book 2, 378, http://elib.biblioatom.ru/text/atomny-proekt-sssr_t2_kn2_2000/go,378/; Oleynikov, "German Scientists in the Soviet Atomic Project," 16.

31. "'Vypiska iz soobshcheniya' o novykh obraztsakh atomnogo oruzhiya SShA" ["Extract from message" on new models of atomic weapons in the USA] doc. no. 17, in *Atomic Project of the USSR*, vol. 2, *Atomic Bomb, 1945–1954*, book 7 (Moscow: FizMatLit, 2007), 38, http://elib.biblioatom.ru/text/atomny-proekt-sssr_t2_kn7_2007/go,38/.

32. Evangelista, *Innovation and the Arms Race*, 73.

33. In the original Russian, the first and fifteenth "programs" are referred to as *napravleniia*, which translates literally as "directions." Because there is no adequate English-language equivalent for this term, however, we have elected to use the word *program* throughout.

34. In either 1956 or 1957, NII-10 and NII-17 were absorbed into NII-16. See Keith Dexter and Ivan Rodionov, *The Factories, Research and Design Establishments of the Soviet Defence Industry: A Guide*, database version 20, Department of Economics, University of Warwick, May 2018, https://warwick.ac.uk/vpk.

35. Tereshkin, "'Dirty Bomb' of Leningrad."

36. A. A. Greshilov, N. D. Egupov, and A. M. Matyushchenko, *Yadernyj shchit* [Nuclear shield] (Moscow: Logos, 2008), 242, http://elib.biblioatom.ru/text/greshilov_yaderny-schit_2008/go,2.

37. E. A. Shitikov. "Division of the Commander-in-Chief of the Navy" in *Yadernye ispytaniya: Kniga 1, Tom 1: Yadernye ispytaniya v Arktike* [Nuclear tests: book 1, vol. 1: Nuclear tests in the Arctic], ed. V. N. Mikhaelov (Moscow: OAO Moscow Textbooks, 2006), 17, http://elib.biblioatom.ru/text/yadernye-ispytaniya_kn1_t1_2006/go,17/; Tereshkin, "'Dirty Bomb' of Leningrad."

38. E. A. Shitikov, "Istoriya yadernogo oruzhiya flota" [History of the Navy's nuclear weapons], in *Nuclear Tests*, book 1, vol. 1: *Nuclear Tests in the Arctic*, 16–17, http://elib.biblioatom.ru/text/yadernye-ispytaniya_kn1_t1_2006/go,16/. Evangelista highlights high-level advocates and decisions taken at the top levels of the military establishment as critical to weapons innovation in the Soviet Union. Evangelista, *Innovation and the Arms Race*, 73.

39. Tereshkin, "'Dirty Bomb' of Leningrad."

40. V. V. Bordukov, "Morskoj sektor na Semipalatinskom poligone" [Maritime quadrant of the Semipalatinsk test site], *ProAtom*, May 22, 2009, http://www.proatom.ru/modules.php?name=News&file=article&sid=1822.

41. Tereshkin, "'Dirty Bomb' of Leningrad."

42. Anatoly M. Kutskov, "K 61-j godovshchine vojskovoj chasti 99795 'Ob"ekt 230 VMF'" [On the 61st anniversary of military unit 99795 "Object 230 of the Navy"], *Krasnaya zvezda* [Red star], April 1, 2014, https://zvezda.press/?p=10832&hilite=%2799795%27.

43. Tereshkin, "'Dirty Bomb' of Leningrad"; and Kutskov, "On the 61st Anniversary of Military Unit 99795."

44. Kutskov, "On the 61st Anniversary of Military Unit 99795"; see also Russkij sled, "Napravlenie No. 15. Zagadka ladozhskix ostrovov" [Direction no. 15: The mystery of the islands of Ladoga], *Moya Planeta* [My planet], March 1, 2016, https://www.youtube.com/watch?v=dgyUCvhdAio.

45. Bordukov, "Maritime Quadrant of the Semipalatinsk Test Site"; Kutskov, "On the 61st Anniversary of Military Unit 99795"; Tereshkin, "'Dirty Bomb' of Leningrad."

46. Some sources suggest that radiological weapons testing was also carried out as late as 1957 at Konovets Island, the location of the navy's chemical weapons test site (polygon 228), which entailed exposing rabbits to radioactive substances

and examining the effects. However, given that other sources put the end of the Soviet navy's radiological weapons development at least a year earlier, these tests may have had a defensive rather than offensive purpose. See, for example, Kutskov, "On the 61st Anniversary of Military Unit 99795"; and Tereshkin, "'Dirty Bomb' of Leningrad."

47. Tereshkin, "'Dirty Bomb' of Leningrad."
48. Ibid.
49. Kutskov, "On the 61st Anniversary of Military Unit 99795."
50. Ibid.; Tereshkin, "'Dirty Bomb' of Leningrad."
51. Shitikov, "Division of the Commander-in-Chief of the Navy," 17.
52. Ibid., 16.
53.. See E. A. Shitikov, *U istokov yadernogo oruzhiya flota* [At the root of the fleet's nuclear weapons] (Moscow: Kurchatov Institute, 1998), 126, http://elib.biblio atom.ru/text/kiae-istoriya-atomnogo-proekta_v14_1998/go,126/.
54. V. A. Logachev et al., "Contamination of the Area in Which Experiments Were Carried Out with Military Radioactive Substances," in *Nuclear Tests of the USSR: Contemporary Radioecological State of Test Sites: Facts, Witnesses, Recollections* (Izdat: Moscow, 2002), 76, http://elib.biblioatom.ru/text/yadernye-ispytaniya-sssr-sostoyanie-poligonov_2002/go,76/. Vitol'd Vasilets claims that prototype bombs were tested at Semipalatinsk between May 1953 and August 1957. Vasilets, "Under the Leadership of Sergei Korolev: How the USSR Tested Radiological Weapons in Rocket and Bomb Form," *Military-Industrial Courier*, February 14, 2007, https://vpk-news.ru/articles/4178.
55. Logachev et al., "Contamination of the Area in Which Experiments Were Carried Out with Military Radioactive Substances," 76.
56. Vasilets, "Under the Leadership of Sergei Korolev."
57. Tereshkin, "'Dirty Bomb' of Leningrad." If this indeed was a Soviet military objective, it is the only instance of which we are aware that a country conceived of RW use against such a naval target.
58. Ibid.
59. Dexter and Rodionov, *The Factories, Research and Design Establishments of the Soviet Defence Industry*.
60. Vasilets, "Under the Leadership of Sergei Korolev."
61. Ibid.
62. Ibid.
63. Tereshkin, "'Dirty Bomb' of Leningrad."
64. V. A. Logachev et al. *Nuclear Tests of the USSR: Contemporary Radioecological State of Test Sites: Facts, Witnesses, Recollections* (Moscow: Izdat, 2002), 52; see also N. A. Kozlov. "Something about Myself and My Security Service," in *Kurchatov Institute: History of the Atomic Project*, No. 5 (Moscow: Russian Scientific Center

180 Notes to Chapter 2

"Kurchatov Institute," 1996), 157, http://elib.biblioatom.ru/text/kiae-istoriya-atom nogo-proekta_v5_1996/go,157/.

65. Pavel Podvig, *Russian Strategic Nuclear Forces* (Cambridge, MA: MIT Press, 2001), 460.

66. Tereshkin, "'Dirty Bomb' of Leningrad."

67. Vasilets, "Under the Leadership of Sergei Korolev."

68. Ibid.

69. Ibid.

70. Ibid.

71. Ibid.

72. Gennady Rostovskiy, *Kapustin Yar: selo, gorod, polygon* [Kapustin Yar: Village, town, test site], electronic book (Moscow: LitRes, 2006); and Evgeny Buyanov and Boris Slobtsov, *Tajna gibeli gruppy Dyatlova* [The mystery of the death of the Dyatlov group], electronic book (Moscow: LitRes, September 5, 2017).

73. V. D. Kukushin, "Rozhdenie raketno-yadernogo oruzhiya" [The birth of nuclear-missile weapons], in *50-ya raketnaya armiya, Kniga 5: Chtoby pomnili. Sbornik vospominanij veteranov-raketchikov* [50th Missile Army, book 5: So that they remember. Notebook of recollections of veteran-rocketeers] (Smolensk, 2004), as published in *Raketnye sistemy RVSN ot R-1 k 'Topolyu-M' 1946–2006 gg* [RSMF missile systems from R-1 to "Topol-M," 1946–2006], ed. G. I. Smirnov (Smolensk: Smolensk Regional Division of the Academy of Military Sciences of the Russian Federation Russian Strategic Missile Forces, Council of Veterans, 2006), 73.

74. Buyanov and Slobtsov, *Mystery of the Death of the Dyatlov Group.*

75. Chertok, *Rockets and People*, 245. It is unclear how many of the tests for the Geran' missile employed actual radiological materials and how many involved simulants.

76. Ibid., 245.

77. Evangelista identifies mobilization as the moment when the "leadership endorses an all-out effort to pursue innovation," noting that it directly precedes mass production and adoption into military arsenals. Evangelista, *Innovation and the Arms Race*, 52. As the documentary record shows, the Soviet RW program was abandoned long before either of these stages.

78. Horowitz and Narang, "Poor Man's Atomic Bomb?," 530.

79. Joachim Krause and Charles K. Mallory, *Chemical Weapons in Soviet Military Doctrine* (Boulder, CO: Westview Press, 1992), 131, 156.

80. The Soviet Union appears to have taken a similar decision by 1962. See ibid., 127.

81. Ibid., 133.

82. Evangelista, *Innovation and the Arms Race*, 45. Michael Horowitz uses a

similar concept—organizational capacity—to explain the propensity of military organizations to innovate. See Horowitz, *The Diffusion of Military Power*, 10, 35. Much of the literature on the relationship between slack resources and innovation can be traced back to the seminal work of James G. March and Herbert A. Simon, *Organizations* (New York: John Wiley & Sons, 1958).

83. Evangelista, *Innovation and the Arms Race*, 48.

84. Shitikov, "History of the Navy's Nuclear Weapons," 17. Vasilets indicates that Soviet research on RW in other military branches stopped only in the third quarter of 1958. Vasilets, "Under the Leadership of Sergei Korolev."

85. Tereshkin, "'Dirty Bomb' of Leningrad."

86. Vasilets, "Under the Leadership of Sergei Korolev."

87. Anatoly Mikhailovich Kutskov, "How It All Started: The Last of the Mohicans," Central Military-Maritime Portal, March 7, 2014, http://flot.com/history/events/99795/.

88. See, for example, D. J. Bradley, "Radioactive Contamination of the Arctic Region, Baltic Sea, and the Sea of Japan from Activities in the Former Soviet Union," prepared for the U.S. Department of Energy, Pacific Northwest National Laboratory, September 1993, 12, OSTI.gov, https://www.osti.gov/biblio/10102627.

89. Evgeny Krutikov, "Top-Secret Project 'Status-6' Recalls an idea of Academician Sakharov," *Vzglyad*, November 12, 2015, https://vz.ru/society/2015/11/12/777703.html.

90. The article mischaracterizes the process by which the stable isotope cobalt-59 would be transmuted into radioactive cobalt-60. The actual process would involve the absorption by cobalt-59 of neutrons from the nuclear detonation. The authors are grateful to George Moore for pointing out this distinction.

91. Krutikov, "Top-Secret Project 'Status-6' Recalls an Idea of Academician Sakharov."

92. An early popular account of Szilard's concept is the subject of an article by William L. Laurence, "Now Most Dreaded Weapon, Cobalt Bomb, Can Be Built," *New York Times*, April 7, 1954.

93. See, for example, Leo Szilard, "Report on 'Grand Central Terminal,'" in *The Voice of the Dolphins and Other Stories* (New York: Simon and Schuster, 1961), 114–122; and Bill Clemente, "The Dolphin Still Speaks: Leo Szilard and Science Fiction," *Hungarian Journal of English and American Studies*, 14, No. 2 (2008): 376.

94. O. I. Leipunskyi, "O knige E. Tellera i A. Lyattera 'Nashe yadernoe budushchee'" [About E. Teller and A. Latter's book "Our nuclear future"], *Atomnaya Energiya*, 4, No. 6 (1958): 112, http://elib.biblioatom.ru/text/atomnaya-energiya_t4-6_1958/go,112/.

95. H. Matsuda and K. Hayashi, *Nuclear Weapons and Man*, trans. G. V. Mel-

nikova (Moscow: Izdatelst'vo Inostrannaya literature, 1959), 270, http://elib.biblio atom.ru/text/matsuda_yadernoe-oruzhie-i-chelovek_1959/go,0/.

96. See, for example, Brian Wang, "Russia's Developing 100 Megaton Dirty Tsunami-Creating Submarine Drone Bomb," *Next Big Future*, March 5, 2017, https://www.nextbigfuture.com/2017/03/russias-developing-100-megaton-dirty.html; Kyle Mizokami, "Pentagon Document Confirms Existence of Russian Doomsday Torpedo," *Popular Mechanics*, January 16, 2018; and Alex Calvo, "Russia's Nuclear Torpedo Promises 'Extensive Zones of Radioactive Contamination,'" *The National Interest*, December 1, 2015.

Chapter 3

The authors wish to thank Martin Everett and Matthew Goldenberg for their research assistance on this chapter.

1. See, for example, Brian Balmer, "The UK Biological Weapons Program," in *Deadly Cultures: Biological Weapons since 1945*, ed. Mark Wheelis, Lajos Rozsa, and Malcolm Dandos (Cambridge, MA: Harvard University Press, 2006), 47–83; and William King, *Nerve Agents in Postwar Britain: Deterrence, Publicity and Disarmament, 1945–1976* (London: Palgrave Macmillan, 2021).

2. The most notable exception is the research on RWs by Barton Bernstein, which includes reference to wartim767e British perspectives. See, for example, Bernstein, "Radiological Warfare."

3. Meyer, Bidgood, and Potter, "Death Dust: The Little-Known Story of U.S. and Soviet Pursuit of Radiological Weapons"; and Samuel Meyer, Jeffrey Lewis, Sarah Bidgood, and William Potter, "Final Performance Report for Addressing the Threat of State-Level Radiological Weapons Programs," Grant No. FA7000-17-0022 (March 5, 2019). See especially pp. 39–46 in the latter report, which was informed by the authors' access to materials from The National Archives in London, UK, hereafter abbreviated as TNA.

4. King, "A Weapon Too Far."

5. Ibid., 3–4. At a meeting on September 24, 1941, the Defense Service's Panel of the War Cabinet's Scientific Advisory Committee invited the Medical Research Council to cooperate with the MAUD Committee and the Experimental Station at Porton "in a fuller study of the range and extent of the radioactive effects of the bomb explosion and the feasibility of obtaining such effects by a more gradual release of the energy." See *MAUD Report*, Defence Services Panel, September 24, 1941, TNA, CAB 90/8. The issue also is discussed by Margaret Gowing, *Britain and Atomic Energy: 1939–1945* (London: Macmillan & Co., 1964), 104.

6. David Holloway, *Stalin and the Bomb* (New Haven, CT: Yale University Press, 1994), 82–83.

7. See Brown, "The Viennese Connection," 189; also cited by King, "A Weapon Too Far," 4. Interestingly, Brown indicates that May also was "apparently employed in the British efforts to extract nuclear knowledge from the Americans" (191).

8. See Chris Hastings, "Deathbed Confession of Spy Who Betrayed Atom Bomb Secrets," *The Telegraph*, January 26, 2003.

9. King, "A Weapon Too Far," 4–5. The document cited by King is "Memorandum on the Use of Radio-Active Fission Products as a Military Weapon," August 30, 1943, TNA, AB 1/608, but the request to ask May to undertake the study occurred on August 14, 1942 at the 8th Meeting of the Technical Committee. See "Minute 68," 4, TNA, AB 1/608.

10. Bernstein, "Radiological Warfare," 44–45.

11. "Use of Radioactive Material as a Military Weapon," ACH1.000003.006.e, DOE OSTI Opennet, 1, https://osti.gov/opennet/servlets/purl/16384400.pdf.

12. A. V. Peterson (principal drafter), "Foreign Intelligence Supplement No. 2," July 31, 1952, *Manhattan Project District History*, 8, DOE Historian, Office of History and Heritage Resources, Germantown, MD, https://www.osti.gov/opennet/detail?osti-id=1127172.

13. King, "A Weapon Too Far," 8. A contrary view is expressed by Bernstein, who suggests that British policymakers initially were probably even more fearful than their U.S. counterparts of an air attack employing radioactive fission products. Bernstein, "Radiological Warfare," 45.

14. See, for example, Richard Rosecrance, "British Incentives to Become a Nuclear Power," in *The Dispersion of Nuclear Weapons*, ed. Richard Rosecrance (New York: Columbia University Press, 1964), 48–65.

15. Gowing, *Britain and Atomic Energy*, 395.

16. Ibid., 433. The close relationship between "the exploitation of nuclear energy for military explosive purposes and for power production" also is discussed in a note by Imperial Chemical Industries Limited, which serves as Appendix VII to the *MAUD Report*, 435–436.

17. Interestingly, however, Appendix VI to the MAUD Report "Nuclear Energy as a Source of Power," in Gowing, *Britain and Atomic Energy*, 434, observes that nuclear energy "may have important applications to military purposes," but it does not specify what they may be.

18. See the January 1946 assessment made by the Atomic Weapons Subcommittee of the Deputy Chiefs of Staff Committee cited in King, "A Weapon Too Far," 11.

19. See section "Problem of Transport" in Alan Nunn May, *Radioactive Poisons*, August 19, 1942, TNA, AB 4/130.

20. In fact, the COS had identified the Soviet Union as the next likely security

threat as early as 1942 but not in nuclear terms. The authors are grateful to William King for calling this point to our attention. Personal correspondence with the authors, May 4, 2022.

21. Matthew Jones, *The Official History of the UK Strategic Nuclear Deterrent*, vol. 1 (New York: Routledge, 2017), 17.

22. Chiefs of Staff Committee, Confidential Annex to C.O.S. (48) 52nd Meeting, Held on Wednesday, 14th April 1948, Strategic Aspects of Atomic Energy, TNA.

23. Ibid., 21.

24. Ibid.

25. Department of Physical Research at the Admiralty to Porton Downs, October 25, 1948, TNA, AB 6/544.

26. "Radiological Weapons: Notes of a Meeting Held by Principal Director of Scientific Research (Defense) in Room 233 Shell Mex House," January 21, 1949, TNA, WO 188/2192.

27. F. J. Wilkins to William Marley, "Use of Fission Products Discussion," December 23, 1948, TNA, AB 6/544.

28. Ibid.

29. William G. Marley, "Preliminary Note on Military Uses of Radioactive Materials Derived from Nuclear Reactors," February 14, 1949, TNA, AB 15/769.

30. Fuchs, "Letter to William Marley, HP/R352."

31. The destruction of approximately 100 folders of Fuchs's documents was discovered by records keepers at the National Archives in 1963. A message by the British scientist Dr. John Corner reporting the loss notes that "they had been put into Penney's safe, and which about the middle 50's existed in the strong room in F6.1." See "PRO ES 1/494," November 29, 1963. Interestingly, Penney also ordered that his own his own papers be burned shortly before his death. See Michael S. Goodman, "The Grandfather of the Hydrogen Bomb?: Anglo-American Intelligence and Klaus Fuchs," *Historical Studies in the Physical and Biological Sciences*, 34, No. 1 (2003): 16.

32. A number of scholars have suggested that that Penney relied heavily on Fuchs for information about American atomic weapons research, especially Edward Teller's theoretical studies on what would become the hydrogen bomb. See Goodman, "The Grandfather of the Hydrogen Bomb?," 14–22; and Frank Closs, *Trinity: The Treachery and Pursuit of the Most Dangerous Spy in History* (London: Allen Lane, 2019), 389–391. Closs (391) speculates that Fuchs is unlikely to have provided the UK with any less information about the U.S. program than he provided Moscow. If so, it is conceivable that Penney and other senior officials engaged in nuclear weapons research were reluctant to leave any records detailing the assistance the UK had received from Fuchs.

33. Goodman, "The Grandfather of the Hydrogen Bomb?," 130–131, 142.

34. See, for example, "Aircraft Bomb Stowage and Shielding," June 2, 1949, TNA, AB 6/544; "Notes of a Meeting Held at Porton on Wednesday, 15th November 1950 to Discuss the Requirements for Protective Clothing for Special Parties," November 29, 1950, TNA, AB 6/544; "Working Party on Protective Clothing for Special Parties," February 15, 1951, TNA, AB 6/544.

35. On this fixation, see Jones, *The Official History of the UK Strategic Nuclear Deterrent*, 21–25. In "A Weapon Too Far," 17, King cites a document to which scholars do not currently have access due to files at the National Archive being retracted in 2018–19 that indicates British Home Office officials met in May 1951 to review possible future nuclear weapons developments. He indicates that their review built upon prior analyses undertaken at Porton Down and "by nuclear scientists such as Marley."

36. Balmer, "The UK Biological Weapons Program," 61–62.

37. "Report on the Military Aspects of Atomic Energy," June 6, 1951, 32, TNA, DEFE 5/31.

38. Ibid.

39. Ibid.

40. Ibid.

41. Ibid. Italics added.

42. Ibid.

43. Kugelmass, "Our Silent Mystery Weapon," 40.

44. Although the event depicted by Kugelmass is likely apocryphal, it is intriguing that the date he provides for the alleged release of "atomic sand" precedes by only fourteen months the actual testing of a British atomic bomb in in the Montebello Islands in Western Australia.

45. Air Ministry, "Radiological Warfare," August 1952, TNA, AB 16/1129.

46. Ibid., 2.

47. Air Vice Marshal E. Davis to Air Marshal, Central Medial Establishment, Royal Air Force, Kelvin House, Cleveland Street, London, December 4, 1952, TNA, AB 16/1129.

48. A. E. Childs, memorandum to Director, A.E.R.E., Harwell, with handwritten text by W. G. Marley, March 11, 1953, TNA, AB 6.1276.

49. Chairman of the OAW Party, "Radiological Warfare," October 26, 1953, TNA, DEFE 32/3; also cited in King, "A Weapon Too Far."

50. Minutes of Meetings, Defense Research Policy Sub-Committee April 13, 1955, TNA, DEFE 10/806, cited in King, "A Weapon Too Far," 20.

51. Major D. B. Janisch, R.A., War Office Representative, Harwell, "A Note on 'Radiological Sabotage,'" February 15, 1956, TNA, AB 6/1731.

52. Rosen, *Winning the Next War*, 45.

53. Notwithstanding this general tendency, the U.S. and UK did meet periodically to discuss RW defenses.

54. Section 10 of the Atomic Energy Act did not address RWs specifically and classified "data concerning the manufacture or utilization of atomic weapons, the production of fissionable material, or the use of fissionable material in the production of power" only as "restricted data."

55. The meeting focused on the establishment of a standardized and integrated list of CW and BW components and equipment. See Colonel William Creasy, Cml C, Subject: Procedure for Establishing the Integrated List, Record Group 373, NARA, June 8, 1948.

56. F. J. Wilkins to William Marley, "Use of Fission Products Discussion," TNA, AB 6/544.

57. These figures included Generals Curtis LeMay, Douglas MacArthur, and James McCormack, Jr.

58. This support is very clearly expressed in the report by the Director of Military Application in Collaboration with the Director of Biology and Medicine, *Application of Radioactive Materials for Military Use*, Atomic Energy Commission, attached to Atomic Energy Commission Decision of the AEC 28/1, *Application of Certain Materials for Military Use*, March 18, 1948, https://www.osti.gov/opennet/servlets/purl/16359831.pdf.

59. As described in the chapter on the Soviet experience, tests of different types of radiological warheads were conducted in the mid-1950s but with inconclusive results.

60. Balmer, "The UK Biological Weapons Program," 50, observes that, in the summer of 1947, the chiefs of staff agreed on the cardinal principle that the UK should "be prepared to use weapons of mass destruction . . . as the best deterrent to war in peace-time." According to Balmer, "WMD were specified as nuclear, biological, and chemical weapons, and BW enjoyed equal priority with nuclear weapons."

61. William King, in his authoritative study of the evolution of the UK's policy on chemical weapons, notes the unusual manner in which the issue of nerve agent acquisition was debated "at the very highest levels of British defense policy." See King, *Nerve Agents in Postwar Britain*, 254.

62. "Preliminary Note on Military Uses of Radioactive Materials Derived from Nuclear Reactors," February 14, 1949, TNA, AB 15/769. In "A Weapon Too Far," 14, King also cites the same passage but interprets it differently, attributing it to cautionary political and moral motives.

63. King, "A Weapon Too Far," 14.

64. Various studies identified the "goldilocks zone" to be between at least several weeks and less than one year. See, for example, Joint NME-AEC Panel on Radiological Warfare, "Radiological Warfare Staff Study, June-August 1948," August 29, 1948, 22–23, DOE OSTI OpenNet, https://www.osti.gov/openet/servlets/purl/16359248.pdf.

65. Chairman of the OAW Party, "Radiological Warfare," cited in King, "A Weapon Too Far," 18.

66. For an examination of the debate over the health effects of nuclear testing in the United Kingdom during the 1950s, see Christoph Laucht, "Scientists, the Public, the State, and the Debate over the Environmental and Human Health Effects of Nuclear Testing in Britain, 1950–1958," *The Historical Journal*, 59, No. 1 (March 2016): 221–251.

67. See King, *Nerve Agents in Postwar Britain*, 256.

68. King, "A Weapon Too Far," 22–23

69. This "substitution effect" among weapons of mass destruction is described by Michael Horowitz and Neil Narang, although their analysis is limited to nuclear, chemical, and biological weapons. See Horowitz and Narang, "Poor Man's Atomic Bomb?"

Chapter 4

1. Leonard Beaton, "A Radiological Arms Race in the Middle East?," *The New Scientist*, No. 332 (March 28, 1963): 679; Leonard Beaton, "Poor Man's Nuclear Warfare?," *The New Scientist*, No. 391 (May 14, 1964): 411 ff.; C. L. Sulzberger, "The Problem of a Garbage Bomb," *New York Times*, November 20, 1963.

2. It is worth noting that Project Ibis might not have been Egypt's only effort at exploring RWs at the time—but it is the only effort on which evidence has emerged. It is not inconceivable that other parts of the Egyptian government (outside the military) contemplated such weapons, especially considering that Egypt had had an operational nuclear reactor since 1961 with the ability to produce various isotopes and a growing cadre of science bureaucracy around it, buzzing with ideas. However, to date, no evidence has come to light regarding such additional efforts.

3. Michel Bar-Zohar, *Spies in the Promised Land* (London: Davis-Poynter Limited, 1972); Roger Howard, *Operation Damocles: Israel's Secret War against Hitler's Scientists* (New York: Pegasus Books, 2014); Sirrs, *Nasser and the Missile Age in the Middle East*.

4. Otto Joklik, deposition to the Chief of the Investigative Agency, March 8, 1963, Zurich Canton Police, 9, Staatsarchiv, Basel, Switzerland.

5. Dan Raviv and Yossi Melman, *Spies against Armageddon* (Sea Cliff, NY: Levant Books, 2012), 217.

6. Meeting [of John F. Kennedy] with Israeli Foreign Minister Golda Meir, December 27, 1962, memorandum of conversation, John F. Kennedy Administration, https://www.jewishvirtuallibrary.org/president-kennedy-meeting-with-israeli-foreign-minister-golda-meir-december-1962.

7. Otto Joklik and Joseph Ben-Gal Judgement, Basel City Criminal Court, June 12, 1963, 2, Staatsarchiv, Basel, Switzerland.

8. Although Joklik alleged such Indian assistance, which was also mentioned in press reports at the time, there is no evidence corroborating it. The India connection might have received undue attention given India's purported intention to assist Egypt's nuclear program at the time. Former Egyptian foreign minister Nabil Fahmy writes: "My father had recounted to me that in the mid-1960s the head of the Indian Atomic Energy Agency had visited Egypt with instructions to develop cooperation in the nuclear field between the two countries. After visiting the Egyptian nuclear facilities and before departing, he informed him that he would report back to the Indian authorities that the nuclear infrastructure in Egypt would not sustain a serious nuclear program." Fahmy, *Egypt's Diplomacy in War, Peace and Transition* (Cham, Switzerland: Palgrave Macmillan, 2020), 116.

9. Sirrs, *Nasser and the Missile Age in the Middle East*, 125.

10. James Walsh, "Bombs Unbuilt: Power, Ideas, and Institutions in International Politics" (PhD diss., Massachusetts Institute of Technology, 2001), 92.

11. Authors studying Egypt's missile and other nonconventional weapons programs in the early 1960s have noted similar challenges in sourcing material, especially on Egyptian internal decision-making. See Sirrs, *Nasser and the Missile Age in the Middle East*; Walsh, "Bombs Unbuilt"; Maria Rublee, *Nonproliferation Norms: Why States Choose Nuclear Restraint* (Athens: University of Georgia Press, 2009).

12. Ray Takeyh, *The Origins of the Eisenhower Doctrine: The US, Britain, and Nasser's Egypt, 1953–57* (Hampshire, UK: Palgrave Macmillan, 2000).

13. Steven A. Cook, *Ruling but Not Governing: The Military and Political Development in Egypt, Algeria, and Turkey* (Baltimore, MD: The John Hopkins University Press, 2007).

14. Michael Sharnoff, *Nasser's Peace: Egypt's Response to the 1967 War with Israel* (New York: Transaction Publishers, 2017).

15. Ibid.

16. Mohamed Heikal, *Secret Channels: The Inside Story of Arab-Israeli Peace Negotiations* (New York: HarperCollins, 1996).

17. Ibid.

18. On the Suez crisis and its implications for Egyptian foreign policy, see Sharnoff, *Nasser's Peace*; Takeyh, *The Origins of the Eisenhower Doctrine*; Mohamed Heikal, *Cutting the Lion's Tail—Suez through Egyptian Eyes* (New York: Abor House, 1987). The Suez crisis also enabled the consolidation of Nasser's regime domestically and the sidelining of local opposition figures. Barnaby Crowford, "Egypt's Other Nationalists and the Suez Crisis of 1956," *The Historical Journal*, 59, No. 1 (2016): 253–285.

19. Takeyh, *The Origins of the Eisenhower Doctrine*.

20. Mohamed Heikal, *The Cairo Documents: The Inside Story of Nasser and His Relationship with World Leaders, Rebels, and Statesmen* (London: New English Library, 1972).

21. Sharnoff, *Nasser's Peace*, 15.

22. Heikal, *The Cairo Documents*, 201 ff. The Balfour Declaration was a public statement issued by the British government in 1917 during the First World War announcing support for the establishment of a "national home for the Jewish people" in Palestine. British Foreign Secretary Lord Arthur James Balfour to Lord Walter Rothschild [The Balfour Declaration], November 2, 1917, https://www.jewishvirtuallibrary.org/text-of-the-balfour-declaration.

23. Ibid., 196.

24. Walsh, "Bombs Unbuilt," 153.

25. Heikal, *The Cairo Documents*, 205.

26. Takeyh, *The Origins of the Eisenhower Doctrine*, xviii.

27. Jesse Ferris, "Soviet Support for Egypt's Intervention in Yemen, 1962–1963," *Journal of Cold War Studies*, 10, No. 4 (Fall 2008): 5–36.

28. Ibid., 8.

29. Ibid.

30. Ibid.

31. Otto Joklik at one point also spoke about a prospective Egyptian radiological threat to "European capitals." "Discovered at the Ben-Gal and Joklik Trial: Egypt Ordered Enough Quantity of Cobalt and Strontium to Exterminate Every Leaving Creature in Israel," *Herut Newspaper*, June 11, 1963.

32. Director of Central Intelligence, "The UAR Missile Program and Its Implications for Israel," Special National Intelligence Estimate, No. 30-4-63, December 4, 1963, https://www.cia.gov/readingroom/docs/DOC_0001173804.pdf.

33. Joseph S. Bermudez Jr., "Pyramid Scheme: Egypt's Ballistic Missile Test and Launch Facility," *Jane's Intelligence Review*, February 9, 2010, 48–52.

34. Sirrs, *Nasser and the Missile Age in the Middle East*, 48.

35. Otto Joklik, deposition to the Chief of the Investigative Agency, March 5, 1963, Zurich Canton Police, 6, Staatsarchiv, Basel, Switzerland.

36. Sirrs, *Nasser and the Missile Age in the Middle East*, 63.

37. Telegram from U.S. embassy in the United Arab Republic to Department of State, June 28, 1963, doc. 283, in *Foreign Relations of the United States, 1961–1963*, vol. 18, *Near East, 1962–1963*, ed. Glenn W. LaFantasie (Washington, DC: United States Government Printing Office, 1995).

38. Intra-Israeli disagreements in assessments of Egypt's missile and RW threat will be detailed further later in this chapter.

39. Dan Raviv and Yossi Melman, *Every Spy a Prince* (Boston: Houghton Mifflin Harcourt, 1990), 62–77.

40. Ibid.

41. Sirrs, *Nasser and the Missile Age in the Middle East*, 106.

42. Heikal, *Secret Channels*, 120. Heikal does not provide a source for this claim.

43. Hassan Elbahtimy, "Missing the Mark: Dimona and Egypt's Slide into the 1967 Arab-Israeli War," *The Nonproliferation Review*, 25, No. 5–6 (2018): 385–397.

44. Walsh, "Bombs Unbuilt," 42.

45. Owen Sirrs offers a detailed account of Robert Komer's exchanges with Nasser, in which the latter laid out his motivations for developing long-range missiles. Sirrs, *Nasser and the Missile Age in the Middle East*, 115ff.

46. Ambassador Jean Badeau to Rusk, telegram (A-767), April 18, 1963, RG 59, CFPF, February–December 1963, POL UR, USNA, cited in Avner Cohen, *Israel and the Bomb* (New York: Columbia University Press, 1998), 246. See also Sirrs, *Nasser and the Missile Age in the Middle East*, 112. That Nasser suspected Israel of being interested in radiological weapons could not be corroborated by further evidence.

47. Badeau to Rusk, telegram, April 18, 1963.

48. "Memorandum of Conversation," Secretary's Delegation to the Eighteenth Session of the United Nations General Assembly, New York, September 30 1963, doc. 331, SecDel/MC/67, *Foreign Relations of the United States, 1961–1963*, vol. 18, https://history.state.gov/historicaldocuments/frus1961-63v18/d331.

49. Nuclear Threat Initiative, "Egypt," NTI Country Profile, https://www.nti.org/countries/egypt/.

50. Walsh, "Bombs Unbuilt"; Rublee, *Nonproliferation Norms*.

51. Hassan Elbahtimy, "Diplomacy under the Nuclear Shadow: Kennedy, Nasser, and Dimona," *Middle Eastern Studies* 59, No. 2 (June 2022): 315–332, https://www.tandfonline.com/doi/full/10.1080/00263206.2022.2083109.

52. Cohen, *Israel and the Bomb*, 244.

53. Ibid., 254 ff.

54. Walsh, "Bombs Unbuilt"; Rublee, *Nonproliferation Norms*.

55. Rublee, *Nonproliferation Norms*, 114.

56. Walsh, "Bombs Unbuilt," 32.

57. Sirrs, *Nasser and the Missile Age in the Middle East*, 1.

58. Ibid., 19.

59. Anthony H. Cordesman, *Arab-Israeli Military Forces in an Era of Asymmetric Wars* (Stanford, CA: Stanford University Press, 2008).

60. Sirrs, *Nasser and the Missile Age in the Middle East*, 78.

61. The Sinai has only few prime roads and passes for use by attackers or defenders, which in theory creates opportunities for area (road) denial by unconventional means, such as chemical weapons. Cordesman, *Arab-Israeli Military Forces in an Era of Asymmetric Wars*.

62. Cordesman, *Arab-Israeli Military Forces*, 201.

63. Beaton, "Poor Man's Nuclear Warfare?"

64. The Egyptian government has always denied the use of chemical weapons in

Yemen. The primary sources of allegations against Egypt were journalists, royalist sources opposed to the Egyptian intervention, and the International Committee of the Red Cross. ICRC, "Practice Relating to Rule 74: Chemical Weapons," Egypt, IHL Databases, https://ihl-databases.icrc.org/customary-ihl/eng/docs/v2_cou_eg _rule74; Nuclear Threat Initiative, "Egypt Chemical Overview," NTI Fact Sheet, January 28, 2015, https://www.nti.org/analysis/articles/egypt-chemical/.

65. Federation of American Scientists, "Chemical Weapons Program," Egypt, FAS Nuclear Information Project, updated October 2, 1999, https://nuke.fas.org/guide/egypt/cw/index.html.

66. "Egypt," NTI Country Profile.

67. Ibid.

68. Ibid.

69. W. Andrew Terrill, "The Chemical Warfare Legacy of the Yemen War," *Comparative Strategy*, 10, No. 2, 1991, 112.

70. Ibid., 110.

71. "Nasser's Nuclear Breakthrough," *The Guardian*, May 4, 1964.

72. "Nasser's Thwarted Hopes," *The Guardian*, May 7, 1964.

73. The source is anonymous, but the description matches Joklik's: he was an engineer and scientist who had worked on Egyptian radiological plans but had ended his association more than one year prior. He is described as having "an evident flair for gadgets" and as having a tendency "to make light of technical difficulties that to most people would seem formidable."

74. The *Guardian* science correspondent was John Maddox, who had coauthored a volume on nuclear proliferation, *The Spread of Nuclear Weapons*, with Leonard Beaton in 1962. Beaton examined the RW revelations with a similarly skeptical eye in "Poor Man's Nuclear Warfare?," *The New Scientist*, May 14, 1964.

75. Egyptian military expert, cited in Maria Rublee, "Egypt's Nuclear Weapons Program: Lessons Learnt," *The Nonproliferation Review*, 13, No. 3 (2006): 555–567, https://www.tandfonline.com/doi/abs/10.1080/10736700601071637.

76. Mohamed Heikal, "Cairo Draws Up Plan for the Construction of the First Atomic Reactor in the Middle East and the Eleventh in the World," *Al-Ahram*, December 6, 1960, cited in Walsh, "Bombs Unbuilt," 145.

77. Sirrs, *Nasser and the Missile Age in the Middle East*.

78. Cohen, *Israel and the Bomb*, 249.

79. Heikal, *Secret Channels*, 142.

80. Heikal, *The Cairo Documents*, 207.

81. James Walsh, cited in Rublee, "Egypt's Nuclear Weapons Program." Similar pledges were repeated to President Johnson in 1964. In one such letter, Nasser declared that Egypt "does not think of bringing that terrifying danger [nuclear terror] to the region she lives in." Walsh, "Bombs Unbuilt," 122. Hassan Elbahtimy, in his

account on the role of Dimona in the 1967 war, similarly argues that between 1961 and 1965, Nasser told several American interlocutors that he would not accept a nuclear-armed Israel, but also that Egypt would not develop its own nuclear weapons. Elbahtimy, "Missing the Mark."

82. "Egypt," NTI Country Profile.

83. Dany Shoham, "Chemical and Biological Weapons in Egypt," *The Nonproliferation Review* 5, No. 3 (Spring–Summer 1998), https://www.nonproliferation.org/wp-content/uploads/npr/shoham53.pdf. It was not until 1990 that a senior Egyptian military intelligence official finally admitted that Egypt had employed CWs during the Yemen civil war. Jack Anderson, "The Growing Chemical Club," *The Washington Post*, August 17, 1990, cited in Shoham.

84. Terrill, "The Chemical Warfare Legacy of the Yemen War," 113.

85. Otto Joklik, deposition to the Chief of the Investigative Agency, March 5, 1963.

86. Rublee suggests that it is conceivable, though it cannot be conclusively shown, that rivalry between Nasser and his defense minister, Field Marshal Abd al-Hakim Amer, kept Nasser from investing decisively in the nuclear weapons option. Rublee, "Egypt's Nuclear Weapons Program." For other accounts on the Nasser-Amer relationship, see Anwar el-Sadat, *In Search of Identity* (New York: Harper & Row, 1977), 157–171; and Raymond A. Hinnebusch Jr., *Egyptian Politics under Sadat: The Post-Populist Development of an Authoritarian-Modernizing State* (Cambridge: Cambridge University Press, 1985).

87. Walsh, "Bombs Unbuilt"; Rublee, *Nonproliferation Norms*.

88. Mark Fitzpatrick, ed., *Nuclear Programmes in the Middle East: In the Shadow of Iran* (London: The International Institute for Strategic Studies, 2008), 19.

89. Rublee, *Nonproliferation Norms*.

90. Bermudez, "Pyramid Scheme." This organization oversaw not only missile design and engineering but also the establishment of a ballistic missile production infrastructure by converting existing arms and aircraft factories, establishing new facilities, and, most significantly, creating the ballistic missile test and launch facility near Jabal Hamzah.

91. Michael Bar-Zohar and Nissim Mishal, *Mossad: The Greatest Missions of the Israeli Secret Service* (New York: HarperCollins, 2012).

92. Andrew Rathmell, "Egypt's Military Industrial Complex," *Jane's Intelligence Review*, 6, No. 10 (October 1, 1994): 455.

93. Unnamed Egyptian source, quoted in Walsh, "Bombs Unbuilt," 165.

94. Cordesman, *Arab-Israeli Military Forces*.

95. Several of Joklik's published works involve applications of cobalt-60. One, collected by Swiss investigators as they were gathering evidence in preparation for Joklik's criminal trial, contains drawn mock-ups of all-terrain vehicles with attached manipulator arms for use in regions that had been contaminated by nuclear or ra-

diological war. Otto Joklik, "Studie über ein strahlengeschütztes Räumfahrzeug mit Manipulatoren, Strahlenmessanlage und TV-Beobachtung Ziviler Luftschutz," 23, No. 7–8 (July–August 1959), Staatsarchiv, Basel, Switzerland.

96. Inspekteur Parzani to Adjutant Maurer, memorandum, March 25, 1963, Staatsarchiv, Basel, Switzerland.

97. Thomas Riegler, "Agents, Scientists, and 'Todesstrahlen': On the Role of Austrian Actors in Nasser's Armament Program (1959–1961)," *Journal of Intelligence and Propaganda Studies*, 8, No. 2 (2014): 44–72.

98. Dan Greenberg, "Washington View: Goods for the Good," *New Scientist*, 58, No. 843 (April 26, 1973): 232–234. Joklik was allegedly involved in other illicit activities throughout his career. Those are summarized in the court documents pertaining to his June 1963 trial in Basel.

99. Otto Joklik, deposition to the Chief of the Investigative Agency, March 5, 1963, 6.

100. Sirrs, *Nasser and the Missile Age in the Middle East*.

101. Dany Shoham, "Chemical and Biological Weapons in Egypt and Libya," *CBW Magazine*, Manohar Parrikar Institute for Defence Studies and Analyses, https://www.idsa.in/cbwmagazine/CBWinEgyptandLibya_DanyShoham.

102. Cook, *Ruling but Not Governing*.

103. Ibid.

104. Rathmell, "Egypt's Military Industrial Complex," 455–460.

105. In his deposition, Joklik claimed that he himself "had nothing to do" with Egypt's missile program, and "never visited the missile factory." Joklik, deposition to the Chief of the Investigative Agency, March 3, 1963.

106. Bar-Zohar and Mishal, *Mossad*.

107. Israeli Mission in Cologne, Germany, letter/telegraph, Report on a meeting between Israeli counsel Leo Savir and unnamed German official, December 1, 1964, State of Israel, National Archive, Hetz (Arrow), Ministry of Foreign Affairs, 585/12, November 1964–June 1965, "Cologne—German scientists in Egypt."

108. Drew Pearson, "Nazi Scientists Busy Preparing Rockets, Nerve Gas for Nasser," *Aiken Standard and Review*, July 27, 1964.

109. Rublee, *Nonproliferation Norms*.

110. Sirrs, *Nasser and the Missile Age in the Middle East*, 35.

111. Otto Joklik, deposition to the Chief of the Investigative Agency, March 5, 1963, 6.

112. Rathmell, "Egypt's Military Industrial Complex."

113. Joachim Joesten, "Those German Rocketeers in Egypt," *New Germany Reports*, No. 62 (November 1963): 14.

114. Otto Joklik, deposition to the Chief of the Investigative Agency, March 5, 1963.

115. Ibid. At the Basel trial, the defense submitted bills and bids for delivery of radioactive materials to Egypt and a shipment certificate aimed at Dr. Isis Khalil, Mansi El-Bakri, in Cairo (Dr. Khalil is the sister of General Mahmoud Khalil). "Discovered at the Ben-Gal and Joklik Trial," *Herut Newspaper*, June 11, 1963. For further claims on Egyptian procurements of cobalt, see "The Orteli Trial and Nasser's Double Game with Moscow and Peking," *Al Ha'Mishmar Newspaper*, September 24, 1965.

116. "Discovered at the Ben-Gal and Joklik Trial," *Herut Newspaper*.

117. Steven Carol, *Understanding the Volatile and Dangerous Middle East: A Comprehensive Analysis* (Bloomington, IN: iUniverse, 2019).

118. For such conflation in press coverage, see Beaton, "A Radiological Arms Race in the Middle East?"; Sulzberger, "The Problem of a Garbage Bomb." This conflation extended to assessment by officials; see "Memorandum of Conversation," Secretary's Delegation to the Eighteenth Session of the United Nations General Assembly, September 30, 1963.

119. Beaton, "Poor Man's Nuclear Warfare?"

120. Ibid.

121. Ibid.

122. Bermudez, "Pyramid Scheme."

123. Soviet-made KHAB-200 R5 aerial bombs (filled with mustard gas) and AOKh-25 aerial bombs (filled with phosgene). Dany Shoham, "Chemical and Biological Weapons in Egypt."

124. Regarding the fallout in Israeli-Austrian relations, see Petra Stuiber, "Gute Geschäfte mit Israels Feinden," *Der Standard*, January 3–4, 2015, https://www.derstandard.at/story/2000009957343/gute-geschaefte-mit-israels-feinden. Regarding Israeli-Swiss relations, see Hannah Einhaus, "Rüstungshilfe für Nasser," *NZZ Geschichte*, January 2017, https://www.worthaus.ch/hannah-einhaus/; Hannah Einhaus, "Basels Rolle bei Angriffsplänen gegen Israel," *Baseler Zeitung*, November 5, 2016, https://www.bzbasel.ch/basel/basel-stadt/basels-rolle-bei-angriffsplanen-gegen-israel-ld.1592026. Regarding Israeli-German relations, see Sirrs, *Nasser and the Missile Age in the Middle East*.

125. "Yesterday's Press: German Scientists," *The Jerusalem Post*, March 22, 1963.

126. "Meir Hits 'Evil Crew' of Nazis," *The Jerusalem Post*, March 21, 1963.

127. "The Arab-Israeli Problem," January 23, 1963, doc. 139, NIE 30–63, in *Foreign Relations of the United States, 1961–1963*, vol. 18, https://history.state.gov/historicaldocuments/frus1961-63v18/d139.

128. Director of Central Intelligence, "The Advanced Weapons Program of the UAR and Israel," Special National Intelligence Estimate, No. 30-2-63, May 8, 1963, 2, https://www.cia.gov/library/readingroom/docs/DOC_0001173804.pdf.

129. Ray S. Cline, Deputy Director (Intelligence), Memorandum for Director of

Central Intelligence, "UAR-Israel Advanced Weapons," April 5, 1963, https://web.archive.org/web/20170123020257/https://www.cia.gov/library/readingroom/docs/CIA-RDP79T00429A001300030005-8.pdf.

130. U.S. Department of State, Memorandum for the Presidential Emissary, Tab B: Scenario with Ben Gurion, May 29, 1963, Folder Israel: Security: Arms Control, 1963, Subfolder Arab-Israeli Arms Control Initiative, JFKPOF-119a-009-p0057, Presidential Papers, President's Office Files, Papers of John F. Kennedy.

131. Otto Joklik, deposition to the Chief of the Investigative Agency, March 3, 1963, Zurich Canton Police, Staatsarchiv, Basel, Switzerland.

132. Beaton, "Poor Man's Nuclear Warfare?"

133. Riegler, "Agents, Scientists, and 'Todesstrahlen.'"

134. Bar-Zohar and Mishal, *Mossad*.

135. Ibid.

136. Meir Amit, *Rosh Be-Rosh [Head On]* (Tel Aviv: Hed Artzi, 1999).

137. For further detail on intra-Israeli divergences on the German scientist affair broadly and Joklik specifically, see Amit, *Head On*; Sirrs, *Nasser and the Missile Age in the Middle East*; and Bar-Zohar and Mishal, *Mossad*.

138. Sirrs, *Nasser and the Missile Age in the Middle East*, 143.

139. For detail on the U.S.-led arms control initiative, see Sirrs, *Nasser and the Missile Age in the Middle East*.

Chapter 5

1. "Tenth Report of the Executive Chairman of the Special Commission Established by the Secretary-General pursuant to Paragraph 9 (b) (i) of Security Council Resolution 687 (1991), and Paragraph 3 of Resolution 699 (1991) on the Activities of the Special Commission," December 17, 1995, S/1995/1038, https://www.un.org/Depts/unscom/sres95-1038.htm.

2. UN Security Council Resolution 687 (1991), April 8, 1991, S/RES/687, https://www.un.org/Depts/unmovic/documents/687.pdf.

3. "Tenth Report," S/1995/1038; "Applications of Nuclear Physics," Atomic Energy Agency, Al-Qa'Qaa' Facility, Muthanna Facility, 1988 (English copy in possession of the authors); William J. Broad, "Document Reveals 1987 Bomb Test by Iraq," *The New York Times*, April 29, 2001, https://www.nytimes.com/2001/04/29/world/document-reveals-1987-bomb-test-by-iraq.html. According to "Applications of Nuclear Physics," the first test was carried out at Al-Haswa, and the second and third in the Western Desert.

4. "Applications of Nuclear Physics."

5. Permanent Representative of Iraq to the United Nations to the Secretary-General, May 5, 2001, S/2001/450, https://digitallibrary.un.org/record/439994?ln=en; "Tenth Report," S/1995/1038.

6. In his work on Saddam Hussein's nuclear vision, Norman Cigar cites Iraqi doctrinal publications that highlighted the operational use of weapons of mass destruction, including those of a radiological nature, at least by 1984. Cigar, *Saddam Hussein's Nuclear Vision: An Atomic Shield and Sword for Conquest*, Middle East Studies Occasional Papers, No. 1 (Quantico, VA: Marine Corps University Press, June 2011), https://www.usmcu.edu/Portals/218/MES/NuclearVision_Web.pdf?ver=2018-10-03-101643-027.

7. Ibrahim Al-Marashi and Sammy Salama, *Iraq's Armed Forces. An Analytical History* (London, New York: Routledge, 2008).

8. Kenneth Pollack, *Arabs at War: Military Effectiveness, 1948–1991* (Lincoln: University of Nebraska Press, 2002).

9. Kevin M. Woods, Williamson Murray, and Thomas Holaday, *Saddam's War: An Iraqi Military Perspective of the Iran-Iraq War*, McNair Paper 70 (Washington, DC: Institute for National Strategic Studies and National Defense University, 2009), https://ndupress.ndu.edu/Portals/68/Documents/Books/saddams-war.pdf.

10. Ibid.

11. Al-Marashi and Salama, *Iraq's Armed Forces*, 57.

12. Pollack, *Arabs at War*, 218.

13. Written exchange with former UN weapons inspector, not for attribution.

14. Pollack, *Arabs at War*, 219; see also Al-Marashi and Salama, *Iraq's Armed Forces*.

15. Interview with Iraqi scholar Ibrahim Al-Marashi, conducted via Zoom, May 27, 2021.

16. Cigar, *Saddam Hussein's Nuclear Vision*.

17. Khidhir Hamza with Jeff Stein, *Saddam's Bombmaker: The Terrifying Story of Iraq's Nuclear and Biological Weapons Agenda* (New York: Touchstone, 2000).

18. Interview with military historian Kevin Woods, conducted via Zoom, June 8, 2021. Iraq always claimed it pursued an RW exclusively for "defensive purposes." See Permanent Representative of Iraq to the United Nations to the Secretary-General, S/2001/450.

19. Interview with former Iraqi Republican Guard General Ra'ad Hamdani, in Woods, Murray, and Holaday, *Saddam's War*, 57.

20. "Applications of Nuclear Physics."

21. Ibid.

22. Ibid. The report merely says: "The container of the radioactive material is pulverized and airborne which effectively spreads its contents of Zirconium dependent upon wind speed and direction. We presume that the explosion can take place in two instances, the first on the earth's surface and the second 30 meters above the surface of the earth."

23. *Chemical, Biological, Radiological, and Nuclear Operations*, Field Manual, No. 3–11 (Washington, DC: Department of the Army, May 23, 2019), https://armypubs .army.mil/ProductMaps/PubForm/Details.aspx?PUB_ID=1007035; *Operations in Chemical, Biological, Radiological, and Nuclear Environments*, Joint Publication 3–11 (Arlington County, VA: Joint Chiefs of Staff, October 29, 2018), https://www.jcs .mil/Portals/36/Documents/Doctrine/pubs/jp3_11.pdf.

24. Cited in Anthony H. Cordesman, "Radiological Weapons as Means of Attack," November 2001, Center for Strategic and International Studies, https://csis -website-prod.s3.amazonaws.com/s3fs-public/legacy_files/files/media/csis/pubs/radi ological%5B1%5D.pdf.

25. "Applications of Nuclear Physics"; "Report of the Secretary-General on the Activities of the Special Commission Established by the Secretary-General pursuant to Paragraph 9 (b) (i) of Resolution 687 (1991)," April 11, 1996, S/RES/258, https: //www.un.org/Depts/unscom/sres96-258.htm.

26. Interview al-Marashi.

27. Interview with General Hamdani in Woods, Murray, and Holaday, *Saddam's War*, 55.

28. Hamza, *Saddam's Bombmaker*. Human-wave attacks describe an offensive infantry tactic in which an attacker conducts an unprotected frontal assault with densely concentrated formations against the enemy line, intended to overrun the defenders.

29. Ibrahim al-Marashi, "Saddam's Iraq and WMD Destruction: Iraq as a Case Study of a Middle Eastern Proliferant," *Middle East Review of International Affairs*, 8, No. 3 (September 2004): 83.

30. Interview with General Hamdani in Woods, Murray, and Holaday, *Saddam's War*, 56.

31. Eric Croddy, "Dusty Agents and the Iraqi Chemical Weapons Arsenal," Nuclear Threat Initiative, September 30, 2002, https://www.nti.org/analysis/articles/ dusty-agents-iraqi-chemical-weapons/.

32. Woods, Murray, and Holaday, *Saddam's War*, 138.

33. Rolf Ekéus, "The Lessons of UNSCOM and Iraq," *The Nonproliferation Review*, 23, No. 1–2 (2016): 131–146.

34. Al-Marashi, "Saddam's Iraq and WMD Destruction," 85.

35. Interview with al-Marashi.

36. Amy Smithson, *Germ Gambits: The Bioweapons Dilemma, Iraq and Beyond* (Stanford, CA: Stanford University Press, 2011), 2.

37. Interview with Hussain al-Shahristani, conducted via Zoom, June 2, 2021. In his memoir, Shahristani recalls that when Iraqi officials approached him to request support for the country's NW program, he was told: "You can contribute to making it, and you should know that it is the duty of every citizen to serve his country,

and those who refuse to serve their country do not deserve to be alive." Hussain al-Shahristani, *Free of Fear* (Author Solutions Inc., 2021), 81.

38. Kenneth Pollack, "Spies, Lies, and Weapons: What Went Wrong," *Atlantic Monthly*, January/February 2004, 22, cited in Joseph Cirincione, Jon B. Wolfsthal, and Miriam Rajkumar, *Deadly Arsenals: Nuclear, Biological and Chemical Threats* (Washington, DC: Brookings Institution Press, 2011), 332.

39. Interviews with multiple Iraqi scholars and historians on the Iran-Iraq war.

40. Målfrid Braut-Hegghammer, *Unclear Physics: Why Iraq and Libya Failed to Build Nuclear Weapons* (Ithaca, NY: Cornell University Press, 2016).

41. Ibid., 78.

42. Walsh, "Bombs Unbuilt," 92.

43. Interview with Shahristani.

44. Interview with a former IAEA inspector, not for attribution, conducted via Zoom, June 2, 2021.

45. Ibid.

46. Interview with Woods.

47. Interview with al-Marashi.

48. Jacques Hymans, *Achieving Nuclear Ambitions: Scientists, Politicians, and Proliferation* (Cambridge: Cambridge University Press, 2012), 102.

49. Ibid., 107.

50. The Al-Qa'Qaa' State Establishment was responsible for developing explosives and high-velocity measurement techniques.

51. "Applications of Nuclear Physics."

52. Braut-Hegghammer, *Unclear Physics*; Hymans, *Achieving Nuclear Ambitions*.

53. *Comprehensive Report of the Special Advisor to the Director of Central Intelligence on Iraq's Weapons of Mass Destruction*, vol. 3 (Central Intelligence Agency, September 2004), https://www.govinfo.gov/app/details/GPO-DUELFERREPORT.

54. Interview with Shahristani. Hymans, *Achieving Nuclear Ambitions*. The accounts of Humman abd-al Ghafur and UNSCOM inspectors Pearson, Barton, Trevan and Ritter equally contain no reference to the RW effort.

55. Interview with a former IAEA inspector; Gary Milhollin, "Comments on the Al Qa'qa Bomb," *Wisconsin Project on Nuclear Arms Control*, May 17, 2001, https://www.wisconsinproject.org/comments-on-the-al-qaqa-bomb/.

56. Hymans, *Achieving Nuclear Ambitions*, 106.

57. Gary B. Dillon, "The IAEA in Iraq: Past Activities and Findings," *IAEA Bulletin*, 44–2 (June 2002), https://www.iaea.org/sites/default/files/publications/magazines/bulletin/bull44-2/44201251316.pdf.

58. Broad, "Document Reveals 1987 Bomb Test by Iraq."

59. "Applications of Nuclear Physics."

60. H. Roth, "Conferences on Radiological Warfare," July 1948, OSTI Net.

61. Interview with a former IAEA inspector, not for attribution, conducted via Zoom, June 2, 2021.
62. "Applications of Nuclear Physics."
63. "Tenth Report," S/1995/1038.
64. Ibid.
65. "Iraq's Full, Final and Complete Disclosure (FFCD) Regarding Chemical Weapons to the United Nations Special Commission (UNSCOM)," 1996.
66. "Report of the Secretary-General," S/RES/258.
67. The Air Force Command, in its suggestions for lessening the weight of the bomb, further notes that it would not be possible to land with the bomb (with its present weight) after the flight if the mission is not accomplished, and that it would be difficult to arm the bomb with its present weight on the fuselage carrier as "there is no loading carriage which can lift such a weight," so an al-Jazzar rocket carriage should be used. It also recommends that the feasibility of using Soviet and Spanish 1,500, 3,000, 5,000 or 9,000 kg bombs for the same purpose be studied. "Applications of Nuclear Physics."
68. Douglas A. Kupersmith, "The Failure of Third World Air Power: Iraq and the War with Iran" (Master's thesis, School of Advanced Airpower Studies, Maxwell Air Force Base, 1993), https://permanent.fdlp.gov/websites/dodandmilitaryejournals/www.maxwell.af.mil/au/aul/aupress/SAAS_Theses/SAASS_Out/Kupersmith/kupersmith.pdf.
69. Interview with Shahristani.
70. Milhollin, "Comments on the Al Qa'qa Bomb."
71. "Applications of Nuclear Physics."
72. Braut-Hegghammer, *Unclear Physics*, 12.
73. Ibid., 9.
74. Interview with a former IAEA inspector, not for attribution, conducted via Zoom, June 2, 2021.
75. Smithson, *Germ Gambits*, 132.
76. Hymans, *Achieving Nuclear Ambitions*, 101, 107.
77. UN Security Council Resolution 687, S/RES/687. Ekéus, "The Lessons of UNSCOM and Iraq."
78. Ekéus, "The Lessons of UNSCOM and Iraq." Gudrun Harrer, *Dismantling the Iraqi Nuclear Programme: The Inspections of the International Atomic Energy Agency, 1991–1998* (New York: Routledge, 2013); Graham S. Pearson, *The Search For Iraq's Weapons of Mass Destruction: Inspection, Verification and Non-Proliferation* (New York: Palgrave MacMillan, 2005).
79. Written exchange with former UN weapons inspector.
80. "Statement of IAEA Director General to the UN Security Council on Inspections in Iraq," November 23, 1992, Iraq Watch, https://web.archive.org/web/

20150814143200/http://www.iraqwatch.org/un/IAEA/iaea-11-23-92.htm; "First Report on the Sixth IAEA On-Site Inspection in Iraq under Security Council Resolution 687 (1991)," September 22–30, 1991, Iraq Watch, https://web.archive.org/web/20150814143600/http://www.iraqwatch.org/un/IAEA/s-23122.htm; Smithson, *Germ Gambits*, 67.

81. Ekéus, "The Lessons of UNSCOM and Iraq." For an overview, see also Harrer, *Dismantling the Iraqi Nuclear Programme*; Pearson, *The Search For Iraq's Weapons of Mass Destruction*; Federation of American Scientists, "Deception Activities," Iraq, FAS Nuclear Information Project, updated November 2, 1998, https://fas.org/nuke/guide/iraq/deception.htm.

82. Smithson, *Germ Gambits*.

83. Ibid., 33.

84. Ibid.

85. Harrer, *Dismantling the Iraqi Nuclear Programme*, 102.

86. *Coalition Warfare: Gulf War Allies Differed in Chemical and Biological Threats Identified and in Use of Defensive Measures*, GAO-01-13 (Washington, DC: Government Accountability Office, 2001), 5.

87. Central Intelligence Agency, *Iraq's National Security Goals*, December 1988, Secret, Source: CIA Electronic Reading Room, released by Mandatory Declassification Review, https://nsarchive2.gwu.edu/NSAEBB/NSAEBB80/wmd02.pdf; Central Intelligence Agency, *Iraqi Ballistic Missile Developments*, July 1990, Top Secret, Source: CIA Electronic Reading Room, released under the Freedom of Information Act, https://nsarchive2.gwu.edu/NSAEBB/NSAEBB80/wmd03.pdf; Central Intelligence Agency, *Prewar Status of Iraq's Weapons of Mass Destruction*, March 1991, Top Secret, Source: Freedom of Information Act, https://nsarchive2.gwu.edu/NSAEBB/NSAEBB80/wmd04.pdf.

88. Interview with a former IAEA inspector, not for attribution, conducted via Zoom, June 2, 2021. The main activation that would have occurred during the irradiation of those targets would have been in the hafnium impurity content of the material, with neutron capture in stable Hf-180 (a very strong neutron absorber) leading to production of Hf-181, which has a six-week half-life.

89. Milhollin, "Comments on the Al Qa'qa' Bomb."

90. Smithson, *Germ Gambits*, 76.

91. Interview with Shahristani.

92. Ekéus, "The Lessons of UNSCOM and Iraq," 142.

93. UNSCOM inspector Rod Barton, quoted in Smithson, *Germ Gambits*, 92.

94. Interview with Gustavo Zlauvinen, conducted via Zoom, September 22, 2022.

95. "Tenth Report," S/1995/1038.

96. On the relationship between UNSCOM and the IAEA, see Harrer, *Dismantling the Iraqi Nuclear Programme*.

97. "Report of the Secretary-General on the Status of the Implementation of the Special Commission's Plan for the Ongoing Monitoring and Verification of Iraq's Compliance with Relevant Parts of Section of Security Council Resolution 687 (1991)," October 11, 1995, https://www.un.org/Depts/unscom/sres95-864.htm. The report does not state the precise date on which the Iraqis issued their ultimatum.

98. Interview with Gustavo Zlauvinen.

99. It should be noted, however, that there had already been some coming forth by Iraq *prior* to Kamel's defection, with the revelation of an offensive BW program in June 1995; that revelation, however, subsequently gave way to Iraqi zigzagging, threats, and ultimatums.

100. "Report of the Secretary-General," S/1995/864.

101. For further detail on the "chicken farm" documents and UNSCOM doubts regarding their completeness and nature of origin, see Federation of American Scientists, "Deception Activities."

102. Harrer, *Dismantling the Iraqi Nuclear Programme*.

103. A former UNSCOM official noted that it might have been the case that initial evidence of work on RWs was found in the trove of documents from the "chicken farm" and that Iraqi officials *then* briefed inspectors further on the evidence that had emerged. It might equally have been the case that Iraqi officials *preempted* the discovery of relevant documents by briefing ahead of an examination of the "chicken farm" files.

104. "Report of the Secretary-General," S/1995/864.

105. Pearson, *The Search For Iraq's Weapons of Mass Destruction*. The conundrum of missing documentation applies to the RW program, too. Although the 1988 Iraqi progress report detailing the test results is available, Iraqi officials claim that a separate report from Hussein Kamel to Saddam on the RWs was lost.

106. Interview with Gustavo Zlauvinen.

107. Written correspondence with unnamed former UNSCOM inspector, June 8, 2021.

Conclusion

The authors wish to express thanks to Jon Pike for his research assistance related to the issue of deterring RW use.

1. While not directly related to our study, there are some parallels between the life cycle of radiological weapons and neutron bombs. For example, although the United States, France, China, and possibly the Soviet Union tested the enhanced radiation weapon (ERW), it was pursued and then ultimately abandoned for some

of the same reasons as those we have observed with respect to RW innovation. These include the presence of a perceived technological imperative and of institutional or individual advocates. In the U.S. context, for instance, Matthew Evangelista has argued that "technological entrepreneurship" brought the neutron bomb from concept to reality fifteen years after its initial conception. He finds that the Army's reluctant advocacy of the ERW in a last-ditch effort to secure "any nuclear artillery at all" ultimately enabled the weapon to move toward production in 1973. See Evangelista, "Case Studies and Theories of the Arms Race," *Bulletin of Peace Proposals*, 17, No. 2 (1986): 199. Likewise, in the case of China's neutron bomb, Jonathan Ray observes that "an ERW coalition led by General Zhang Aiping championed the program from 1977 to 1984 but fell apart before the ERW's completion." Correspondingly, he finds that, "consistent with [Scott] Sagan's 'domestic politics' model, leaders from the military and labs were key ERW advocates." See Ray, "Red China's 'Capitalist Bomb': Inside the Chinese Neutron Bomb Program" (Washington, DC: National Defense University, 2015), 2, 18. In contrast to the case of RWs, however, normative considerations appear to have played a much larger role in the demise of the neutron bomb. For instance, in the United States the tremendous international backlash against the Reagan administration's plans to deploy the neutron bomb in Europe led to the decision to produce but limit the stationing of neutron bombs to the United States. See, for example, Leslie Gelb, "Reagan Orders Production of 2 Types of Neutron Arms for Stockpiling in the U.S.," *The New York Times*, August 9, 1981, https://www.nytimes.com/1981/08/09/us/reagan-orders-production-of-2-types-of-neutron-arms-for-stockpiling-in-the-us.html. Similarly, France decided to forego plans to manufacture ERWs in 1986 in part because of West German concerns that the new weapon would probably be used only on German territory. See "France Rules Out Manufacturing a Neutron Bomb in Near Future," *The New York Times*, July 11, 1986, https://www.nytimes.com/1986/07/11/world/france-rules-out-manufacturing-a-neutron-bomb-in-near-future.html. In China, meanwhile, Ray observes, "By the time the Central Committee called for the ERW's completion in 1986 . . . a taboo against the weapon was well established." See Ray, "Red China's 'Capitalist Bomb,'" 29. It is worth considering whether normative considerations such as these would have played a similarly significant role in the demise of RWs had there been more robust public debate around the potential for RWs to be deployed.

2. See Evangelista, *Innovation and the Arms Race*, 52.

3. See King, "A Weapon Too Far," 8.

4. Niobium formerly was known as columbium.

5. Perhaps more surprisingly, there is no evidence that the U.S. intelligence community was aware of the United Kingdom's exploration of RWs, although it is far from certain if they would have cared had they been aware.

6. Also noteworthy was the role played by writers and other influencers of pop-

ular culture, who helped to create an environment conducive to the propagation of the concept of RWs.

7. See, for example, Ridenour, "How Effective Are Radioactive Poisons in Warfare?," 200; and Parker, "War without Death."

8. This point is noted by King, "A Weapon Too Far," 15.

9. While this general finding applies across all the cases, there were some notable dissenters in the United States, including Ernest Lawrence and Joseph Hamilton.

10. Horowitz and Narang, "Poor Man's Atomic Bomb?"

11. In the Iraqi case, RWs initially were seen as a potentially useful additional nonconventional weapon to deploy against Iran. Results from the tests of the prototype RW, however, were discouraging.

12. It is difficult to discern the degree to which there was high level support for the Egyptian RW program. As we have indicated in the Egyptian case study, President Nasser and his senior military commanders generally welcomed military innovation but tended to promote a variety of projects without setting clear priorities or committing the financial resources and political capital necessary for their achievement. This often led to the initiation of research but not sustained development.

13. Smith, *American Biodefense*. As noted previously, neutron bombs rely on bursts of high energy neutrons rather than radioactive fallout to achieve their lethal effects.

14. King, "A Weapon Too Far," 22.

15. Bernard Brodie, "The Anatomy of Deterrence," U.S. Air Force Project RAND Research Memorandum RM-2218, July 23, 1958, https://www.rand.org/content/dam/rand/pubs/research_memoranda/2008/RM2218.pdf.

16. Ibid., iv.

17. Ibid., 25.

18. Ibid.

19. Ibid., 26

20. *Conference on Methods for Studying the Psychosocial Effects of Unconventional Weapons*, research memorandum, RM-120 (Santa Monica, CA: RAND Corporation, January 26–28, 1949), https://apps.dtic.mil/sti/citations/tr/AD0108425.

21. Ibid, 55.

22. This assessment is based on one of the author's conversations with senior U.S. government officials and with particular respect to the DPRK.

23. One can point to a similar failure by the U.S. intelligence community to recognize the possible attractiveness to Iraq of a technology long discarded by the U.S. to enrich uranium: calutron electromagnetic isotope separation. See Federation of American Scientists "Nuclear Weapons," Iraq, FAS Nuclear Information Project, updated May 31, 2012, https://nuke.fas.org/guide/iraq/nuke/program.htm.

24. The authors are grateful to Jeffrey Lewis for his insights about these cases.

25. Quoted in Benjamin Buch and Scott D. Sagan, "Our Red Lines and Theirs: New Information Reveals Why Saddam Hussein Never Used Chemical Weapons in the Gulf War," *Foreign Policy*, December 13, 2013, https://foreignpolicy.com/2013/12/13/our-red-lines-and-theirs/.

26. Ibid., 1; and Kevin M. Woods, David D. Palkki, and Mark E. Stout, *The Saddam Tapes: The Inner Workings of a Tyrants Regime, 1978–2001* (Cambridge, UK: Cambridge University Press, 2011), 221–222.

27. "Obama Warns Syria Not to Cross 'Red Line,'" *CNN*, August 21, 2012, https://www.cnn.com/2012/08/20/world/meast/syria-unrest/index.html. For an in-depth analysis of Syrian chemical weapons use, see Joby Warrick, *Red Line: The Unraveling of Syria and America's Race to Destroy the Most Dangerous Arsenal in the World* (New York, Doubleday, 2021).

28. See Wyn Bowen, Jeffrey Knopf, and Matthew Moran, "The Obama Administration and Syrian Chemical Weapons: Deterrence, Compellence, and the Limits of the 'Resolve plus Bombs' Formula," *Security Studies*, 29, No. 5 (2020): 797–831.

29. On this issue, see Jeffrey William Knopf, "Russia Isn't Likely to Use Chemical Weapons in Ukraine—Unless Putin Grows Desperate," *The Conversation*, April 12, 2022, https://theconversation.com/russia-isnt-likely-to-use-chemical-weapons-in-ukraine-unless-putin-grows-desperate-180534. See also Hanna Notte, "Why Deterring Russian Use of Chemical Weapons Is a Challenge," *Washington Post*, April 18, 2022, https://www.washingtonpost.com/outlook/2022/04/18/chemical-weapons-deterrence-russia-ukraine/.

30. Scott Sagan, "The Commitment Trap: Why the United States Should Not Use Nuclear Threats to Deter Biological and Chemical Weapons Attacks," *International Security*, 24, No. 4 (2000): 85–115.

31. Robert Jervis, *The Meaning of the Nuclear Revolution: Statecraft and the Prospect of Armageddon* (Ithaca, NY: Cornell University Press, 1990), 215.

32. Alan Cullison, "Inside Al-Qaeda's Hard Drive," *The Atlantic*, September 2004, https://www.theatlantic.com/magazine/archive/2004/09/inside-al-qaeda-s-hard-drive/303428/.

33. See Goldenberg and Potter, "Russian Misinformation about Ukrainian Radiological Weapons Capabilities and Intentions."

34. We are aware of only one article prior to 2022 that discusses the possibility of Ukrainian interest in a radiological weapon. It is by Sergey Goncharov and was published in 2016 in the journal of the Center for Energy and Security (Moscow). It maintains that work on RWs was conducted during the Soviet period on the territory of the Ukrainian republic and asserts that the current regime retains "all the 'ingredients' to create a full-fledged combat radiological weapon, starting with stocks of highly radioactive substances" (23). See Goncharov, "Radiological Weapons for the Armed Forces of Ukraine: Propaganda and Political Bluff or Potential Reality

in the Near Future?" (in Russian), *Yaderny Klub*, 3–4, No. 31–32 (2016): 22–24.

35. See William Potter, "The Fallout from Russia's Attack on Ukrainian Nuclear Facilities," *War on the Rocks*, March 10, 2022, https://warontherocks.com/2022/03/fallout-from-russias-attack-on-ukrainian-nuclear-facilities-military-environmental-legal-and-normative/.

36. The military rationale for the seizure is discussed in more detail in Potter, "The Fallout from Russia's Attack on Ukrainian Nuclear Facilities."

37. Mary Glantz, "Russia's New Nuclear Threat: Power Plants as Weapons," United States Institute of Peace, August 24, 2022, https://www.usip.org/publications/2022/08/russias-new-nuclear-threat-power-plants-weapons.

38. "The Main Topics of the Hour: 9:30," *Radio Sputnik*, March 6, 2002, https://radiosputnik.ria.ru/20220306/1776887012.html.

39. See also Alexei Ivanov, "Our Soldiers Liquidated the 'Nuclear Ukraine Project' in Time," *Zavtra*, March 6, 2022, https://zavtra.ru/events/nashi_vojska_svoevremenno_likvidirovali_proekt-yadernaya_ukraina?; and "RF Ministry of Defense: SBU Is Preparing a Provocation with a Radioactive Contamination in the Vicinity of Kharkiv," *TASS*, March 6, 2022, https://tass.ru/armiya-i-opk/13989709.

40. "Russia's Defense Chief Warns of "Dirty Bomb" Provocation, *CNBC*, October 23, 2022, https:www.cnbc.com/2022/10/23/russias-defense-chief-warns of-dirty-bomb-provocation.html. General Valery Gerasimov, chief of the Russian general staff, also called on his U.S. and British counterparts to make the same case. See Tom Nichols, "Russia's 'Dirty Bomb' Ploy," *The Atlantic*, October 24, 2022, https://www.theatlantic.com/newsletters/archive/2022/10/russias-dirty-bomb-ploy/6771854.

41. David Sanger, "The State Dept. Warns That 'Dirty Bomb' Claims Could Be a Pretext for Russian Escalation," Russia-Ukraine War, *New York Times*, October 25, 2022, https://www.nytimes.com/live/2022/10/24/world/-russia-ukraine-war-news#dirty-bomb-russia.

42. Neil MacFarquhar, "Putin Repeats Unfounded Accusations That the West Has Labeled Disinformation," Russia-Ukraine War, *New York Times*, October 26, 2022, https//www.nytimes.com/live/2022/10/26/world/russia-ukraine-war-news#putin-dirty-bomb-disinformation. For more on President Putin's remarks, see "Russia Comments on Ukrainian 'Dirty Bomb' Allegations: Moscow Knows Roughly Where the Weapon Is Being Produced, the President Claimed," *RT*, October 27, 2022, https://www.rt.com/russia/565473-putin-dirty-bomb-details/.

43. Office of the Spokesperson, "Joint Statement on Ukraine: Media Note," U.S. Department of State, October 23, 20022, https://www.state.gov/joint-statemntohn-lukriane-2/. The statement also notes that the defense ministers of France, the United Kingdom, and the United States conveyed a similar message to Russian Defense Minister Shoigu.

44. The letter is reproduced in Matthew Bunn, "Russia's 'Dirty Bomb' Disinformation, Annotated," *Bulletin of the Atomic Scientists*, December 1, 2022, https://thebulletin.org/2022/12/russias-dirty-bomb-disinformation-annotated. A few months later, in the context of Western states pledging the delivery of advanced battle tanks to Ukraine, Russia's accusations regarding Ukrainian acquisition of a "dirty bomb" took yet another form. A senior Russian official claimed that Leopard 2 tanks, alongside Bradley and Marder fighting vehicles, are "armed with APCR shells with uranium cores" and that Russia will view Western shipments of such "depleted uranium ammunition" to Ukraine as "use of dirty bombs." See "Diplomat predupredil Zapad o posledstviyakh postavok VSU boepripasov s uranom," *RIA Novosti*, January 25, 2023, https://ria.ru/20230125/snaryad-1847362826.html. The statement was disingenuous since depleted uranium (DU), a byproduct of making fuel for nuclear reactors and nuclear weapons, is considerably less radioactive than natural uranium. DU has been commonly used in the manufacture of munitions designed to pierce armor plating and as a component of tank armor. See "Depleted Uranium," International Atomic Energy Agency, https://www.iaea.org/topics/spent-fuel-management/depleted-uranium. According to the International Coalition to Ban Uranium Weapons, numerous countries have developed or imported depleted uranium munitions including the United States, Russia, the United Kingdom, India, Pakistan, France, China, Bahrain, Jordan, Israel, Taiwan, Saudi Arabia, Turkey, and South Korea. See "Depleted Uranium Weapons—State of Affairs 2022," International Coalition to Ban Uranium Weapons, www.icbuw.eu/depleted-uranium-weapons-state-of-affairs-2022/.

45. Bunn, "Russia's 'Dirty Bomb' Disinformation, Annotated."

46. Ibid.

47. "Address by the President of the Russian Federation," Kremlin.ru, September 21, 2022, cited by Simon Saradzhyan, "Putin's Increasingly Loose Talk on Use of Nukes," *Russia Matters*, November 10, 2022, https://www.russiamatters.org/analysis/putins-increasingly-loose-talk-use-nukes.

48. See, for example, Michael E. O'Hanlon and Bruce Riedel, "The Russian-Ukraine War May Be Bad News for Nuclear Nonproliferation," Brookings Institution, March 29, 2022, https://www.brookings.edu/blog/order-from-chaos/2022/03/29/the-russia-ukraine-war-may-be-bad-news-for-nuclear-nonproliferation/; and Andreas Umland, "Putin's War Is a Death Blow to Nuclear Nonproliferation," *Foreign Policy*, March 21, 2022, https://foreignpolicy.com/2022/03/21/nuclear-weapons-war-russia-ukraine-putin-nonproliferation-treaty-npt/. A retrospective variant of this argument is that had Ukraine been able to retain the nuclear assets it inherited at the time of the Soviet Union's collapse, Moscow would have been more wary about intervening militarily. This argument, however, ignores the fact that Ukraine never had full operational control over the nuclear weapons on its territory. Moreover, had

Kyiv sought to achieve such control in the face of both Russian and U.S. opposition, it might well have precipitated Russian military action long before the current war. For an analysis of Ukraine's denuclearization decision-making, see Mariana Budjeryn, *Inheriting the Bomb: The Collapse of the USSR and the Nuclear Disarmament of Ukraine* (Baltimore, MD: Johns Hopkins University Press, 2023); and William C. Potter, *The Politics of Nuclear Renunciation: The Cases of Belarus, Kazakhstan, and Ukraine*, Occasional Paper No. 21, Stimson Center, Washington, DC, April 1995.

49. Jeffrey W. Knopf, "Why the Ukraine War Does Not Mean More Countries Should Seek Nuclear Weapons," *Bulletin of Atomic Scientists*, April 12, 2022, https://thebulletin.org/2022/04/why-the-ukraine-war-does-not-mean-more-countries-should-seek-nuclear-weapons/.

50. This evidence is discussed in William C. Potter and Jeffrey Lewis, "Cheap and Dirty Bombs," *Foreign Policy*, February 17, 2014, https://foreignpoliocly.com/2014/02/17/cheap-and-dirty-bombs/.

51. In this regard, it should be noted that Russian propaganda about Ukraine's alleged pursuit of RWs, while widespread in February and March 2022, was mainly confined to Russian and apparently intended to justify the invasion to a domestic audience. We are grateful to Matthew Goldenberg for calling our attention to this distinction.

52. United Nations, Conference on Disarmament, "Agreed Joint USSR-United States Proposal on Major Elements of a Treaty Prohibiting the Development, Production, Stockpiling and Use of Radiological Weapons," CD/31, July 9, 1979, https://www.un-ilibrary.org/content/books/9789210579834s027-c011. For a detailed analysis of the negotiations leading to the 1979 draft accord, see Kucharski, Bidgood, and Warnke, "Negotiating the Draft Radiological Weapons Convention."

53. See, for example, Nina Tannenwald, "Is Using Nuclear Weapons Still Taboo?" *Foreign Policy*, July 1, 2002, https://foreignpolicy.com/2022/07/01/nuclear-war-taboo-arms-control-russia-ukraine-deterrrence/. It is important to note that the line between conventional and nuclear weapons use has been blurred by formal Russian declaratory policy as well as recent saber-rattling.

54. See Goldenberg and Potter, "Russian Misinformation about Ukrainian Radiological Weapons Capabilities and Intentions"; and "The War in Ukraine: Implications for the Use and Proliferation of Chemical and Biological Weapons," Center for Nonproliferation Studies webinar featuring Dr. Jeffrey Knopf, Dr. Filippa Lentzos, Dr. Philipp Bleek, and Dr. Hanna Notte, April 25, 2022, https://nonproliferation.org/cns-webinar-series-nuclear-threats-and-the-war-in-ukraine/#webinar04.

55. It is beyond the scope of this study to explore the variation across societies of the transmission link between education and popular culture and policy decisions regarding military innovation.

56. According to one caption (December 26, 1947), "This darkness was caused

by atomic rubbish, dumped over your valley.... This may take a thousand years [to clear up].... We Boys at Oak Ridge are mighty sorry about this—but—Chin up!! Keep smiling!!" At its peak, *Lil' Abner* was estimated to have a daily readership of over 60 million. The relevant episodes are available at https://www,gocomics.com/lilabner/1947/12/11.

57. See Brians, *Nuclear Holocausts: Atomic War in Fiction, 1895–1984*.

58. Tony Shaw, "The BBC, the State and Cold War Culture: The Case of Television's *The War Game* (1965)," *The English Historical Review*, 121, No. 494 (December 2006): 1351–1384, https://doi.org/10.1093/her/cel282.

59. *Threads*, a 1984 British-Australian television dramatization of the effects of a US-Soviet nuclear exchange, also had a very wide viewership and has been called "Britain's answer to *The Day After*." See quote by Leonard Maltin in "Threads (1984 film)," *Wikipedia*, https://en.wikipedia.org/wiki/Threads_(1984_film)#Production_and_themes.

60. Jesse Beckett, "The Movie 'The Day After' Put Ronald Reagan in Damage Control over Nuclear Weapons," *War History Online*, October 25, 2021, https://www.warhistoryonline.com/war-articles/ronald-reagan-the-day-after.html.

61. It is unclear what impact a public relations campaign mounted by the Reagan administration to counter the film's anti-nuclear weapons narrative had on public opinion.

62. Stanley Feldman and Lee Sigelman, "The Political Impact of Prime-Time Television: 'The Day After,'" *The Journal of Politics*, 47, No. 2 (1985): 575.

63. See, for example, Parker, "War without Death"; De Roos, "What Are We Doing about Our Deadly Atomic Garbage?"; Kugelmass "Our Silent Mystery Weapon"; Armagnac, "What You Should Know about 'RW'"; "Radiological Warfare," *Officers' Call*; and Louis N. Ridenour, "How Effective Are Radioactive Poisons in Warfare?," 199–202, 224.

64. See, for example, a clip from Russian state television of May 1, 2022, at https://twitter.com/visegrad24/status/1520850902915108869. See also Mary Illyushina, Miriam Berger, and Timothy Bella, "Russian TV Shows Simulation of Britain and Ireland Wiped Out by a Nuke," *The Washington Post*, May 3, 2022.

65. MacDonald, "Solution Unsatisfactory," 86. Italics in the original.

Index

Abdel Rahman, Ibrahim Hilmy, 87
Action Team (IAEA), 109, 126, 127, 128–29
Ad Hoc Committee on Chemical, Biological and Radiological Warfare (United States), 37–38
adoption-capacity theory, 12
Advisory Committee on Human Radiation Experiments, 8
Advisory Committee on Uranium, 23
Air Force (United States), 34
Air Force Command, 199n67
Al-Basra (Iraq), 113
Aldrin, Andrew, 42
Al-Faw peninsula (Iraq), 112
Allison, Graham, 10–11
Almquist, Peter, 42
Al-Muthanna complex (Iraq), 119
Al-Qa'Qaa (Iraq), 119
Al-Tuwaitha Nuclear Research Center (Iraq), 108–9, 121, 122, 127–28
americium-241, 163n17

Amit, Meir, 104
animals, testing on, 47–48
Arab-Israeli War, 111
area denial: chemical weapons for, 115; goldilocks zone for, 31–32; against Iranian human-wave attacks, 113–15; of Iraq, 113–15, 139; isotopes for, 31; radioactive dust for, 20–21; radiological weapons (RWs) for, 28, 89–92; weapons for, 114
Armed Forces Special Weapons Project (AFSWP) (United States), 26–27, 36
Army Chemical Corps (ACC) (United States), 28–29, 30, 35, 36, 97, 140
Assad, Bashar al-, 147
Astounding Science Fiction (magazine), 19, 20, 21
Aswan High Dam (Egypt), 81
atomic bomb/warfare, 18–20, 22, 28–30, 45, 58–59, 60–62, 64–69
Atomic Energy Act, 70

209

Index

Atomic Energy Agency (Iraq), 121
Atomic Energy Commission (AEC) (Iraq), 26–27, 97
Atomic Energy Establishment (Egypt), 92
Atomic Energy for Military Purposes, 43
Atomic Energy Research Establishment (United Kingdom), 15
atomic fission, 22, 23–24, 59
Atomnaia Energiia (Atomic energy), 55–56
Australia, 66
Aziz, Tariq, 129–30, 147

Baghdad Pact, 81
Baker, James, 146–47
Balfour Declaration, 189n22
ballistic missiles, 84–85, 88–89, 103–4
Balzer, Harley, 42
Banerjee, Anindita, 41
Barker, M. E., 33
Barton, Rod, 128
Beaton, Leonard, 90
Benford, Gregory, 21
Ben-Gal, Joseph, 76–77, 91, 100
Ben-Gurion, David, 16, 76, 104
Bernstein, Barton, 59
Biang, Michel Havier, 150
Biden, Joseph, 156
biological weapons (BWs), 71, 97–98, 128
Bradbury, Ray, 158
Braut-Hegghammer, Målfrid, 117–18, 125
Brodie, Bernard, 144–45
Bulletin of the Atomic Scientists (journal), 27, 37, 159
Bunn, Matthew, 150
Burgess, Guy, 58

Cairncross, John, 44, 58–59
californium-252, 163n17
Campbell, John W., 1, 2, 19–20, 21–22, 135, 160
Capp, Al, 27–28, 158
Center for Nonproliferation Studies, 163n17
Central Intelligence Agency (CIA) (United States), 38–39
cesium-137, 100, 122, 163n17
Chemical Defense Research Department (United Kingdom), 62
Chemical Institute of the Red Army (Soviet Union), 43
chemical weapons (CWs): for area denial, 115; deterrence of, 146–47; of Egypt, 88, 90–91, 97–98; of Iraq, 91, 112, 119, 128, 147; radiological weapons (RWs) and, 70–71; radiological weapons (RWs) comparison to, 143; as special weapons, 116; of Syria, 147; threat of, 53; of the United States, 34, 35–36; of Yemen, 91
Chernobyl nuclear power plant, 149
Chertok, Boris, 41, 51
Chiefs of Staff (COS) committee (United Kingdom), 60–61, 65–66
China, 81
Cline, Ray, 103
Clinton, Bill, 8
cluster munitions, 49–50
cobalt, 90
cobalt-59, 55, 181n90
cobalt-60, 100–102, 122, 163n17, 181n90, 192–93n95
Cockcroft, John, 62–63
Cohen, Avner, 87
Cold War, 81, 155–56
Colliers (magazine), 27, 159

Commission for Conventional
  Armaments (United Nations), 38
Committee on Disarmament (CD),
  155–56
Compton, Arthur, 23–25
contamination, purpose of, 113. *See also*
  area denial
Cook, Stephen A., 98
Cordesman, Anthony, 89–90
Corner, John, 184n31
Cornog, Robert, 20
Coronet (magazine), 27, 159
Creasy, William, 70
Czechoslovakia, 81

The Day After (film), 158–59
Dayan, Moshe, 85
Defense Research Policy Committee
  (United Kingdom), 61, 65–66
Defense Services Panel (United
  Kingdom), 58
Department of Defense (United
  States), 28, 114
depleted uranium (DU), 206n44
deterrence, 144–49, 154–55
diffusion, 6
Dimona reactor (Egypt), 85–88
dirty bombs, 6, 150, 152, 206n44
Dugway Proving Ground (United
  States), 20, 29, 32–33, 35

economics, weapons innovation and,
  11–12
Egypt: accusations against, 102–3; air
  force of, 88–89; area denial and,
  89–92; Aswan High Dam of, 81;
  Atomic Energy Establishment
  of, 92; ballistic missiles of, 84–85,
  88–89, 103–4; biological weapons
  of, 97–98; bureaucratic political
determinants of, 94–100; challenges
  of, 106; chemical weapons and,
  88, 90–91, 97–98; China and, 81;
  cobalt-60 and, 100–102; comparative
  perspective regarding, 105–7;
  deterrence of, 88–89; exploratory
  phase of, 77; fallout from Otto
  Joklik affair within, 102–5, 106; Free
  Officers' coup in, 80, 81; influence
  of, 81; international security
  imperatives within, 80–83; Israel
  and, 83–88, 89–90, 104–5; Izlis of,
  97–98; Jabal Hamzah launch facility
  of, 84; mustard bombs of, 90–91;
  nonconventional weapons within,
  92–93; nuclear program of, 87–88,
  95; political prioritization within,
  94–98; Project Ibis of, 15–16, 76, 83–
  84, 88, 94–98, 100–102, 103–5, 187n2;
  radiological warheads for missiles
  of, 84–85; radiological weapons
  (RWs) development by, 2, 137,
  187n2; radiological weapons (RWs)
  drivers in, 80–88; radiological
  weapons (RWs) inhibitors in, 98–
  102; radiological weapons (RWs)
  overview of, 15–16, 75–80; role of
  prestige within, 141; Soviet Union
  and, 82–83; Suez crisis within, 81;
  technical constraints within, 100–
  102; topography of, 89–90; trash
  bomb of, 96; warhead development
  by, 16; weaponization challenges
  within, 100–102; weapons of terror
  of, 83–88
Egyptian Atomic Energy Commission
  (Egypt), 87
Egyptian General Aero Organization
  (Egypt), 95
Eichmann, Adolf, 104

Index

Einstein, Albert, 19
Ekéus, Rolf, 128
Elbahtimy, Hassan, 87
Eliot, T. S., 1
enhanced radiation weapon (ERW), 201–2n1
Evangelista, Matthew, 4–5, 42, 53, 131, 202n1
Experimental Design Bureau 240 (OKB 240) (Soviet Union), 49

Fahmy, Nabil, 188n8
Fermi, Enrico, 23–24, 71
Ferris, Jesse, 83
15th Program (Soviet Union), 46
1st Program (Soviet Union), 46
fog of war, 147
food, radiological weapons (RWs) poisoning of, 23, 24
France, 202n1
Free Officers (Egypt), 80, 81
Fuchs, Klaus, 2, 14–15, 44, 64
full, final, and complete disclosures (FFCD) (Iraq), 124

gamma-emitters, 31
General Accounting Office (United States), 127
Generator (Soviet Union), 51
George, Alexander, 4
Geran' series (Soviet Union), 51–52
Germany, 2, 22–23, 59, 69, 104, 138
Goercke, Heidi, 77
goldilocks zone, 186n64
Goncharov, Sergey, 204n34
Goncharov, V. P., 50
Görcke, Paul, 97
Gorshkov, S. G., 48, 53
Groves, Leslie, 23–24
GSKB-47 (Soviet Union), 49

Guardian (newspaper), 91
Guterres, António, 150

Hakim Amer, Abd al-, 94, 192n86
Halperin, Morton, 10–11
Hamdani, Ra'ad, 113, 115
Hamilton, Joseph Gilbert, 24, 25, 26–27, 28, 29, 36, 62, 71, 72
Hamza, Khidhir, 112, 115
Hanford reactor (United States), 32, 136
Hankey, Maurice, 58
Harel, Isser, 76, 85, 104
Harrer, Gudrun, 127
Hatcher, Jack, 20
Hayashi, Kashiba, 56
Heikal, Mohamed Hussein, 80, 81, 82, 92, 93
Heinlein, Robert, 1, 2, 14, 19–22, 135, 158
Heinsenmaa (Suri) (Soviet Union), 47
Hines, John, 42
Hiroshima, 140
Holland, Albert, 32
Holloway, David, 58
Horowitz, Michael, 12, 52, 143
Hussein, Saddam, 2, 16, 93, 111–13, 120, 126–27, 146–47
Hutchinson, William, 26–27

Ibrahim, Ghassen, 121
India, 188n8
innovation. *See also* military innovation
innovation, defined, 6
Institute of Organic Chemistry of the Academy of Sciences of the Soviet Union (Soviet Union), 43
International Atomic Energy Agency (IAEA), 8–9, 109, 126, 127, 128–30, 150–51, 157–58
international security: changes in, 142; considerations regarding, 137–39,

142; Egypt and, 80–83; Iraq and, 111–13, 138–39; military innovation and, 10; overview of, 10; Soviet Union and, 138; United Kingdom and, 68–69; United States and, 138
invention, defined, 6
Iran, 116
Iran-Iraq War, 111–13, 116, 118
Iraq: aerial bomb of, 120; Al-Basra in, 113; Al-Faw peninsula of, 112; Al-Muthanna complex of, 119; Al-Qa'Qaa of, 119; Al-Tuwaitha Nuclear Research Center in, 108–9, 121, 122, 127–28; area denial by, 113–15, 139; Atomic Energy Agency within, 121; Atomic Energy Commission (AEC) of, 26–27, 97; biological weapons of, 128; bureaucratic political determinants of, 117–19, 120–21; chemical weapons of, 91, 112, 119, 128, 147; comparative perspective regarding, 131–33; domestic determinants of, 139; foreign intelligence failures regarding, 126–28; full, final, and complete disclosures (FFCD) of, 124; impunity of, 116; international community and, 126–31; international inspectors in, 128–29; international security considerations of, 138–39; international security imperatives of, 111–13; Iran-Iraq War and, 111–13, 116, 118; LD-250 aerial chemical bomb (Muthanna-4) of, 124; Military Industrialization Corporation (MIC) of, 108, 119, 121, 140; near-immunity and, 115–17; nonconventional weapons of, 117, 121; normative considerations of, 115–17; Nuclear Research Center of, 108; obstruction by, 126–28, 131–32; Operation Karbala V, 113; Osirak reactor of, 156; overpromising by, 125; Qa'Qaa'-28 (Nasser 29 bomb) of, 120, 123, 124; R-400 of, 124; radiological weapons (RWs) development by, 2, 133, 136; radiological weapons (RWs) drivers of, 111–19; radiological weapons (RWs) inhibitors in, 120–24; radiological weapons (RWs) origin in, 118–19; radiological weapons (RWs) overview of, 16, 108–11, 131–33; radiological weapons (RWs) program ending in, 125; radiological weapons (RWs) program reveal by, 129–31, 132; radiological weapons (RWs) support in, 143; scientific work within, 120–21; Tammuz-2 in, 122; technical constraints within, 122–24, 131; uranium and, 203n23; weak state capacity of, 117–18, 122, 125; weaponization challenges of, 123–24; weapons use of, 116; WMD program of, 109, 120, 146; zirconium-95 use within, 122–23
Iraqi Atomic Energy Commission (IAEC), 110
iridium-192, 163n17
"Is Death Dust America's Secret Weapon?" (Campbell), 21–22
Islamic Revolution, 111
isotopes, types of, 31
Israel: civil defense exercises by, 2; disagreements regarding, 103–5; Egypt and, 83–88, 89–90, 104–5; Germany and, 104; nuclear pursuit of, 83–88; reaction to Joklik affair by, 102–3; rocket testing of, 86; Shavit II of, 86
Izlis (Egypt), 97–98

Jabal Hamzah launch facility (Egypt), 84
Jafar, Jafar Dhia, 119
Jervis, Robert, 148
Joklik, Otto: characteristics of, 96; departure of, 79; fallout from, 102–5; leadership of, 96–97, 98, 107; overview of, 75–77; Project Ibis and, 94–98; published works of, 192–93n95; quote of, 84; testimony of, 15, 84–85, 90, 91–92, 93, 100–101, 103–4, 140, 188n8; work of, 86

Kamel, Hussein, 16, 110, 111, 112, 115, 118–19, 125, 129–30, 131, 132, 133, 136
Kanyon (Russia), 56
Kapustin Yar (Soviet Union), 51
Kennedy, John F., 76, 81–82, 91
Kesarev, Vasillii Vladimirovich, 46
Khalil, Mahmoud, 86, 94
Kharkiv Institute of Physics and Technology, 149
Khlopin, Vitaly, 42–43
Khrushchev, Nikita, 40–41, 83
Khuzestan Province (Iran), 111
kinetic frame, 35
kinetic warfare, 35, 143
King, William, 58, 59–60, 72, 73, 74, 144
Kit vessel, 47
Knopf, Jeffrey, 152
KOBALTRON, 97
Komer, Robert, 86, 103
Konovets Island (Soviet Union), 178–79n46
Korolev, S. P., 50–51
Kosolov, V. V., 50
Krause, Joachim, 52–53
Kugelmass, J. Alvin, 66

Laboratory B (Snezhinsk) (Soviet Union), 44, 46
Lake Ladoga (Soviet Union), 47, 48
Latter, Albert, 56
Lavrov, Sergey, 150
Lawrence, Ernest O., 22, 25, 27, 29, 30, 32, 33–34, 38, 71, 115
LD-250 aerial chemical bomb (Muthanna-4) (Iraq), 124
LeMay, Curtis, 25, 33, 34
Li'l Abner (Capp), 27–28, 158, 170n58, 207–8n56
Lilienthal, David, 27, 36
liquid air bombs, 49, 50
Logachev, V. A., 50

MacArthur, Douglas, 33
MacDonald, Anson (Robert Heinlein pseudonym), 21, 160
Mahmoud, Mohamed Sedky, 94
Makarinsaari (Malyi) (Soviet Union), 47
Mallory, Charles, 52–53
Manhattan Project, 18, 20, 24–25
Marashi, Ibrahim Al-, 112, 116, 119
Marley, William G., 62, 63–64, 65, 67, 70, 72
Maslov, V., 42
Matsuda, Hajime, 56
MAUD Committee (United Kingdom), 58, 60
May, Alan Nunn, 2, 14, 43, 44–45, 59, 138, 141
Mayak plant, 46
McCloy, John, 85
McCone, John, 103
McCormack, James, 26, 27, 29, 33, 36–37
Meir, Golda, 76, 85, 87

Metallurgical Laboratory (Met Lab) (University of Chicago), 22–23, 24, 25
military, change capacity regarding, 11–12
Military Industrialization Corporation (MIC) (Iraq), 108, 119, 121, 140
military innovation, 9–13
Military Unit 99795 (Soviet Union), 48
Minder, Walter, 100
Ministry of Chemical Industry (Soviet Union), 43
Mukerikku (Myuarka) (Soviet Union), 47
mustard bombs, 90–91

Nadim, Elsayed, 94
Nagasaki, 140
Narang, Neil, 52, 143
Nasser, Gamal Abdel: concerns regarding, 93–94; Israel and, 80–81; leadership of, 81–82, 83, 87, 91, 92, 96, 98–99; quote of, 191–92n81; viewpoint of, 2, 141, 203n12
National Defense Research Council, 20
Navy (Soviet Union), 45–46, 47
Navy (United States), 34
near-immunity, perceptions of, 115–17
Nebenzia, Vassily, 150
neutron bombs, 7, 201–2n11
neutron ship, 22
The New Scientist, 101
New York Times, 109
Nichols, K. D., 26
NIIChimMash, 49
niobium-95, 46, 122, 137
non-state actors, 3, 7
North Korea, 2, 153
Noyes, Albert, 27, 28

Noyes Committee, 31
nuclear deterrence, 144–49, 154–55
nuclear physics, developments in, 19–20
Nuclear Research Center (Iraq), 108
nuclear war, avoidance of, 157
nuclear waste, processing of, 31
nuclear weapons, 6–7, 12, 14, 115–16, 153. *See also specific weapons*
Nuclear Weapons and Man (Matsuda and Hayashi), 56

Oak Ridge National Laboratory, 27
Obama, Barack, 147, 148
Object 230 (Soviet Union), 47, 48
Ocean Multipurpose System Status-6 (Russia), 56
Officer's Call (journal), 27, 33–34, 159
Omega Plan, 81
Operation Damocles (Israel), 76
Operation Karbala V (Iraq), 113
Operation Peppermint, 24, 43
Oppenheimer, Robert, 23–24, 71
organizational slack, 53
orphaned sources, statistics regarding, 163n17
Osirak reactor (Iraq), 156
Our Nuclear Future (Teller and Latter), 56

P-5 Process, 156, 157
Pavlov, Nikolai Ivanovich, 50
Penney, William, 64
Peres, Shimon, 76
Perrin, Michael, 64
Pertsev, Lev Aleksandrovich, 46
Pilz, Wolfgang, 84, 97
plutonium-238, 163n17
plutonium-239, 136
poisoning, 23–25, 31, 45

Pollack, Kenneth, 112, 117
polonium-210, 136
pop culture, 27–28, 158–60
Popular Science (magazine), 27
Poseidon (Russia), 56, 145
prestige, as weapons acquisition factor, 12, 141
Privetninskoe (Soviet Union), 47
Project Ibis (Egypt), 15–16, 76, 83–84, 88, 94–98, 100–102, 103–5, 187n2
Putin, Vladimir, 150, 151, 152, 156

Qa'Qaa'-28 (Nasser 29 bomb) (Iraq), 120, 123, 124

R-400 (Iraq), 124
radiation emission device, 162n13
radioactive dust, 20–22
"Radioactive Poisons," 22
radioactive sources, statistics regarding, 163n17
radioactive waste, 47, 61–62
radioisotopes, 163n17
radiological dispersal devices (RDDs), 7, 114
radiological weapons (RWs): challenges regarding, 65–66; contamination effects of, 65; defined, 6; development variations of, 136; domestic determinants regarding, 139–40; domestic impediments regarding, 142–43; drivers regarding, 135–41; future of, 149–54; as gas warfare instrument, 23; inhibitors to, 141–42; international security considerations regarding, 137–39, 142; legal restraints regarding, 155–56; life cycle of, 134–35, 201–2n1; military advantages of, 26; mitigating strategies regarding, 154–60; as "more humane," 140–41; non-state actors and, 3, 7; normative considerations regarding, 140–41, 143–44; normative restraints regarding, 157–58; offensive use of, 23–24; popular culture and education role regarding, 158–60; preventive measures regarding, 154–60; role of prestige regarding, 141; in science fiction, 1–2; scientific exploration of, 2; state-level programs of, 7; as terrain contaminating material, 23; uses for, 44, 61

RAND report, 144
Rathmell, Andrew, 95
Ray, Jonathan, 202n1
Reagan, Ronald, 158–59
Report of the MAUD Committee (United Kingdom), 58
Rickover, Hyman, 34
Ridenour, Louis, 37
Roberts, Brad, 12
Roosevelt, Franklin D., 1–2
Rosen, Stephen, 10
Royal Air Force (RAF) (United Kingdom), 67
Rublee, Maria Rost, 87, 88
Russia, 3, 56, 145, 148, 149–54, 155–56

S-1 Committee, 23
Sagan, Scott, 148
Sakharov, Andrei, 41, 55
Salama, Sammy, 112
salted bombs, 6–7, 55–56
Sänger, Eugen, 97
science, 72–73, 135–41
science fiction, 1, 19, 30, 36, 40–41
Scientific Research Institute 88 (NII 88) (Soviet Union), 50–51

Seaborg, Glenn, 29
Semipalatinsk Test Site (Soviet Union), 48–49, 50
Serebristaya pil' (Silver dust), 14, 40, 41, 51, 159
71st Air Force Test Base (Soviet Union), 50–51
Shahin, Fa'iz al-, 121
Shahristani, Hussain al-, 117, 124, 197–98n37
Shavit II (Israel), 86
Shoigu, Sergey, 150
Shpinel, V., 42
Sinai, topography of, 89–90
Sirrs, Owen, 89, 99, 101
60th Detachment (Soviet Union), 48
Skardon, William, 64
SK (Spetskomitet) (SK preparation) concentrate, 46–47
Smith, Frank, 35, 143
Smithson, Amy, 116–17, 127, 128
Smyth, Henry, 22, 43, 138
Solution 904, 46
"Solution Unsatisfactory" (MacDonald/Heinlein), 21, 160
South Korea, 153–54
Soviet Council of Ministers (Soviet Union), 43, 138
Soviet Union: accidents within, 49; changes in perceived threats to, 53; Chemical Institute of the Red Army, 43; chemical weapons and, 53; cluster munitions development within, 49–50; domestic determinants of, 139, 140; Egypt and, 82–83; Experimental Design Bureau 240 (OKB 240) of, 49; 15th Program of, 46; 1st Program of, 46; Generator of, 51; Geran' series of, 51–52; GSKB-47 of, 49; health and safety concerns within, 54; Heinsenmaa (Suri), 47; Institute of Organic Chemistry of the Academy of Sciences of the Soviet Union, 43; international security considerations of, 138; Kapustin Yar, 51; Konovets Island, 178–79n46; Laboratory B (Snezhinsk), 44, 46; Lake Lagoda, 47, 48; leadership changes within, 54–55; liquid air bombs of, 49, 50; Makarinsaari (Malyi), 47; military effectiveness lack within, 52–53; Military Unit 99795, 48; Ministry of Chemical Industry, 43; Mukerikku (Myuarka), 47; Navy, 45–46, 47; Object 230, 47, 48; organizational slack lack within, 53; preparatory measures of, 176n20; Privetninskoe, 47; radioactive waste of, 47; radiological weapons (RWs) development by, 45–52, 135, 137; radiological weapons (RWs) diffusion within, 6; radiological weapons (RWs) genesis of, 42–45; radiological weapons (RWs) overview of, 13–14, 40–41; radiological weapons (RWs) program demise within, 52–55; radiological weapons (RWs) pursuits of, 38–39, 41–52; radiological weapons (RWs) support within, 143; radiological weapons (RWs) testing within, 178–79n46; salted bombs and, 55–56; science fiction within, 40–41; Scientific Research Institute 88 (NII 88) of, 50–51; Semipalatinsk Test Site, 48–49, 50; 71st Air Force Test Base, 50–51; 60th Detachment, 48; SK (Spetskomitet) (SK preparation)

Soviet Union (*cont.*)
concentrate of, 46–47; Solution 904 of, 46; Soviet Council of Ministers, 43; technological impediments within, 142; testing locations of, 47–49, 51; as threat, 60–61; Topelov Design Bureau, 50–51; TSNII12 (12th Central Scientific Research Institute of the Ministry of Defense), 50; Tu-4s of, 50–51; uranium use of, 42; Vasilyevsky Island, 46; weapons innovation stages within, 5; zirconium usage by, 122
state capacity, 117
Stone, Robert, 24, 25, 71
strontium-90, 100, 163n17
substitution effect, 107, 142–43
Sulzberger, C. L., 16
super-dirty bombs, 144–45
Syria, 146, 147
Szilard, Leo, 22, 24–25, 55

Taher, Selim, 94
Taiwan, 153–54
Tammuz-2 (Iraq), 122
tantalum-182, 31–32, 73
technology, as catalyst, 11, 72–73, 135–42
Teller, Edward, 19, 21, 23–24, 25, 56
Tereshkin, Victor, 54
Thirring, Hans, 36
Time (magazine), 27, 159
Topelov Design Bureau (Soviet Union), 50–51
Transcontinental Atomic Company, 97
Transcontinental Oil Company, 97
trash bomb, 96
Treaty on the Non-Proliferation of Nuclear Weapons (NPT), 152
Tsar Bomba, 55

TSNII12 (12th Central Scientific Research Institute of the Ministry of Defense) (Soviet Union), 50
Tu-4s (Soviet Union), 50–51
Tupelov, Andrei, 54

Ukraine, 3, 148, 149–54, 204n34, 206–7n48, 206n44
United Arab Republic (UAR), 79, 82, 92
United Kingdom: atomic bomb and, 65–68; biological weapons and, 71; Chemical Defense Research Department of, 62; Chiefs of Staff (COS) committee of, 60–61, 65–66; comparison perspective of, 68–74; Defense Research Policy Committee of, 61, 65–66; Defense Services Panel of, 58; domestic determinants of, 140; external threat perceptions of, 58–60; international security and, 68–69; key scientist impact within, 62–64; MAUD Committee report of, 58, 60; postwar threat environment within, 60–62; radioactive isotope usage within, 73; radiological weapons (RWs) overview of, 14–15, 57–58, 73–74; radiological weapons (RWs) program demise of, 67–68; radiological weapons (RWs) support within, 143; radiological weapons (RWs) threat regarding, 135–36; research sources within, 8; Royal Air Force (RAF) of, 67; Soviet Union threat to, 60–61; threats to, 69; weaponry of, 63; Windscale (Sellafield) plutonium reactor of, 73; World War II and, 58–60
United Nations, 6, 38

United States: accusations against, 43; Ad Hoc Committee on Chemical, Biological and Radiological Warfare, 37–38; Air Force, 34; area denial and, 28; Armed Forces Special Weapons Project (AFSWP) within, 26–27, 36; Army Chemical Corps (ACC) within, 28–29, 30, 35, 36, 97, 140; atomic weapons program of, 32; Central Intelligence Agency (CIA), 38–39; chemical weapon development within, 34, 35–36; consensus building phase of, 25; Department of Defense within, 28, 114; domestic determinants of, 139–40; Dugway Proving Ground within, 20, 29, 32–33, 35; Egypt policy of, 81; General Accounting Office of, 127; Hanford reactor of, 32, 136; intelligence of, 155; international security considerations of, 138; Iraq WMD program and, 127–28, 146; kinetic warfare and, 35; lack of perceived threat within, 37–39; military rationale within, 33–35; Navy, 34; neutron bomb development within, 202n1; normative considerations within, 35–37, 140; nuclear doctrine of, 145–46; nuclear weapon development within, 34–35; promotion phase within, 30–31; radiological weapons (RWs) anxiety of, 59–60; radiological weapons (RWs) conceptualization within, 18–25; radiological weapons (RWs) development by, 2, 25–33, 136–37; radiological weapons (RWs) diffusion within, 6; radiological weapons (RWs) overview of, 13, 18; radiological weapons (RWs) program demise within, 33–39; radiological weapons (RWs) secrets of, 69–70; radiological weapons (RWs) in pop culture within, 27–28; reaction to Joklik affair by, 102–3; research sources within, 8; Russia and, 155–56; technocratic initiative phase of, 25–26; weapons innovation stages within, 5; zirconium usage by, 122

University of California at Berkeley, 26
UN Security Council, 126
UN Security Council Permanent Five, 117
UN Special Commission on Iraq (UNSCOM), 8–9, 108, 109, 126–30
uranium, 42, 203n23
uranium-192, 122
Urey, Harold, 22
"Use of Radioactive Material As a Military Weapon," 23
Uspenskij, K. F., 50

Vannikov, V. L., 44, 46, 54, 72
Vasilets, Vitol'd, 49, 50
Vasilyevsky Island (Soviet Union), 46
Volodin, I. F., 50
von Braun, Wernher, 19
von Neumann, John, 27
Voskoboinikov, M. I., 51
Vostochniy Mining and Processing Plant, 150–51
Vzglyad, 55

Waitt, Alden, 28
Walsh, James, 87, 88, 93, 96
The War Game, 158
warheads, 16

weapons: action-reaction process regarding, 138; domestic factors regarding, 70; innovation stages of, 4–5; scientific and technological breakthroughs regarding, 11; technological entrepreneurship regarding, 71–72. *See also specific types*
weapons of mass destruction (WMD), 38, 88, 109, 120
weapons substitution theory, 164n21
Weapons System Evaluation Group, 30, 33
Wells, H. G., 18–19
White, E. B., 37
Wigner, Eugene, 22, 24–25
Wilkins, F. G., 62–63
Wilkins, F. J., 70
Wilson, Carroll, 27, 36–37
Windscale (Sellafield) plutonium reactor (United Kingdom), 73

Woods, Kevin, 119
The World Set Free (Wells), 18–19
World War II, 14–15, 21–22, 58–60, 93–94

Yemen, 91
Yost, Don M., 20

Zadginedze, G. A., 46
Zaporizhzhia nuclear power station, 149
Zavenyagin, A. P., 45, 54
Zawahiri, Ayman al-, 148
Zhikharev, C. C., 46
zirconium, 196n22
zirconium-95, 46, 122–23, 137
zirconium-columbium, 31
zirconium-niobium, 137
zirconium oxide, 122
Zlauvinen, Gustavo, 128–29, 130

Printed in the USA
CPSIA information can be obtained
at www.ICGtesting.com
JSHW020301191023
50329JS00001B/1